WE WANT FALMER!

"We want Falmer and we want Falmer!
We want Falmer and we want Falmer!
We want Falmer and we want Falmer!
We are the Falmer Wanters!
WE WANT FALMER!
WE WANT FALMER!"

Sung to the tune of *Tennessee Wig Walk* by thousands of
Brighton fans at Withdean Stadium and grounds up and
down the country 1999-2009

WE WANT FALMER!

How Brighton & Hove Albion and its fans united to build a stadium

Paul Hodson and Stephen North

To all of the Falmer For All campaigners

There was no official membership of the Falmer For All campaign. Anyone was welcome to help, and invitations were issued from time to time. Some people "popped in and popped out again". Others stayed the course.

All statistics, facts and figures may be incorrect as they are a recollection of memory from the interviewee.

© Paul Hodson and Stephen North

Paul Hodson and Stephen North have asserted their rights in accordance with the Copyright, Designs and Patents Act 1988 to be identified as the authors of this work.

Published by: Stripe Publishing Ltd, First Floor, 3 St. George's Place, Brighton, BN1 4GA

Email: info@stripepublishing.co.uk | Web: www.stripepublishing.co.uk | Twitter: twitter.com/#!/StripePub

First published 2011

10-digit ISBN: 1-907158-16-2
13-digit ISBN: 978-1-907158-16-2

Manufacturing managed by Jellyfish Print Solutions Ltd
Editor: Dan Tester www.copymatters.co.uk
Photographs: Gloss insert pages - Roz South, Stewart Weir and JJ Waller. (Images on text pages are from many sources, including Brighton & Hove Albion, the authors, the Albion Collectors' and Historians' Society, the subjects of the photos and various bottom drawers around Sussex. We apologise to anyone we haven't mentioned.)
Design: Bill Swallow

Contents

Acknowledgments

Many thanks to:

To everyone at Stripe Publishing for their hard work, Paul Camillin, Tim Carder, Juliet Pickering from AP Watt, Paul Samrah, Bill Swallow, Dan Tester, Anders Swaffield, Jessie Hodson, Roz South, Stewart Weir, JJ Waller, Tim Colville, Ian Green and Tim Herbert who all helped us in different ways.

As well as... Brighton & Hove Albion Football Club, Brighton & Hove Albion Supporters' Club, Northstandchat.com, *Albion Almanac*, *The Argus*.

And to all the people who got us out of a deep hole with the transcribing of the hundreds of hours of recorded interviews; Gina North, Anders Swaffield, Sue Lapwood, Kate Paskin, Jackie Blake, Janet Sate and Carol Brailsford.

Also to all the interviewees... thank you for your time, your tea and your stories.

And finally thanks and love to Gina North and Beth Fitzgerald for being so understanding when we were missing in action.

Authors' preface

In October 1997, *Build a Bonfire – How Football Fans United to Save Brighton & Hove Albion* was published, a verbatim account of Brighton fans' fight to save their club after the Goldstone Ground was sold by Bill Archer. The book ended with the confirmation that Dick Knight's consortium had gained the controlling share in the club, with Dick taking over the reins as club chairman. The club had survived, but were deeply in debt, in the bottom division, about to start a ground share forced upon them at Gillingham, with no tangible sign of getting home.

Fourteen years later and the Albion have a multi-millionaire chairman financing a multi-million pound squad, playing in a brand new state-of-the-art stadium back in Brighton.

This has been an extraordinary journey, uniting fans and Board in fights to bring the club back from exile in Kent, to gain planning permission for a permanent home, and to raise finance for, and build, a new stadium.

In putting together this book, we have interviewed around 50 people who we felt represented all aspects of the campaign: life-long supporters of all ages, people involved in the construction of the stadium, the key members of the campaigning team, journalists, a press officer, two lords, council officials, a chief executive and two chairmen were all approached and agreed to be recorded and then transcribed.

All very different people, but united in their aim to see Brighton & Hove Albion playing in a permanent home in the city.

As with *Build a Bonfire*, we have let the people who made the story tell the story, rather than writing a factual account of events. A by-product of this is that sometimes the book has contradictory views or memories of the same incident, which is hardly surprising as the story covers over 14 years. (Although one interviewee had difficulty remembering the day of the opening fixture against Doncaster Rovers a few weeks previously, but that may have been due to the amount of Harveys they consumed.)

We decided to interview only people who were involved in the campaign (rather than include those who were against). If Anne De Vecchi, Norman Baker MP and Melanie Cuttress wish to write their accounts, I am sure we will all queue up to read them, but our aim was to celebrate the pro-Falmer campaign by hearing from the people who made it happen; share their highs and lows, see their minds at work dealing with the latest crisis and coming up with the next imaginative solution.

The key members of the Falmer For All team, to whom this book is dedicated, clearly have centre stage throughout; we apologise to the members of the team we didn't have the time or resources to interview.

The story breaks down into three clear sections: Gillingham and the fight to bring home the Albion; Withdean and the struggles to gain planning permission to build a stadium at Falmer; and then, finally, the financing, building and opening of the Amex.

The book ends with the first professional league game at the new stadium and for this we asked everyone included in the book to write their own accounts of that amazing day – if you shed a tear or two whilst reading them, then you'll pass us in the queue for the tissues; thank you to all who contributed, we included as many as we could.

The way that the supporters and the (then future) Board joined together from 1996 to fight the various campaigns was remarkable and could (and should) be an inspiration to any football club in a similar situation in the future. Dick Knight and Martin Perry have to take enormous credit for involving the fans in the inner workings of the football club in a unique way, allowing them to come up with ideas and tactics and lead the campaign from the front. Many of the key members of the Falmer For All team were among the most vociferous campaigners against Archer and Bellotti and the seeds of the Amex were planted in those times.

It is hard to single out any individual supporters but special mention has to be made of Tim Carder and Paul Samrah, without whose incredible efforts we may not have had a stadium.

The arrival of Tony Bloom to finance the building of the stadium has to be one of the greatest things ever to happen to the Albion; but from way back in the dark old days when the first suspicion was raised about Bill Archer, the campaigns, initially against the Board and then for the new stadium, have always been team efforts.

So, while this book is dedicated to the group of fans at the heart of the campaign, perhaps it should also be for anyone who ever signed a petition, wrote a letter, wore a ribbon, voted for a Seagull, wrote to *The Argus*, sent flowers, went to Gillingham, road bikes, posted postcards, sat in the rain at Withdean, bought a player, posted on the internet, delivered Valentine's cards, went to a gig, argued in pubs, walked to Sheepcote and countless other events and campaigns along the way in support of Brighton & Hove Albion's fight for a permanent stadium at Falmer.

The fans, united, will never be defeated.

Oh, and one more thing.

Archer and Bellotti – we will never forget.

Paul Hodson and Stephen North
November 2011

Introduction

Paul Hayward

The first book was about defiance. This one tells of deliverance. From descent to ascent and the Amex Community Stadium, one theme stands out.

The longer it dragged on the more implacable Brighton's supporters became. New grounds are monuments to money, certainly, but this one memorialises a refusal to surrender to bureaucracy, cynicism and low ambition.

Forgive any smugness on the part of the Falmer For All gang, those relentless lobbyists who gave up endless hours to right a wrong. The sale of the Goldstone Ground was an outrage that lodged itself in the gut and refused to shift. It united the community against the profiteer. A grander vision worked alongside the urge for revenge: a new home that would raise the life of the city, glow on winter nights and draw swarms of Sussex folk to a place they could feel they shared.

Over the course of the long struggle to build the club's spectacular new ground at Falmer I heard many people in positions of influence dismiss the idea that Brighton and Hove needed a sporting church. "Brighton's not a football town," they would say, or "the bird has flown – they'll never make it to the Premier League," or "this is an arts and culture city now – and the kids all support Chelsea and Arsenal, anyway."

These grumbles were offensive on many levels. First, they sought to disenfranchise people whose upbringing in the area had led them to see the Albion as a community institution to which they felt they belonged. At Brighton games you encounter many families who have watched the Seagulls for generations. The faint disdain for all things football from sections of the 'city by the sea' expressed a kind of arrogance about Brighton's social history.

Equally, it ignored a truth seen easily by the likes of Dick Knight, Paul Samrah, Liz Costa, Tim Carder and Tony Bloom, who finally made it happen with his wealth and boldness. The mistake was to examine the 7,500 crowds at Withdean and say Brighton were merely a lower league club with a small hardcore following. The campaigners saw the club not as it was at Withdean but how it could be in a new stadium with inspiring architecture.

Let's be humble, and clear. Not every Football League club could afford the high-spec and luxurious feel of the Amex, with its rolling cylindrical structure, its posh facilities and comfy seats. But the Amex, as we inevitably call it, confirms an old belief about grounds. If it can be avoided (and often it can't), they need to be more than flat-pack, identikit arenas with a club crest nailed on a wall.

The Goldstone was magnetic for a different set of reasons. It was decaying, charismatically. It had charm and presence. It would never let you down. Even the floodlights cast an old, ghostly glow. The echoes were of mass crowds, creaking terraces, sheepskin coats and dodgy haircuts. Ripped out of its natural setting, the club went homeless, first in Gillingham, then suburbia, where the Withdean grass thickens and the metallic tannoy din of Sussex by the Sea is heard no more.

When Gus Poyet's promoted side moved into the Amex in the summer of 2011, the first buzz was the stadium itself. A new team was inspiring its audience with slick carpet football and the stage they played on suggested a new world of possibilities: the Premier League, chiefly, to which Swansea, Burnley and Blackpool have all graduated in recent years.

Falmer closed the gap between the sleeping-giant rhetoric and the reality on that lush new turf beside the A27. It rendered upward mobility credible in a way no impassioned chairman's speech ever could (even one from Dick Knight, the king optimist). It was not flash or blingy. Instead, it spoke of a new kind of seriousness. Brighton were no longer hoping for something good to turn up. It already had. Each department was expected to do its bit and support the big push. There could be no passengers.

You saw the excitement in the eyes of people attending a match for the first time, in the scurry from car parks and train station. And what about that wonderful noise? At Withdean, passion and song floated through the trees and dissipated. At the Amex it shakes the Downs. A generation of Sussex children have been plugged into football's live energy – in the Championship, where big name clubs jostle to escape, and every game is a contest.

A new cast of gladiators have replaced the men who kept Withdean in drama. Many a pint should be raised to players from the Micky Adams-Steve Coppell-Peter Taylor-Mark McGhee eras. Now. Albion fans who once studied David Cameron (the soldier-footballer, not the Prime Minister) now watch Craig Mackail-Smith pull on a Scotland jersey days after scoring for Brighton. Seagulls fans are no longer applauding the struggle, the fight for survival, and have fixed their eyes instead on the performers, the sport, the team.

This takes some getting used to. This book marks the end of anxiety. It records the feelings, experiences, fears and sacrifices of people who saw football reinvent itself as a political cause. It gave them something to rally around – and threw together an eclectic mix of characters, who might have written their own sitcom to break up the agony of campaigning and waiting.

Brighton are no longer skint and no longer desperate. They have ceased to be the object of football's sympathy. That role has passed to others, most recently Plymouth Argyle. This volume could be the last word on an episode that affirms the power of community action in an age when politicians privatise and attack collectively-owned institutions. To borrow an American phrase, the Falmer For All movement fought City Hall and won.

To live in a society of corporate greed and starved public services is to feel disempowered. They want you to give up and go away. Brighton & Hove Albion were going nowhere. Cancel that: they were always going home.

Paul Hayward
Chief Sports Writer, *The Daily Telegraph*

The cast list

Unless otherwise stated, the people listed are supporters of Brighton & Hove Albion.

All were interviewed by the authors by recording them onto audio which was then transcribed. Everyone had the right to read the transcription of their own interview and remove anything they did not want published. The words you are reading have not been re-written or changed from the original interviews, only edited.

Steve (Lord) Bassam Leader of Brighton & Hove Council up to 1999 and chief whip for Labour in the House of Lords

Ed Bassford Falmer For All campaign activist, Seagulls Party candidate

Attila the Stockbroker (John Baine) Falmer For All campaign activist

Aaron Berry

Tony Bloom Chairman of the Albion 2009 - present

Bob Bruce Brighton & Hove City Council solicitor

Paul Camillin *Scars & Stripes* fanzine founder, Albion head of communications

Tim Carder Falmer For All Campaign activist, Seagulls Party secretary, Supporters' Club chairman 1998-2008, *Albion Almanac* editor

Derek Chapman Chairman of Adenstar Construction, Albion director, stadium project manager

Roy Chuter

Liz Costa Falmer For All Campaign activist, Supporters' Club vice-chairman

John Cowen Falmer For All campaign activist

Claire Byrd (Newnham) *The Argus*

Ian Hart Presenter of the Seagulls Phone (Moan) In, BBC SCR 1998-2009

Paul Hayward Chief Sports Writer, *The Daily Telegraph*

Tim Herbert

John Hewitt Falmer For All campaign activist, Supporters' Club chairman 2008 to present

Ian (Hiney) Hine Northstandchat.com moderator

Jessie Hodson

Adrian Holdstock KSS project architect

Tim Johnson

Dick Knight Chairman of the Albion 1997-2009

Kerry Mayo Albion player, 1996-2009

Ian Morley Chair of the 'Yes Yes' Campaign

Richie Morris

Andy Naylor Brighton & Hove Albion reporter for *The Argus* (Brighton)

Adrian Newnham Founder of Bring Home the Albion, Falmer For All campaign activist, Seagulls Party Deputy Leader

Martin Perry Chief Executive of the Albion 1999 - present

John (Lord) Prescott Deputy Prime Minister 1997-2008, Hull City supporter

Graeme Rolf Jack Straw on Northstandchat

Paul Samrah Chair of Falmer For All campaign, leader of Seagulls Party

Andy Simons KSS Design Director

Roz South Falmer For All campaign activist, Seagulls Party communications officer and candidate

Nigel Summers

Anders Swaffield

Dave Swaffield

Sam Swaffield Co-editor of *The Seagull Love Review* fanzine

Bill Swallow Falmer For All campaign activist

Jan Swallow Falmer For All campaign activist

Stefan Swift Co-Editor of *The Seagull Love Review* fanzine

Dan Tester *Scars & Stripes* fanzine founder, managing director Stripe Publishing

Alan Wares

Sarah Watts Falmer For All campaign activist, Supporters' Club secretary

Paul Whelch Falmer For All campaign activist

PART ONE

Gillingham

August 1997 – May 1999

1. THE END OF THE BONFIRE
Genesis of salvation

MARTIN PERRY: In 1996 I was working for Alfred McAlpine. We had developed
an expertise in building football stadia. We built the Stretford End for Manchester
United, stands for Coventry, Everton, replaced most of Ewood Park for Blackburn
Rovers and built Molineux for Wolverhampton Wanderers. We had also won the
contract for building the new stadium at Huddersfield, which had gone exceptionally
well. It was then that Ivor Caplin rang and said: "I have heard about what you are doing
at Huddersfield, it sounds fantastic. Would you come down to Brighton to talk to us
because we've got a problem?"

Which was when I uttered those immortal words; "Ivor, I am a Brighton fan, I was brought up there as a boy, I went to the Goldstone, I've always followed Brighton, so it would be wonderful to come down and sort out their new stadium, they are a sleeping giant – but I don't want to end up running the football club!"

I well remember that first meeting. It was in Liam Brady's living room. And Liam said: "I've got someone who wants to take over, would you come and meet him? His name is Dick Knight."

It was very obvious from Dick's and Bob Pinnock's point of view that they knew what they were trying to achieve and how they were going to do it, but they had no construction expertise whatsoever. So we agreed: "Let's work together…"And that's where it all started. In Shirley Drive, Hove. What I saw was a huge club that was in the doldrums. From that moment onwards, I never lost the belief, I always thought the club had absolutely massive potential. If there was a club that could rebuild itself and build a new stadium it was this one, because it would have the support.

Dick then had an alignment with Alfred McAlpine which gave the consortium credibility, because here was a company who clearly knew what they were doing when it came to football stadiums, aligned with Dick's passion and love of the club… put those two together and you've got a pretty potent mix. The consortium had to have the backing of the fans. And when it was explained and they understood what it was all about, they got behind us.

That gave the momentum to be able to put ourselves into a negotiating position with Bill Archer who had control. And, so for me, that's where it all started, in 1996, while the battles were still going on…

The arbitration meetings were held in the offices of the Centre for Effective Dispute Resolution, CEDR for short. I went to those meetings with Dick; they were difficult, but ultimately we got an agreement the night before the last game at the Goldstone.

We were trying to get control of the club and the discussions had become deadlocked. Bill Archer did not want to step away completely but, for Dick and his partner Bob Pinnock to put in the money that was needed for the club to survive, Dick clearly wanted to be the major shareholder, in other words to have at least 51% of the shares. It was only right that in putting this money in at risk he should be able to control how it was used. Bill Archer, however, was insisting he retained 51% of the shares so there appeared to be no way forward.

The way that CEDR worked was that they put Bill Archer and David Bellotti in one room and Dick, Bob and myself in another. CEDR used to shuttle between the two rooms, talking the issues through and trying to find common ground on which we could move forward - that's how mediation works.

I remember sitting late one evening, and I said to the guy who was mediating; "Can I go and see Bill?" And he said; "Yes if you want to." And I walked in to see Bill Archer and said: "Bill, what it seems to me is - the two of you both want control, so how about a compromise? How about if you have 45%, Dick has 45% and someone who both of you trust in the middle has 10%… Would that work?" I honestly did not think that he would go for it. But to my astonishment he agreed. So I said: "Are you happy for me to put that to Dick?" And he said he was.

When I put it to Dick he said; "Yes I will agree to that on one condition, that you hold the 10%." And I said; "He'll never agree that." But Dick insisted and told me to "Go and try." So I went and said to Bill; "I've spoken to Dick and he will agree to it on the condition that McAlpine hold the 10%," and Bill said; "Yes I agree to that." And that actually is the point where a statement was made that we had reached an agreement.

The arrangement then got fine tuned and in the end it was agreed that McAlpine would not hold any shares, but I would hold the shares personally, so finally it came down to Bill Archer 49.5%, Dick 49.5% and me 1%. That agreement was reached at a meeting the night before the game against Doncaster Rovers, the last ever game at the Goldstone.

The following morning I came down to Brighton, I met Dick and we walked to the Goldstone Ground. We didn't even know where the directors' door was! We actually went on a tour around the Goldstone, which was about to be demolished of course. Most of it went that afternoon!

Up until then the directors' box had either been empty or Bellotti had been there, and now it was full with Dick and his family, Bob and his family, me… and this huge rousing welcome we got, and all the emotion of the Last Post – and the game! The sending-offs, and the goal… and then as soon as the final whistle went, to our absolute amazement we were surrounded by police in full riot gear and taken into the Boardroom while the Goldstone Ground was ripped apart around us. We were held in the Boardroom with this noise going on, incessant noise of people ripping up seats and grabbing souvenirs – and it was pretty scary. And that was my first football match as a director of a football club!

And, of course, seven days later there we were travelling to Hereford, for our league survival, the drama of the Hereford game – the first half, Kerry Mayo's own goal, Reinelt… So we had all of that emotion and tension – and that was my second game as the director of the football club! And I thought is this what it's going to be like every day?

Those eight days were just extraordinary. I remember the sheer ecstasy on the faces of the Brighton fans and total abject misery of the Hereford fans – it's one of those images of the whole story that's quite unforgettable.

DICK KNIGHT: The Football League called an EGM in the July before Gillingham to vote on whether Brighton should be allowed to stay in the League – this was unprecedented because it was not for financial reasons but because of the way the club was being run by Archer. I was allowed to go to that but I wasn't allowed to speak. Archer spoke at this meeting – it was not a very convincing performance on his part, shall I say…

There was one chairman of another club who spoke strongly in favour of Brighton as a club, and that was Dan McCauley of Plymouth, because he knew what it meant to the community. He spoke not in support of Archer but simply in support of the club. They had this vote, and 17 clubs in the Football League voted to throw us out… They have to have a 75% majority with any Football League motion and we scraped through. There were a lot of people who stood up at this meeting, some well-known chairmen, who put the knife into Brighton.

The club's reputation was dirt in football. I thought: "I've got an awful lot of rebuilding to do."

MARTIN PERRY: So that's where it all really kicked off. Attempts to ground share with Millwall, Woking and Crawley Town had all failed. In the end we had no choice. Reluctantly, we went to Gillingham…

2. DISLOCATION
"Every game was an away game"

DICK KNIGHT: The most ludicrous ground share in the history of football, anywhere in the world.

ATTILA: My first memories of going to Gillingham were just feeling totally alienated.

ANDY NAYLOR: Gillingham was just hell really, to think that you are driving there every fortnight to cover a home game.

TIM CARDER: I refused to go to Gillingham at the start because it was my club playing in a foreign county under a regime which still offered no future for the club.

LIZ COSTA: It is a horrible place to have to go but it served its purpose.

MARTIN PERRY: There were attempts to ground share with Millwall, Woking and Crawley Town. All of those had failed and we were stuck with Gillingham.

DICK KNIGHT: I said to David Dent, who was the Football League secretary: "Do you realise what my predecessors have done? And you are trying to insist we fulfil this ground share at Gillingham? We will have many away games nearer to Brighton than our home games." It is 75 miles to Gillingham from Brighton. I had an absolute imperative to get out of Gillingham as soon as we could.

ED BASSFORD: There was something upsetting about Gillingham, as well as something to feel a sense of relief about; the relief was obvious, we'd survived. I felt almost as though I wanted to boycott Gillingham, I didn't want to go until the Albion were back home. And for the first half of that first season at Priestfield we did not go and watch matches, we listened to it on the radio, followed the team… God, that was a depressing thing to do in its own right wasn't it?

AARON BERRY: I probably managed, I don't know, maybe a dozen games each season. But it was awful.

PAUL SAMRAH: Grim, time consuming, but thank God we've still got a club, thank God we're still in the Football League and thank God there's been a regime change.

TIM HERBERT: I remember being chuffed to bits that we were actually playing at Gillingham. Despite it being a terrible, terrible place, just the fact that we were playing somewhere, it was fantastic.

TIM JOHNSON: You can never get over that feeling of arriving at quite possibly one of the most desolate towns I think I have ever been to in my life; every brick and every pavement just smelt of loneliness and desperation, which quite possibly fitted into how we were feeling at the time. The season-ticket holders who went there week in week out, they have got to be applauded in their own right. Quite why they bought a season ticket I don't know because we were never going to fill the place, we could have just tipped up and it would have been fine.

PAUL SAMRAH: When Bellotti turned up there was almost a riot. *The Sun* headline was 'Is this the most hated man in football?' and the national press could not believe what Brighton had been through to get to Gillingham and to find that the ex chief executive was still there.

DAVE SWAFFIELD: I saw David Bellotti there on the first day, selling tickets behind a Perspex cover and nearly got arrested because I was just banging on this Perspex, wanting to get my hands round his throat. I just saw that face and I went for it and got dragged off by the police, away, which was probably just as well.

ANDERS SWAFFIELD: I was never taken. It's too far away. I don't think it's a particularly nice place to go for a two or three year-old.

PAUL HAYWARD: It was very strange to watch your own club in exile in that way, particularly in such an environment that didn't feel like Brighton and Hove whatsoever. You weren't really there for the game, no-one would have paid to go and watch that football, they would have only paid to express their sort of allegiance to the club.

ANDY NAYLOR: You know, it was just a soul-destroying experience for everyone, I think. You used to look at the fans coming up there in the coaches and the crowds were down to a couple of thousand.

KERRY MAYO: It just felt like every game was an away game. Originally, when we started, they wanted us to all travel together and put a coach on for the games, and after about two or three matches we ended up sacking that off and just driving. The last thing you wanted to do after a 70 mile, 80 mile trip on the A23 is go and sit in the dressing room for an hour and a half and go out and play. If there was traffic it was even worse.

SAM SWAFFIELD: When we left the Goldstone I was just about to turn 13 and Stefan had got me to migrate to the North terrace from the top of the East. I had done that for maybe a season and a half, and we would stand at the front of the North Stand and the crowds were quite big towards the end. We got to experience some really good atmospheres in the North Stand but then suddenly, boom, it was taken away from us.

That progression and a sort of maturity you get as a young football fan, especially in your teens, was taken away from us completely and suddenly – we were thrown into this Gillingham world. We were just learning about a more adult football culture, and singing, and terracing, and big crowds, and great atmospheres on our doorsteps, then suddenly it was very strange disjointed trips to a town we had never heard of.

STEFAN SWIFT: That first season there was just so dull, so boring compared to the previous seasons, both in terms of on-the-pitch, and fan, events.

IAN HINE: We got something like 15 points less at that first season at Gillingham than the last season at the Goldstone and it was only because Doncaster were so rubbish we didn't go down that year.

ADRIAN NEWNHAM: Dick Knight had a suspicion for a few weeks that the attendances given out at Gillingham were not representative of the number of people who'd come through the turnstiles... So either people had come through and hadn't paid or there were people who had paid to go in but hadn't been clicked through. You wouldn't do that to your own. You were tenants in every sense of the word.

PAUL SAMRAH: I went to every other game at Gillingham. The gates started falling off until, I think, Bonfire Night 1997. We played Barnet, lost 3-0 at home, and the crowd was just over a thousand, I think it was 1,025.

TIM HERBERT: You just think it can't get any worse than this really.

DAN TESTER: I'd gone for a piss and I came back to see Rod Thomas – our nippy winger – tip the ball over the bar to concede a penalty, possibly against Plymouth. I remember thinking "What the fuck was that?" and just sat on the terrace and wept.

SARAH WATTS: It really was hell but I think that is why more Brighton fans started going away and not going to the home games. We enjoyed that, and it was the fun side of it, but we had maybe ten/12 wins over the two years in the league there – horrendous!

ROZ SOUTH: It gradually created a sort of siege mentality. The fan experience was oddly a combination of grim, but sort of solid, in a funny sort of way, and I wouldn't have wanted to miss out on Gillingham. It was a long, long trek to watch some pretty abysmal football, but I think everyone was buoyed up with the idea that this can't last for long anyway.

PAUL SAMRAH: Had we continued in that first season not having anything developing, the club would've just gone down; the football was dire. I think we were so relieved to have survived the regime change that everything else carried us through to Christmas 1997 and then from early 1998, Withdean was on the cards with the 'Bring Home the Albion' campaign and the planning application. But, had it gone on like the end of that first season, with nothing emanating from the Board of what they were going to do, then I dread to think what would have happened.

3. THE PRIESTFIELD P.A.
The great double act is formed...

ATTILA: Early on at Gillingham the Gillingham PA announcer was doing our games, in a very lacklustre fashion, and the music he was playing was absolute vomit. Dick said "Isn't that PA rubbish?" and I said "I could do that" and he said "Right, you're on". I said "I promise I'll play some decent music and announce the team with some passion, to make our fans feel a tiny bit more at home, it'll be a Phil Collins-free zone and we'd get punk rock".

I used to go to the pub at 12 o'clock and have a lot of beer, then do the PA, and that made for interesting times for two reasons: 1) obviously being that I was pissed and 2) I'd have to dash to the loo during the game. Paul's not a drinker so I said; "Hey Samrah could you come and help do the PA?" That's how he got involved.

PAUL SAMRAH: I remember when we were 3-0 down at half-time and then one of our players scored a hat-trick. I had a bottle of bubbly that I'd put on the window sill of the PA box and when we scored a goal – our first goal for eight games – I cracked it open. The next thing this police commander, in charge of crowd control, rushed into our PA box and John was about to have a drink. This bloke grabbed the glass from him and says: "If you don't stop drinking in here I will turn the whole PA off and the game will be called off". The reason he gave was "You can't have alcohol in view of the pitch" which was the first I'd heard about it!

ATTILA: I thought I'd wake everyone up and play Anarchy In The UK and half way through a gentleman in a blue uniform ran into the box saying "Take it off! Take it off!" I said "Why?" and he said "It's on the banned list!" and I took it off and put The Clash on instead and I said "Officer, why is it on the banned list?" He said "That's obvious, it incites violence in the crowd" and I said "I bought it when it first came out, black cover, it never incited me to violence and no-one I knew was moved to violence either – but I have been to all 92 league grounds and every time I've heard In The Air Tonight by Phil Collins it had made me feel like an axe-murdering psychopath!!" He obviously wasn't very happy with this and Kent Constabulary issued a formal letter to the club saying they should relieve me of my job of PA announcer. Dick Knight stood up to them and it all quietened down.

Another time we'd lost 4-0 to Darlington, Marco Gabbiadini had scored a hat trick and of course there had to be our Man of the Match, which someone gave to Kerry Mayo. He'd had an awful game so I announced "And the Man of the Match is… KERRY MAYO????" Of course, it wasn't professional of me at all – but it was just really funny.

ATTILA: I've played the music for 14 years and I'm retiring now we've got the new stadium. I've done my bit! I've loved doing it. I am a scratchy punk DJ, most certainly not the jolly corporate announcer type, and that's what they want at Falmer! I guess the music will be different, but that's up to the club. Just one thing: NO MUSIC AFTER GOALS! (Photo taken at Priestfield.)

4. TAKEOVER
In safe hands at last

DICK KNIGHT: After all the other shenanigans Archer pulled between having agreed in principle to step down in April, it took nearly five months – from April, the last game at the Goldstone, to the following season in early September – to finally get the ink on the contract, which finally meant that he was no longer the chairman and no longer the owner of the club. The deal was 49.5% for myself, 49.5% for Archer, and 1% for Martin.

TIM CARDER: I refused to go until the Board changed, and that happened to be September 2nd 1997, which was my birthday, so I couldn't have had a nicer present.

ADRIAN NEWNHAM: Talk about burying news on a busy news day. The announcement of the takeover was the Tuesday after Princess Diana died so every newspaper is full of the funeral and one sidebar in the paper was saying that Bellotti was finally going and the takeover goes through. If ever there was an example of someone waiting for an opportune moment to sneak that one through.

IAN MORLEY: The club was struggling financially even after Dick had come in. I read the company accounts going back over that period of time. They were constantly relying on more and more directors' loans to prop the business up as the reality of the slashed turnover as a result of being at Gillingham.

PAUL CAMILLIN: I think back to that game, it was quite a significant evening. I

NEW BOARD TAKES OVER   2 September 1997

All parties are pleased to announce that the shareholding restructure of the Club envisaged by the FA-backed mediation agreement has been finalised, all legal matters have been completed, and the new board of Brighton and Hove Albion is now in place.

In compliance with the FA agreement, the employment of David Bellotti has been terminated on completion of the legal procedures and he has now left the Club.

Greg Stanley has resigned as a director and shareholder and all monies owed to him by the Club have been repaid.

The new board comprises Dick Knight as Chairman, Bill Archer, Bob Pinnock, Martin Perry and the non-executive directors, Sir John Smith and Richard Faulkner. The board will rapidly seek a new senior executive responsible for the day-to-day running of the Club and it is intended that a supporters' representative will also be appointed.

The new board are unanimous in their thanks to the FA who brokered the mediation deal, and in particular appreciate the untiring efforts of David Davies and CEDR towards its successful conclusion.

Dick Knight said, "If I pause a moment to reflect, it is not in celebration, but rather my mood is one of determination to ensure that this Club, its supporters and staff will never again have to face the traumas of the past two years.

We must all put those problems behind us. They are history. It is time to move on, to rebuild the Club, to restore confidence, pride and a sense of purpose.

The new board is dedicated, first and foremost, to getting the Club back on an even keel. Our objectives include establishing a sound financial footing for the next few years as we face the economic hardships of playing away from our Brighton home, to develop the already encouraging relationship with our Local Authority towards the ultimate goal of a superb new stadium in the Brighton area. And yes, within sensible parameters of our overall financial position, making money available to Steve Gritt to strengthen the playing side.

Above all, we are committed to rebuilding bridges with the most important people of all, the fans, without whom none of this would have been possible.

On a personal note, I take up the mantle of Albion Chairman with much humility and pride. After all those years on the terraces, I am finding a seat in the Directors box a little awesome! But I'll get used to it and trust that my new board colleagues and I can lead the Club to a better future."

remember leaving the ground that night, I think we drew 2-2, and there was a sort of sense of a new era kicking off. It's frightening how far we've come. It's frightening when you think what we had to do at that stage, but I don't think that dawned on anybody.

STEFAN SWIFT: Archer still had the 49.5% stake so he wasn't quite out of it, but it was just a matter of time before he was going to be bought out so it kind of felt like the victory was won. Support in the club lost a bit of something that season, suddenly there was no intensity like there had been.

5. AWAY SUPPORT
"Brighton & Hove Albion away, away, away…"

TIM CARDER: If there was a positive to come out of the whole situation, it was the supporters got used to travelling to matches; they had to travel 75 miles, on buses and coaches, and got to know people and they actually had quite a nice day – until the time between 3 o'clock and a quarter to five! I think it sowed the seed for the phenomenal away support that we experience now.

PAUL SAMRAH: Ironically, Gillingham increased our away attendance going forward, I have absolutely no doubt about that, a 20-30% increase, I'm convinced of it. There were many fans that thought actually we can easily do Milton Keynes, Southampton or anywhere in the south.

ROY CHUTER: The away support began to boom and it's been like that ever since. And I put it down initially to the fact that there were large numbers of people who would not go to Gillingham.

DAN TESTER: The Gillingham experience brought everyone together. Lifelong friendships were formed and no other club has really had to go through what we have. It doesn't make us better than anyone else but it does make us different.

We had to travel nearly two hours each way for home games. That's a lot of talking time you don't normally get for a home game and you got to know people really well. This weird Dunkirk spirit was fostered. So many Albion fans simply wouldn't let the club die.

KERRY MAYO: Honestly it's a different class with away games being better than home games… you get all the diehard singing fans. The atmosphere is always better at away games than home games.

LIZ COSTA: We took three coaches every week to Gillingham. All those people were then part of the bigger team when we wanted petitions handing out because they were all friends. They were part of an exercise, if you like, to save the club and they knew if they could do their little bit, even if it was only getting signatures on a piece of paper. As far as I'm concerned that is really where it all started.

GRAEME ROLF: Gillingham did, in a sense, feel like home. All the supporters you got to know over the years, they were all there, all the hardcore support where there, the average was 3,500, which for an away game is just phenomenal really. A lot of those supporters also went away. When you go to all away games, you certainly know who the really hardcore supporters are.

6. SCARS & STRIPES
Voice of the people

PAUL CAMILLIN: Myself, Kieron Moorman and Paul Hazlewood were the three original founders, if you like. I think I stumped up the £500 for the first copy, bankrolled it, bashed together on a computer at home.

IAN MORLEY: The fanzine *Gulls Eye* packed up the day the Goldstone turnstiles stopped turning and it was probably brave for Paul and the other guys (Darren McKay, Kieran Moorman, Paul Camillin, Dan Tester) to start a fanzine.

DAN TESTER: It came out for the Darlington game at Priestfield and momentum gathered. People would say we were doing well and Bill and Jan Swallow got in touch offering to help. They turned a 28-page black and white publication into a full colour 42-page colour fanzine! It was better than the programme!

IAN MORLEY: They took fanzine making to a whole new level producing a 42-page, glossy, high res full colour fanzine – I mean, seriously good. Paul Camillin, of course, went on to be the club press officer and the Swallows, who designed the fanzine, designed the club programme as well.

PAUL CAMILLIN: We were turning out a decent fanzine, which was actually voted 'best fanzine ever' in *When Saturday Comes* at some point.

DAN TESTER: Before email, I had to save my articles on a floppy disc and then go to Worthing on the train! It was ridiculous! It was my first proper attempt at writing and my first article was about Rupert Murdoch taking over Man United, and Sky taking over football.

IAN MORLEY: I started to write a monthly article called, The Biggest Battle is Yet To Come – "You think you've had a big battle so far, removing Archer and Bellotti from the club, that's nothing". I guess looking back I don't think I ever realised when I started writing those, and I probably wrote about 30-40 articles for the fanzine, that it would be 14 years until we found a permanent home.

What I wrote about was really my reading of local politics, my reading of the various planning processes, analysis of the financial challenges of football at this level and trying to convey this in a simple way to the ordinary fan. So it wasn't typical fanzine satire, it was just a very factual account that I started to write.

I went to a public meeting in the early days of the Dick and Martin era at Hove Town Hall. Martin gave one of his typically strong performances where he updated about getting back from Gillingham, and the bigger long-term vision of getting a permanent home. I'd never met Martin before, but during his piece he said: "If you want to know simply what's happening, read Ian Morley's article in Scars & Stripes." It spurred me on to do more.

After the event I made contact with Martin. I used him for tips on things I was writing, so he was like my source in the club, so material I would write I would email and he'd point me in the right direction where necessary.

DAN TESTER: For most of the two years at Gillingham we outsold the programme and gave all the money to the club, apart from a massive end-of-season piss-up for all our contributors. They were cracking nights in Worthing. All the contributors – about 30-odd people – would congregate in a restaurant, have a great laugh receiving personalised presents from the fanzine crew, and then go back to play football in Darren's lounge. His house wasn't really designed for five-a-side matches and a few things were broken!

In October 1998, Tony Hylands and I went to a meeting at the Paradox nightclub on West Street with Phil Leppard, Alan Davies, Alan Perry (from Bad Manners) and Nick Rowe. The idea was to have a gig - Fans and Bands United - to raise some much needed funds for the Albion. We had two weeks to sort everything! We didn't really have the internet in those days so the marketing machine went into overdrive. We had 5,000 flyers printed and myself and a friend, Scott Goble, went around town dropping them into loads of pubs, shops and the club shop. We had one game at

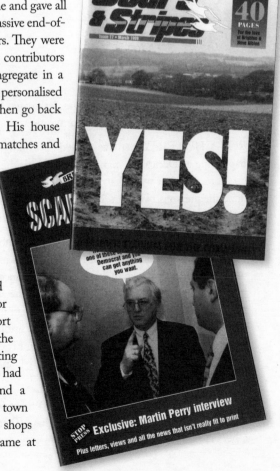

Gillingham too and handed them out on the terraces. *The Argus* helped us push it and *Scars & Stripes* plugged it big time.

On the night, we did one last sweep of town and headed to the venue at six. There was already a queue. The Levellers, Fish Brothers, Fly Kicking Badgers and Too Many Crooks played and it was absolutely amazing. Over a thousand people paid £4 each to get in. The atmosphere was electric and all the bands wore Albion shirts. The Levellers did a cover of Abba's SOS and changed the words to 'Save Our Seagulls'.

A truly fantastic night and we got to present a £4,000 cheque to Dick on the pitch at Gillingham.

Scars & Stripes ran until the first season at Withdean. I didn't have the time anymore. It had done its job. We'd got back to Brighton. It is still the best thing I've ever done; it was exciting, an amazing time.

7. FANS UNITED 2
The Heart of Football

TIM CARDER: Fans United 2 was designated for Valentine's Day 1998. It was called the Heart of Football – a slightly corny title, trying to relate it to Valentine's Day.

ROY CHUTER: When we started at Gillingham, we were finding out what was happening at Doncaster, making friends with them, and the following month we went up there, and that was what triggered their campaign exactly the same way as we had done the previous two years. So, really, the campaign never stopped, it just moved on to other clubs.

ADRIAN NEWNHAM: If ever there was a club that was much more poorly run than we'd ever been it was Doncaster Rovers. They actually had a chairman who was accused of burning down his own main stand for insurance purposes (Ken Richardson was jailed for four years for conspiring to burn down the stand – although no firm motive was proven, it was believed to be financial). He had installed his best mate as the manager and the manager was picking the players he wanted, including somebody who was the relative of a taxi driver who ended up playing in goal for them. He was running the club into the ground. And here we were, actually helping them because we weren't as badly off as they were.

TIM CARDER: There was about 6,400 there for that match, which was by far the largest crowd that we ever had at Gillingham. There were loads of supporters there from other clubs.

ADRIAN NEWNHAM: There was another thousand people at that game thanks to free buses from *The Argus*, who were totally supportive of what we were trying to do. That was surreal as well.

TIM CARDER: The Doncaster fans were quite happy with Attila playing a lot of 'fire' related songs – their owner had been convicted of burning down their main stand – Lynne Truss in *The Times* thought we were having a dig at the Doncaster fans. The Donny fans understood!

ATTILA: We were awful but, of course, Donny did us a favour by being so unbelievably shit, even we couldn't do worse. The goalkeeper for Donny was an enormous bald bloke who looked like a 50-year-old who had managed to empty the whole Greggs franchise in the south of England. It was the worst 0-0 I've ever seen – we had to do a Man of the Match…? Couldn't!

DAN TESTER: For the love of Christ, that is, without doubt, the worst game of football I've ever seen. Michael Mahoney-Johnson? I could have done better than him, with one of my legs chopped off.

TIM CARDER: It was never going to be quite like Fans United 1, but it was certainly the best atmosphere at Gillingham. No 5-0 thumping this time though. But, from the point of view of the bottom of the table it was a decent result.

ED BASSFORD: It was only when the Fans United 2 game was announced that I got my head around the idea of going to Gillingham. Roz and I and the kids went up there which was appalling but it was a campaigning game so you felt that things hadn't changed. From that point onwards we went regularly to Gillingham and we went up on the train, and as a family day out. It developed into something that was actually very, very good.

ADRIAN NEWNHAM: It really helped us, in football circles, that we were helping other people. When you start wanting to get people to support a planning application they are no longer looking at you – 'Poor Brighton' – it was actually, 'here's Brighton, doing something for the benefit of somebody else'.

ROY CHUTER: Portsmouth had a Fans United game. Chester had one against us. York City had one, Bury had similar and at all of them, there were coach loads of Albion fans going… Wrexham was another one. Wrexham, last game of the season in 2004, we went up there and the ground was under real threat at the time and within two minutes all the Albion fans behind the goal were singing: "He's fat, he's round, he only wants the ground, Guterman." He was their chairman and the whole thing just exploded. All the Wrexham fans around us heard us all singing anti-Guterman songs and there was a huge round of applause and they started as well. You've got to get involved in these things.

GRAEME ROLF: No-one will ever forget that awful 0-0 draw we got on Valentine's Day, the worst match of football between two of the worst teams we have ever seen. Then the following year it all started to get a bit better and news of going back to Brighton broke…

8. BRING HOME THE ALBION
Get back to where we started from

MARTIN PERRY: It was so obvious from the moment we got to Gillingham – with the attendances so low – there were great sections of the fan base who were excluded, young people, the elderly, who just couldn't make it. I remember us putting on buses to run people up there – and two of our buses ran into each other!

DICK KNIGHT: Realistically, I thought it was going to take four or five years to build a new stadium, but my first objective was to get the club back in Brighton within three years, inside three years because I wanted that £500,000 back! (£500,000 was a returnable guarantee – a bond – to the Football League that the Albion would be back in Brighton and Hove within three years.) The pyrrhic victory I had was getting Archer to pay half of it, but at the same time it was £250,000 of my money that was better off in the bloody football club.

I had to bring the club back home quickly and as far as I was concerned it had to be within the borders of Brighton and Hove.

LIZ COSTA: Once Dick got really involved then we used to start having meetings with him and he used to come and talk to us quite regularly, telling us how he saw the future, what he wanted to do and how we were going to go about doing it.

ADRIAN NEWNHAM: I used to belong to the old Seagulls mailing list (if you wrote an email it went to everyone on the mailing list). There was a guy on there in the States who had got hold of a consignment of Seagull badges he was trying to sell and he said "Actually, it would be a good idea if we made a pound out of every sale for the club", and I came up with the name "Bring Home the Albion" based on this concept.

We were just festering at Gillingham and it was surprising how little public outcry there was that this football team, with two towns in their name, wasn't playing in either of them.

I went to a midweek game at Cambridge and I spoke to a few people at the game – people like Tim Carder and Liz Costa and some people who were working on *Scars & Stripes* fanzine and said "I've had this idea that perhaps we need to get an awareness campaign – a positive one – getting a roll of pressure in support of the club because at some point the club are going to put an application in to return to Brighton, and if the club have only got 2,000 people at Gillingham we're off to a bit of a poor start".

TIM CARDER: Our supporters, led principally by Adrian Newnham, formed a campaign called Bring Home the Albion, the initial letters, BHA, of course we all are familiar with. That campaign sought to show that the economic wellbeing of the town would improve with the return of the Albion. They went round businesses seeking their views on the subject and the overwhelming feeling was: 'Yes, let's Bring Home the Albion because it will boost our trade'.

ADRIAN NEWNHAM: We had a meeting in The Eclipse with a number of fans' representatives and they said 'Yes, we'll get behind it'.

We picked an away game at Scunthorpe United to put the idea out there on a flyer to everyone who went to the game saying we need your help: we need to mobilise and the intention is to get the people of Brighton and Hove to support the concept.

We picked a day when we didn't have a game and we got banners and flyers printed up and went round to loads of pubs and shops, businesses in Brighton, and tried to get people to put up this poster that displayed 'Bring Home the Albion'.

Somebody mentioned the concept of tying a yellow ribbon, when people have gone off to war you tie a yellow ribbon up somewhere until they come back. Why don't we tie a blue and white ribbon? Tim Carder said; "Have you spoken to anyone in the media?" And I said; "No, who would you speak to in the media? I've got no idea."

Tim arranged a meeting with Adrian Faber who had only just become the editor at the time and somebody called Claire Byrd. Basically, Tim and I went into this meeting pitching to get a few paragraphs in *The Argus* for publicity. Tim said; "Wouldn't it be great if we could get an article."

And I said; "Let's ask for the moon and see what we get."

CLAIRE BYRD: It was a great campaign for someone to bring to the paper and Adrian Faber was really fired up about it and started talking about Battle Buses and convoys. He went into tabloid overdrive.

ADRIAN NEWNHAM: He said "I can see it now... Magnificent Seven ride again" and painted the words in the sky with his hand. He was thinking headlines, angles.

We told them we were looking to go round the town and get people to display posters and that we would create a list of them called

Friends of the Albion which we will circulate through fanzines and supporters' networks.

They wanted to know what else we were going to do and, on the spot, I said we were going to put blue and white ribbons on the monuments. I could see Tim Carder look at me and think "How we going to do this? We haven't even planned for this".

SARAH WATTS: The image of the blue and white ribbons being tied around the statues – I think it was Liz Costa who mounted Steve Ovett.

ADRIAN NEWNHAM: We put some round Steve Ovett's statue in Preston Park. Someone said they would put one round the Peace statue but we thought that was going a bit too far. It was giving picture stories that *The Argus* could use.

LIZ COSTA: There wasn't an agenda, it happened and everybody seemed to fall into whatever this week's campaign or plan was. Somebody came up with an idea and we ran with it. The ultimate aim was – get us home and then we have a base from which to work.

GRAEME ROLF: My Nan, bless her, who died a few years ago, spent ages making those blue and white cross ribbon things and I remember taking a big box up to the club shop for them to give away.

A chap who worked for Gunn's Florists in Sydney Street, I went and saw him and said, "Can you make us a massive great big blue and white ribbon?" I got up at five in the morning on the Saturday. As you come into Brighton you have got those big brick pillars and I got a ladder, put my fluorescent top on, climbed as far as I could go, then used a big splodge of 'grip-fill' to plonk the little cube of wood that this ribbon was attached to, so that as you came into Brighton you could see this huge great ribbon that was stuck on the pylon. (If you look 12 foot up right in the middle, there is a big sort of strange discolouration, that's the grip-fill which is still there to this day.) I went up to Withdean Stadium and tied other ribbons to lamp posts and signs and stuff like that; I sort of worked independently on that.

ADRIAN NEWNHAM: We heard from a lot of businesses that the perception of the anti-Archer campaign was that it was an aggressive, almost a negative campaign and to try and win people over to the Albion returning it needed to be a positive sales campaign. It was about pulling together a plan that had a beginning, a middle and an end, with steps in it that would hopefully build up.

DICK KNIGHT: During the time we were in Gillingham, some people in Brighton & Hove Council hoped that the football club would die, in my view. They thought they'd washed their hands of it. They treated me, and then Martin who came with me, like used car salesmen – not the politicians but the officers in the council. They looked down their authoritarian noses thinking that this football club doesn't belong here… they had the attitude that football belonged to the north of the country, it doesn't sit comfortably here, you know the Downs and southern England.

PAUL HAYWARD: A lot of people who were in positions of power just thought the football club was irrelevant and a relic and the mindset in the town was that the glory days were over, this club was just sort of hanging around on the fringes and could be ignored.

I spoke to councillors who perhaps weren't from Sussex who thought; "Why are you making such a fuss about the football club? Why does it matter so much?" And, you had to explain to them over and over again it was in the fabric of the town and the county, and all they needed to do was to recognise its importance and give it a chance to grow again. I doubted personally that it ever would…

DICK KNIGHT: Steve Bassam was the leader of the council at that time and it was only when Tim Carder presented a petition of 34,000 names in support of the club coming back to Brighton that he began to realise that this was a powerful force that I had at my disposal. I said: "If you think this is impressive you wait to see what I can conjure up, to make your people understand this is an important part of the culture of these towns." Steve got on board quite quickly. He was a cricket man, but he began to believe that the Albion was so much more in this community than he had realised.

MARTIN PERRY: We said to ourselves there is absolutely no way we are going to survive even the three years in Gillingham – we had put up a bond with the Football League to say we would be back in Brighton within the three years, so there was a chunk of money tied up there… But, it was very obvious in terms of attendances that we had to get back as soon as possible. And, so it was agreed that the first job was to start looking around Brighton and see if we could find a temporary solution for us to play. We looked at various sites: the cricket ground, Withdean, the Greyhound Stadium, Waterhall, Sheepcote Valley.

ADRIAN NEWNHAM: It quickly became clear that the favourite was Withdean Stadium. I went to Withdean when the Brighton B52s played the University of Los Angeles and there were 12,000 there, I went to a school sports day there and I also remember going to see the Wombles there when I was kid. As a site it is well known in Brighton and capacity should never have been a problem, given what we had put up with previously.

MARTIN PERRY: I remember coming to Withdean and it was a crumbling athletics track, weeds growing up between the seats, it wouldn't comply with any safety regulations but, the pitch was big enough, and it was a football pitch – of a sort! None of the other sites had any of the facilities; we would have had to start from scratch. And I remember looking at Withdean, with my then girlfriend, and saying "Can we do it?" And she said: "You've got to do it, you've got to bring the club back otherwise it will go under".

We thought it was going to be relatively simple – it needed upgrading, but it least it's a stadium. And we talked to Steve Bassam, and he thought it was going to be relatively simple – he agreed we had to come back. And, when he put it to the council members, I think he honestly thought that nobody would argue with it, so we were all completely taken by surprise when the local residents were up in arms.

STEVE BASSAM: I have got a feeling it might have been against someone like Brentford, at half-time I was in the sort of Gillingham Boardroom talking to various people including Martin and Dick and I said: "The club has got to go back to Brighton, it can't go on like this, it's going to die and the answer is Withdean." I think they had been thinking along the same lines, is there anywhere we can put a temporary stadium to bring the club back? And I think it was at that stage I said let's have a look at Withdean then, let's do it so we went on a little site visit. When we looked at Withdean Stadium they went "Well, we could be able to make this work". And we did.

BOB BRUCE: I am the principal solicitor of Brighton Council, I deal with all the major projects; my core job is dealing with the big things, like the football club, Amex building, the Dome, Jubilee Library all that sort of stuff. When Steve Bassam was leader of the council of Brighton before it merged into Brighton and Hove – he is a passionate football fan of BHA – he said that if, as it seemed likely at the time, he became leader of the city council, one of his number one projects was to get a ground for the football club. So I sort of found out about how things had gone wrong on the Goldstone Ground, how people like Archer and Bellotti took the ground from under the feet of the club, so I was involved from, I suppose, it would have been about 1996.

There weren't any other serious contenders for the temporary ground other than Withdean, not that the club discussed with the council anyway. There wasn't anything else we could offer – it's our only suitable facility really.

ADRIAN NEWNHAM: One thing that really shocked me, though, was how many of the councillors were against it initially. I remember going to an open meeting of the Labour Party and three Labour councillors spoke out against it. One, allegedly an Albion fan, spoke out very vociferously. He kept saying; "It's a council owned property. We are not going to do anything to support a commercial venture."

TIM HERBERT: I never thought we would not return to Brighton. We were always going to do it, even if it took 15 years. I would trek around wherever we had to go to, nomadic style, if we were a nomadic club for a few years – fine, we will end up back in Brighton at some point. I don't know how Wimbledon fans must have felt, did they always have that feeling of doom, or did they have that feeling that I always had, that it was always only temporary?

TIM CARDER: Adrian and I had a meeting with Ivor Caplin (Labour MP for Hove at the time), to discuss tactics on how we could help the campaign to Bring Home the Albion. Ivor suggested a petition.

ADRIAN NEWNHAM: I met with Steve Bassam and told him we were doing a petition. He said; "It's easy to object to a planning application. We get stacks of objections to them, but nobody ever supports them."

So I said; "Well, OK, if we can get six or seven thousand that would be great."

TIM CARDER: Some people questioned it at the time, how are we going to collect so many signatures? We only get 1,500 people at Gillingham.

ADRIAN NEWNHAM: We ended up with 32,000 signatures which at the time was the biggest ever petition in support of a planning application. Tim Carter did some analysis using postcodes and worked out every ward would go marginal if everybody who signed the petition voted purely on whether the councillor they voted for was in favour of the stadium. We had enough to overturn everybody's vote. Even the most popular councillors would lose seats if everybody would switch their allegiance – you've got that sway in every ward.

TIM CARDER: All the forms were handed back to me, and me and my Mum used to analyse them. We used to divide them into areas: wards around Withdean Stadium, the rest of Brighton and Hove, Sussex, southern England, etc, etc. And we were pleased to find there was a fair proportion of residents in Withdean signing our petition to bring the Albion home.

I was working for a printing company at the time, so it was actually very useful throughout the campaigning, to have ready access to printing materials. I arranged them in binders with an insert in the front that we were able to spell out the words 'Bring Home the Albion', so it made a nice picture of us presenting 32,000 signatures to Lord Bassam.

ADRIAN NEWNHAM: At that point I met Chris Jones for the first time. He was getting involved with the club about producing a survey of the fans which would dismiss the myth that all football fans were working class, factory workers or unemployed with low IQs. 'Actors to architects, undertakers to underwriters, deacons to decorators', that there was a complete spectrum of Albion supporters. People who would read the *Daily Sport*, and people who would read the *Daily Telegraph*. It covered everything from occupation, spending habits. There were 1,200 responses, which is more than enough to make it statistically relevant.

From that we were able to come up with financial statements about what bringing home the Albion would deliver. I think we said it would deliver something like £3m to the town in one year. And that was based on proper stats of what would be spent by away fans in hotels, what would be spent in bars and restaurants, what would be spent in shops and what people would be spending if they were going elsewhere, and how that money then recycled into the economy. It starts to create a really compelling financial argument for what a football club can deliver.

SWEAT

TIM CARDER: We were actually quite pleased, in some way, when we heard of the existence of the Save Withdean Environment Action Team, SWEAT, because at least it embodied opposition with the Withdean area. They made arguments in *The Argus*, they delivered leaflets around the area and we, and the club, were able to respond to their arguments.

ADRIAN NEWNHAM: They'd started off on the premise that all football fans were thugs and there were stories about how people will urinate in your gardens and decapitate your dogs and it was quite vicious stuff. What really annoyed me was they had said that Preston Park station was Brighton's very own Hillsborough in the making. That it was inadequate to cope with the number of football fans who were going to use it and that crushes would ensue. For anybody to use what is the worst disaster in British football history as some kind of gain for their own public ends was just repulsive.

PAUL WHELCH: There were a lot of Withdean residents that I think thought that Manchester United were coming to town, or something, and they got very, very aggravated about it. There was a meeting at Hove Town Hall where Martin was sort of saying that the time spent at Withdean by the local football club will be less than 1% of the year, at which one local resident jumped up and said, that is 1% too many and there was a lot of sort of bitching about it.

I decided that the most important thing was to counter it because my parents' home was in Withdean, ten minutes from the ground, so I was clear there would be a lot of people in Withdean who wanted to support the club. So what we did was to form a little pressure group called

Withdean Invites the Seagulls Home, or WISH, and our objective was to just really get the publicity to explain that actually there is another view here.

ADRIAN NEWNHAM: There was a meeting of WISH that was held at the Preston Park Hotel and it was like a meeting of Alcoholics Anonymous. There were all these people who had come along, not knowing who else was going to be there. Actually, about a hundred turned up to this meeting and Tim Carder put a map of Withdean on the wall showing a red dot for all the signatures of people who had supported the petition. It was like Withdean had been given an attack of measles with all these red dots on the map. You could see these people beginning to feel quite good that they were no longer this lonely person.

PAUL WHELCH: So we established WISH as the positive face really, when it came to the whole planning issue it was important to have a counterweight to the local residents in SWEAT, to show there were divided views amongst local residents.

Planning Application

JAN SWALLOW: There was a councillor on the City Council who said everyone will want to park very close to the ground as "the ladies will have their hairdos ruined if they have to walk too far". She had this wonderful image of coiffeured ladies with handbags. tripping along to the ground. They're living in another planet these people, they really are.

TIM CARDER: In the spring of 1998 the planning application was with Brighton & Hove Council. There were two aspects to our campaign at the time. There was the petition, which was ongoing in support of the application, but we also felt we had to write letters to the council in support of the application.

It transpired that we were being out-written by the opponents of the Albion moving to Withdean – something like two to one against the Albion's application. We knew that we had to ramp up the letter writing. So, although it seemed a bit harsh at the time perhaps I came up with this leaflet which accused supporters of killing the Albion unless they wrote a letter to the council.

Let's face it, it took five minutes, an envelope, and then I think it was then 20 pence for a stamp. We handed leaflets out at matches, which garnered a bit more support for the campaign. In the end, what we decided to do was to provide pre-printed letters, with stamped envelopes in case the 20p was putting supporters off the task in hand.

TIM HERBERT: I got writer's cramp from writing so many letters too. Well, I can't even remember who I wrote them to now! It felt like it was the same old thing, that was the frustrating thing, that you were banging on writing the same letter to somebody else and then somebody else again, but the fact that so many thousands of people did it really helped out I think. I felt quite politically empowered because I'm not a very political person. That was the core goal to get the Albion back home first and foremost, and then to get them a new stadium.

ADRIAN NEWNHAM: In June 1998 the first council planning committee hearing took place and all of the planning committee councillors are there. The Withdean residents turned up in absolute droves, tried to disrupt the meeting, tried calling points of order, holding banners, protesting. There were all these football supporters in suits and ties, sitting there nicely and politely and all these Withdean residents hurling abuse at the councillors, being threatened with being kicked out the chamber. It was quite surreal to watch. Monty Pythonesque.

The club had already started to think about the benefits of community involvement, particularly in education, to the planning application – education through football has got so many facets to it. It can be used to support Maths lessons, can be used to support English lessons. So much was put through into the education side that councillors who normally showed no interest at all in the Albion – like Pat Hawkes, who was chair of the Education Subcommittee – started to think there is something to this application. It's not purely around a football club.

TIM CARDER: It was quite a tense day at Hove Town Hall. Councillors who decide applications are not allowed to express an opinion on the matter until the time of the meeting, so until you actually hear them speaking you're not clear which way they're going to go.

STEVE BASSAM: When the thing went to planning committee I recommended to the council that there needs to be a three-year deal, but I did smile as I said it because I knew it would take longer than three years to get a permanent site and get planning permission and I was not wrong.

It wasn't universally popular amongst the council and I wasn't universally popular for wanting to do it, but once we decided that was what we wanted to do, we made it happen. The Labour group was fine, the council itself was less fine. You get blockages amongst officers from time to time. There was some opposition, too, from Withdean Councillors and the Tory group, they didn't like it being there. I think some saw it as a deliberate Labour ploy to put the problem into their backyard.

ADRIAN NEWNHAM: The colour of the council was quite significant. If we hadn't been able to persuade the Labour Party, with the petition and the business focus, then I suspect we would have needed a Seagulls Party a lot earlier than we did.

TIM CARDER: There were actually four council meetings. The planning application was itself important, and we won that ten votes to two. But, we also needed the permission of the council as the landlord for the use of Withdean Stadium – and that vote was actually a little bit closer, so this was the council saying "Yes, you have permission to use our stadium for league football". And that was also a little bit tense – there were more councillors this time speaking against the proposal. I think they tended to be the ward councillors for the area, but we got past that hurdle.

So, it got through the council, everything was looking rosy again, but the question at that time was would SWEAT take it to a judicial review? They did, they lodged papers in the High Court, perhaps three weeks later, and it certainly went before a judge, but in July 1998, we learnt that they had withdrawn the application. I think it was for financial reasons; the council were prepared to defend, and the matter was dropped, so that gave the green light for the Albion to enter into agreements with the council.

Converting Withdean

STEVE BASSAM: The original idea was that the Albion would come back halfway through the season but I think Martin and co decided that actually it wasn't such a clever idea to do that, even though they were desperate to come back and have more fans watch. The economics of it made sense to finish out a season and I think there were some technical issues with the stadium that they had to resolve.

MARTIN PERRY: We then went into negotiations with the company who then ran Withdean, Ecovert, and those negotiations were extremely difficult. And I remember Steve Bassam getting very frustrated and bringing us all together and banging our heads together. The basis of the deal was that we wouldn't pay rent for the stadium, but we would upgrade. We would eventually hand back to the council a legacy in the form of a much-improved stadium – which it is! So we paid for actual running costs, not rent – and that was the deal. And it was a good deal, it got us back within two years of leaving, so we got the release of the bond.

Then we were faced with the task of actually getting the stadium ready. McAlpine came in and sorted everything, One of their main sub-contractors was Adenstar, which is Derek Chapman's company, and they performed absolutely brilliantly.

ADRIAN HOLDSTOCK: We were the ones who converted the athletics track into the football stadium and I think we were appointed in 1997 for that. My director, Andy, was the architect who did all the planning work, and the design work, for the permanent North Stand, and all the temporary stands that used to be dismantled every summer and shipped off to Scotland for the golf.

The brief was obviously to conform to Football League requirements, the minimum Football League requirements because they didn't have a lot of cash.

MARTIN PERRY: January to July 1999 was an incredibly short period to convert the stadium and a couple of weeks before we were due to complete people were asking whether we'd make it or not, but I knew we would, though it would be tight. It was absolutely flat out. One day Dick turned to me and said: "Would you like to come full-time?" And, I suppose I felt my job at McAlpine was done, and I was thinking what's next for me? And there were various other reasons why a life change actually suited me and so I said that I would love to come. And, I can honestly say that I have never once regretted that decision; it's been a rollercoaster ride, it's been fantastically hard work and it's been frustrating but immensely rewarding. My favourite expression has always been "you'll never guess what's happened now…"

TIM CARDER: The dates got put back until the start of the 1999/2000 season. It was frustrating. Jeff Wood became manager, the form nosedived and we ended up plummeting down the table, and the end of that season was pretty dire. Jeff Wood was sacked after, I think, 11 matches and Micky Adams took over. He made his first public appearance with a 'Yes Yes' T-shirt on at Hove Town Hall, to fantastic applause.

We saw out the season. The last bus to Gillingham was a bit of a party bus, it was quite good fun, the last time we would have to do 75 miles there and 75 miles back, we had made it through two years and now we were going to come home to Withdean.

9. LOOKING FOR A PERMANENT HOME
Home is where the heart is

PAUL WHELCH: We realised from an early stage while we were at Gillingham that the club had to get on with finding a new permanent home.

MARTIN PERRY: The search for Withdean taught us how to do it – we'll look at a number of sites, we'll have to demonstrate why we chose the one we want – it's a process in planning terms that we call the sequential analysis, comparing sites and working out which is the best one.

DICK KNIGHT: For our new permanent home, we carried out this huge evaluation of all the potential sites, 16 I think, out as far as Lancing, Shoreham cement works and Newhaven. For the good of our identity, I really needed it to be in Brighton and Hove.

TIM CARDER: If I had a magic wand and you asked me where I would want the stadium, I would have said next to Brighton station. I do like city centre locations for stadia like Newcastle. I'm not in great favour of edge-of-town sites. But I think ours is the best site we could have got – it has been proven it is the only site we could have developed a stadium on, but had things been different I think next to Brighton station was my choice… it was a serious site at one time.

TIM HERBERT: I always thought Waterhall was the best because every time I drove down to Hove you'd pass this big bowl that had nothing in it and I thought let's stick the ground in there; I didn't really know about any of the intricate details. But once Falmer was the preferred option I was 100% behind it.

STEFAN SWIFT: Throughout my time of watching the Albion, there was always some sort of plan. Even in 1992 there was a plan in *The Evening Argus* for a new stadium at Waterhall. In fact, a friend of ours found a supplement that came with the 1983 Cup Final edition. I think the headline was 'Bamber's Waterhall Dream'. It was enclosed, had a roof and was going to have ice-skating in the evenings and a shopping mall but that never came to anything. My Dad says that all through the 1970s there was always a new plan that was being mooted in *The Argus* every so often – possibly just to sell papers. It was always Waterhall and Toad Hall Valley that came up.

ANDY NAYLOR: I never saw Falmer as being the perfect site. I was actually brought up in Woodingdean and it always struck me that from the point of view of road links and stuff that it wouldn't be the perfect place. I always thought that Waterhall seemed the most logical place for the stadium.

DEREK CHAPMAN: Waterhall, you'd think, is the absolute logical place until you start looking; for instance, it's on the railway line but Network Rail said they could never build a station on the line because it's the busiest line in the country – so when people say "you build a railway station, you put the park and ride there, you put the stadium and a supermarket pays for it, easy isn't it?" It's not!

I would say the three best sites in Brighton are Waterhall, Falmer and Sheepcote. If you did a proper scoring matrix on matters of accessibility, cost, who owns the land then probably none of them would get ten out of ten. Falmer is probably eight, Waterhall is probably seven and Sheepcote is probably six so that's the sort of situation we were in.

I knew the Falmer site because I am from here. I lived in Coombe Road when I was small, went to school at Stanmer and I live a mile away now so it's really right where I have grown up.

DICK KNIGHT: Waterhall was in the designated part of the new South Downs National Park. Falmer on the other hand had a train station and a good 'A' road running right past it… it was the only sensible choice.

MARTIN PERRY: A lady called Maggie Deacon said; "I know where the stadium should be." We went up to Village Way and looked across the site and I said to her, and these are my actual words: "You must be fucking joking!" But she said; "Look where the station is, look where the buses are, look at the access – put the park-and-rides in, it would be great". I pointed out that it would overlap onto university land but she said the university need to redevelop their buildings, university funding is tight, so there is a deal to be struck.

I went back several times and I thought she might be right. And I talked to our architects, and they came down and they produced a sketch and they said yeah, it could work, and they said you'd need that land by the university.

ADRIAN HOLDSTOCK: We started a sequential test of the major sites in and around Brighton to determine which were likely to be the most appropriate without any favourites at all.

We looked at Waterhall, we looked at Falmer, we looked at Toad's Hole, we looked at Shoreham Harbour, we looked at the railway station site, we looked at the Greyhound track. We did eventually look at Shoreham Airport as well and there was a suggestion in the second public inquiry to go to the quarry north of Shoreham – Upper Beeding.

Essentially we had to ask 'is a site big enough?' And, 'can you get people to and from it?' So some of the sites were actually quite easily dismissible; we actually looked at Withdean as well but Withdean obviously had some difficulties with capacity with the railway arch, there is a maximum number of people you can get through there, you need the access. Falmer came up on top simply because it is within the A27 corridor within the conurbation of Brighton, it has excellent transport links in terms of the A27 and trains, it also has a

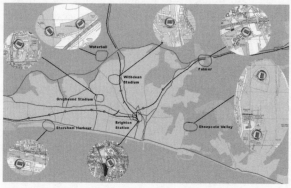

reasonably good connection with the local communities of Bevendean, Coldean, Moulsecoomb.

The trouble with things like Shoreham is you couldn't gain access to it. Waterhall is in the middle of a green belt, and there is no train link, very little pedestrian links and there is only one little tunnel at the end of the road on the way in. The railway station site was about to be given consent for apartments and retail, Toad's Hole was quite good but there was no railway access etc. The site of the Greyhound Stadium was too small, there is no railway access to the racecourse. It became relatively clear fairly early on that Falmer was going to be the best option.

We prepared diagrams and there were other consultants, transport consultants and planning consultants that put together a list of all the policy issues and the transport issues related to each of the sites.

ED BASSFORD: Part of my job at work was to comment on the planning application. The first planning application I saw at East Sussex County Council relating to the new stadium was Bellotti's infamous back of the envelope job, which we frankly laughed at. It was simply not a planning application; the club had done absolutely not enough to get it taken seriously. But, that actually sullied the waters as far as the local authority was concerned because their experience of the Albion and these planning applications were set by that early one and they thought 'who are these people, their track record is bad, bad for planning?' So they started, I think, with a bit of an obstacle to climb.

DICK KNIGHT: What I inherited was not only the immediate baggage of Archer and his regime. In the council's eyes it went way back to, dare I say it, the Mike Bamber days all the way back – because of what happened then. First of all there was never any dialogue between the club and the council – then he wanted them to build the Albion a stadium when the club was in the top division, but they were having none of it.

MARTIN PERRY: We were starting to prepare the planning application for Falmer. And a planning application of that nature is pretty big. When we got the scheme worked up our planning consultant said: "This is going to be interesting... We think we ought to run this across a planning barrister." And so they brought down Jonathan Clay. I walked Jonathan around the
site and he stood and looked at it from all sorts of angles for more or less the whole day... We were stood down by the station and he looked across, and he was very quiet, then he said: "It's very bold isn't it?" And, I said "Yeah... But, can we do it?" And, he said: "Yeah, we can win this one, but I don't think it's going to be easy."

And so we took the decision to go for it – I don't think any of us thought it was going to be quite as difficult as it really was! But, we knew we were breaking new ground here. And so it started...

So we went to the council and said "I think we have found the site", and we showed them and they said can you plot it and we will take it to our members. So we did.

BOB BRUCE: The Local Plan is the council planning document; so, basically, if you have got a planning proposal one way you can help develop it to have a chance of getting permission is give it an allocation in the Local Plan, so by allocating the Falmer site in the Local Plan it effectively meant that, from a planning point of view, it was a strong starting point.

MARTIN PERRY: Somebody in the council leaked the plan and the next thing we knew it was in *The Argus* and my heart sank... It was another 'You'll never guess what's happened now'. One of the things about working in a football club is that you do work in a goldfish bowl, it's not like running a normal business, everything that you do is analysed, and so the moment we stick something in that's a bit controversial there are headlines.

DICK KNIGHT: Martin and I were a very good team because he could deal with these interminable meetings we had with the council, his experience of these committee-type gatherings was one of the reasons I brought him in… and we often played good-cop/bad-cop in these meetings – usually I was the bad cop. We needed them to gain respect for the club and what we were trying to do. Martin gradually got to know certain council officers – who were all important as far as we were concerned – and that worked.

MARTIN PERRY: The reaction to the idea generally wasn't too bad. We said it's the only site that's good… look at the public transport, we could come up with a sustainable plan that will work, and they said we'd have to produce a report which shows how this works, a brief paper that looks at all sites – and we did. And we submitted it, and in fairness to them they said "Yeah, it's good" and they showed us how they wanted the report tweaked and we adjusted it and they helped us build the paper, and people were swung over, they were now backing us.

DICK KNIGHT: We were dealing with a planning system that is incredibly inefficient. We couldn't put our planning application for Falmer together until we resolved big issues, for example with the University of Brighton over the land.

ED BASSFORD: I saw the Falmer planning application in its first form, and some of the supporting papers on transport, and I was asked to comment. There were a couple of us who were involved in looking at them who were Albion fans and we did have a conversation that started as a transport professionals conversation saying 'its not very convincing is it', 'they need to do a lot of work', 'is this the transport infrastructure there', 'it's all very well saying Falmer is next to the railway station, but is it going to work?'

I have to say that I think those of us who read the documentation weren't very convinced at that stage. But, as I got more and more involved in the campaigning, and in the debates and discussions that were going on within the club, and conversations through the Falmer For All team, it became quite clear to me that, genuinely, the club realised that it did have to overcome the objections that were being formulated about the plans and they were seriously committed to doing that.

10. THE YES YES CAMPAIGN
Listen to the people

TIM CARDER: There was also a leaflet printed by myself, backed by the Supporters' Club, BISA, *Scars & Stripes* fanzine and it was called 'Time To Turn Up The Heat' – this was a letter that we printed out for fans to send off to Lord Bassam, who was the council leader at the time, requesting, asking, pleading the council to find a permanent solution for the Albion's homelessness problem. As a result of that Lord Bassam invited myself and Adrian Newnham along to a meeting at Brighton Town Hall and said: "I'm thinking of holding a referendum into the idea…" Because, essentially, that would give the council public backing to their quest to find the Albion a new home and to ask the public what they thought about the Albion's preferred option of constructing a stadium at Falmer.

ADRIAN NEWNHAM: Tim and I walked out the room absolutely gobsmacked. I remember Tim saying: "This is winnable but it will be hard work."

TIM CARDER: Bassam's idea of the referendum went ahead; it was going to be held on local council polling day which was May 6th 1999.

IAN MORLEY: The news came as a bolt out the blue. The council had historically been slow to really embrace the Albion cause. On top of this, there were different voices in both the ruling Labour group, and the Opposition Conservative group, on both the extent to which the council should take an overt role in helping the Albion, and, more importantly, to what extent Falmer was the right site. Therefore the referendum allowed Bassam to achieve two objectives; get support of the public, and take the councillors with him.

STEVE BASSAM: The question of whether the council should be involved with this is very important too, because it meant then that if it was 'Yes', the council really had a stronger than moral obligation, it had a political obligation to work with the club to ensure that the stadium was developed. It enabled us to get a clear message over to the people, the city. This was their moment and if they wanted a club that badly, then they had to vote for it. It was a risk, but it was a risk well worth taking.

IAN MORLEY: The government, in that day, had decided to provide a vehicle for local councils to get feedback from the electorate by doing 'advisory referendums'. And, of course, Steve Bassam, Leader of the Council, being the opportunist politician, obviously leapt upon this to help the Albion, but also to get a great headline for him as being the first authority in the UK that ran a referendum for people to show their feelings.

ADRIAN NEWNHAM: Tim and I went to see Dick Knight, to find him absolutely up in arms. "How dare they have a referendum over something as important as this? This is our planning application!

Let there be a Cathedral of Sport in the City by the Sea.

Permanent stadi… wanted… local he… Vot… Yes, Y…

Let our youngsters fulfil their field of dreams. Vote Yes, Yes.

FALM… FOR A…

You can make The Referendu…

FALMER FOR ALL

You can make The Referendum count - 6th May.

Why are people playing politics with our application?"

Tim and I sat there very quietly and decided it wasn't a good idea to let on that we had heard about this two days previously. The message did sink home that it was the right thing to do – you have got what is fundamentally a huge political decision because there is so little land in Brighton and Hove that any site is going to have to be very carefully viewed.

STEVE BASSAM: We'd decided to have a referendum in that set of local elections, on two questions, and I think the fact that it was two questions was right.

1) Do you support Brighton & Hove council's policy of giving a home to Brighton & Hove Albion?

2) Do you support that being at Falmer?

We were criticised to limiting it to one site and I said; "No, it makes it much better to focus, we can deal with other sites if they reject it."

TIM CARDER: We felt that most people would support the first question. The second was much more controversial… Even at that time people were expressing opposition to the prospect of a stadium at Falmer; the local Green Party had supported the homecoming to Withdean but were against the building of a stadium at Falmer. Friends of the Earth, and the majority of Falmer villagers, were against it, Lewes District Council had come out against it.

DICK KNIGHT: After the council realised we had this huge support, Steve Bassam called a referendum in May 1999 to gauge feelings towards a permanent home in Brighton, and specifically at Falmer… and also to boost the turnout in Brighton and Hove for the local elections. Steve, no fool, realised that if they stuck a referendum about the Albion on the back end of the voting form he'd get more people to turn out, and that's what happened.

ADRIAN NEWNHAM: Then somebody said; "Actually, how do you fight a referendum?" And nobody had ever fought one before. We were only just coming to terms with how to understand planning applications. So, Paul Samrah and myself, and I think it might have been Martin Perry, went to meet the council solicitor and sat down with her and asked what is the law about fighting a referendum? And, basically, she told us there is no limit on funds, as there is on a normal election. You can set yourself up as a campaign but please be careful on what colours you pick. Don't fight as blue because that upsets the Conservatives and then we couldn't even use purple at that time because a councillor had defected from Labour to Scottish Nationalist and he was fighting under purple.

As we left the room she said: "Please be sensible. The last thing I want as a council solicitor is a legal challenge on this at the end of the day."

TIM CARDER: The referendum campaign was really an extension of the meetings between supporters – representatives, if you like – and the Board. It was called the 'Yes Yes' campaign because we wanted two 'yeses' to the answers to the two questions.

The chair of that campaign was *Scars & Stripes* fanzine writer Ian Morley. He was backing up the initiatives of the letters and the forms regarding the Local Plan by writing why we needed to do this; he was very good in what he was doing, and he took the initiative and took the chair at these meetings.

IAN MORLEY: It was clear to me that this was a huge challenge for the supporters who were, by this point, weary after years of battles with Archer and Bellotti and, more recently, fighting to get approval for the move to Withdean.

I decided to step forward and try and organise a group of people to run the campaign. I got in touch with Martin and started to discuss my ideas. Having, from a very young age, hung around local politics doing stuff for my Dad – posters, knocking on doors, canvassing etc. etc. – I thought I had something to add.

I arranged to get the key people around the table. I can remember that day really well, it was a Sunday at Liz Costa's office near Brighton station and anybody that was anybody who'd been on the edges of helping the campaign was there, there was probably about 20 of us in a room.

The club and the fans were one organisation. It was fascinating seeing how Dick and Martin worked with the different fans' leaders.

ADRIAN NEWNHAM: By the time we came to the referendum campaign I think there was an understanding of what we as fans could do, and that we could be trusted to work for what was the best interest of the football club. That there was a business logic to what we were doing, that we were business people who knew how to organise things without doing silly things.

Ian had this military brain for how things could and should happen. His Dad was a Labour councillor and knew how to get people out canvassing. What works? Does a van with speakers on the roof work? Actually, it does if you go round at the right time and in the right locations. How do you get permission from Asda to turn up on their doorstep and hand out leaflets? How do you get into George Street to leaflet? He knew all of these things and had an absolute brass neck as well. It was superb. He just got that campaign by the scruff of the neck and got people organised and got them running it. He was brilliant.

IAN MORLEY: It wasn't about just winning because I guess we thought we'll get over 50%, but we knew that we needed to win convincingly. We thought we needed to get 80% in the first one, and two thirds in the second.

We had to try to educate the whole population of Brighton and Hove on what the referendum stood for, and, more importantly, why we needed for them to vote 'yes'. The turnout for these local elections is diabolical so that was the challenge ahead of us; the

45

plan was essentially to utilise our best asset, our fanbase. Plus, win the hearts and minds by some pretty creative campaigning.

We decided at quite an early stage to be ambitious. We will leaflet drop the town twice, organise set piece events in the town and also make sure we drove home a positive message via the media throughout the campaign.

We also needed to raise money. This level of campaigning did not come for nothing. Given that we had lost most of our fanbase because we were now playing at Gillingham – this was a tall order. However, the fans – yet again – put their hands in their pockets, to such an extent that one of the leaflet drops we were able to pay for via the Post Office.

TIM CARDER: The principal tools were two leaflets that the club had printed explaining the proposals for the stadium at Falmer, explaining why the club needs a permanent home and secondly, why that permanent home needs to be at Falmer. Now, we could have employed the Post Office to deliver all those leaflets for us but we chose not to. We knew that supporters were champing at the bit to help out, so we asked supporters to deliver those leaflets for us. I took it upon myself to organise that part of the campaign. I drew maps, hundreds and hundreds of maps for leafleting rounds, roughly 100 to 200 leaflets a round which I reckoned would take an hour's walk.

IAN MORLEY: Tim is one of the most diligent and organised men I have ever worked with. He masterminded how to cut up Brighton, off a map of the whole of Brighton, the roads that needed doing. Two hundred people turned up on a Sunday morning and got bundles of leaflets, and this was like proper political campaigning.

PAUL SAMRAH: Tim managed the whole thing, it was fantastic – it was a work of art. It would've cost thousands to pay the Post Office to deliver stuff. It's phenomenal – that's what we had within our campaign group, we had someone that would deliver every bloody time.

TIM CARDER: We met at the Excelsior Hotel on Hove seafront, which has now been demolished, on Sunday mornings; we would give people the right number of leaflets by weight! (It was a lot easier than counting them.) We would give the supporters a map of what round we wanted them to do and send them off. It was a real communal event. Some people were coming on the Sunday morning, doing a round, then coming back and doing another round!

ADRIAN NEWNHAM: We opened at 9 o'clock in the morning. We had people queuing up at 8 because they wanted to get certain routes. By about 11 am, somebody is going to have to do Elm Grove, whether you like it or not.

We had 400 people come through the door. Political parties don't get 400 people coming through the door, but here were people saying; "We want to do this. This is what we can do."

STEFAN SWIFT: I remember just delivering leaflets, loads of leaflets. I've got the T-shirt still somewhere but I looked a bit too much like Liz Costa when I put it on.

ROY CHUTER: I was in London Road, handing out green balloons and leaflets and this military looking old chap came marching up towards us and I thought he's not going to want a balloon, so I tried to give him a leaflet and he said: "Is that about Association Football?" "Yes, it's about bringing the Albion back to Brighton and eventually playing at Falmer." And he said: "I disapprove of this entirely. If it was rugger, or cricket, or golf, then rather, but not Association Football."

IAN MORLEY: The other thing we did a hell of a lot of was PR and publicity, so we used the local media really cleverly. This is where you get Dick's expertise being a media man, a master of marketing. 'Falmer For All' was the campaign catchphrase and, of course, that came from Dick. The notion of making the logo green to take on the sceptics head on was, of course, naturally Dick's.

PAUL CAMILLIN: I remember sitting in the Grand Hotel with Micky Adams, who Dick had just brought in as manager, who was being unveiled at a Hove Town Hall public meeting that evening, wearing a Yes Yes T-shirt, which was on the front page of *The Argus* the next day. Typical Dick, the old PR engine, full steam ahead.

IAN MORLEY: The week leading up we had a full-on schedule: we had an aeroplane flying across Brighton, we had banners going up across the town. The spirit was fantastic and, I guess, all of it would have been on top of our day jobs. I haven't got a clue how I did it. Certainly, for a couple of months, the vast majority of our time in our day jobs was spent on this.

TIM CARDER: As the actual day of the referendum approached, we started to be out on the streets campaigning. We hired an old, open-top South Downs vintage bus and we took the team around on the top of this bus. Adrian Newnham had a loudhailer and he called out 'vote Yes Yes on 6th May!' We went around Whitehawk, Moulsecoomb, several council estates where we were trying to get people out that we thought would be supportive of the cause and who might not otherwise come out to vote in council elections. But, the poor old bus struggled up Coldean Lane. We had to modify the route in the end to get it to go up slightly less steep hills.

The advert on the side of the bus said 'Come and visit the beautiful South Downs!' I would argue that we're not building on the beautiful South Downs itself, we were building on the fringe of the beautiful South Downs. The fact that this bus was adorned with this advert I found slightly ironic. We found a big 'Yes Yes' banner which we managed to drape over the advert.

ADRIAN NEWNHAM: People had written to all the managers of the Football League saying can you give support for the new stadium. From some of them you got standard letters – 'Sam Allardyce has asked me to respond in support of the planning application…' Then we got the most fantastic letter from Alex Ferguson, who wrote this superb letter about how important a football club was to the local community. Now, if ever there was a guy who could have said 'I am too busy' it was him!

PAUL SAMRAH: We managed to get hold of a minibus that got rigged out with loud speakers, so we spent four days touring Brighton and Hove with a megaphone, including round to Woodingdean, somewhat ironic going all the way into enemy territory.

ADRIAN NEWNHAM: Then during the week of the referendum we hired a video van. Basically, a van with a giant video on the side – and we played the planning application video – Right Here, Right Now by Fatboy Slim with the stadium, in its first guise of appearing out of thin air.

We managed to get this new technology (at that stage) and get it into Asda car park, and outside Churchill Square.

IAN MORLEY: We decided that we needed to wake Brighton up on the morning of the referendum and called it 'Operation Morning Surprise'. So the idea was 'how do you get the news headlines on the day?' You've got to think what our biggest asset was and our biggest asset was the number of people we had. So we told a whole load of people there was a secret undercover mission. We did this in the weeks leading up via the people who had been leafleting but also at games. There was a little bit of suspense and intrigue around it, which obviously helped.

The plan was to ensure that when everyone in Brighton and Hove woke up on the morning of the referendum day, all they they saw was a mass of green balloons with 'Vote Yes' on them.

We even managed to get hold of biodegradable balloons, because we couldn't have the headlines the next day saying we'd made some environmental crisis. And we had really clear instructions saying where you could and could not put them.

LIZ COSTA: Everybody was asked to turn up with either a stool or a set of steps, a pair of scissors and a piece of string. Nobody knew what the hell they were going to be in for and they were all given a map and a bag of balloons and told to go and hang them up. At 9 o'clock at night they were told to put them up; not before, because all the political campaigning from all the various parties had stopped by then. So we were going around absolutely everywhere, every street had these 'Yes Yes' balloons.

IAN MORLEY: We even worked out where the local radio presenters lived that did the breakfast shows and their route to work. We did the same for the editors of the local press.

JAN SWALLOW: I did Seven Dials, the Sixth Form College, up to the big roundabout by the Dyke – tying a balloon to every lamppost. About midnight – I got some very funny looks.

IAN MORLEY: It was a publicity game and, of course, it was all over *The Argus*. We were number one item on the news, on Radio Sussex, and on Southern FM.

Who knows whether it made any difference or not, but what I would say was, we had a hell of a lot of fun, at midnight, traipsing around the streets of Brighton putting up balloons.

ADRIAN NEWNHAM: Adam Trimingham was on Southern Counties talking about the local elections and said; "It's a side show. The local referendum – that's the big one. Have you seen the balloons? They are everywhere."

CLAIRE BYRD: The buzz all round those results was all about the referendum. The level of anticipation at *The Argus* and the sort of interest and excitement was not akin to anything we had had for a local election. Everyone hanging on it.

TIM CARDER: There were all sorts of initiatives on the day. I went out with Adrian, he had our loudhailer speaking out of a car window asking people to vote 'Yes Yes'.

SARAH WATTS: I was up at Brighton station meeting the commuter trains in the evening, handing out the leaflets saying vote. Some people said; "I don't agree with it." Well, unlike the others, I was like; "Well go and vote anyway because you can't complain unless you have voted."

LIZ COSTA: I was driving this blooming van with John Baine (Attila) sitting behind me with a megaphone on my shoulder and he is yelling out all round Hollingbury and Patcham, and up and down all those hills. You could see people standing back in horror and at the end I had a headache. Then the microphone broke… I thought 'this is justice', we couldn't get it to work again so we just went round with the posters on it.

IAN MORLEY: We didn't get the result until the next day, the Friday. It was 84% in favour of the council's policy of giving a home to Brighton & Hove Albion! We were just delighted, of course we were.

ADRIAN NEWNHAM: And, then there was 68% who were in favour of the question 'Do you support that being at Falmer?'

TIM CARDER: Our opponents said it was a flawed referendum, saying that there was no choice given where the site of the stadium should be – our argument was that people were perfectly entitled to vote 'Yes No' and I would extrapolate from those figures that something like 16% did vote 'Yes No'. Over two thirds of the people who voted were in

favour of the Falmer site and that gave us the moral high ground.

IAN MORLEY: The referendum gave a mandate to the Labour group that says we've got a mandate to build the stadium at Falmer; but it also provided a mandate for a relationship between the club and the council that said they were in this together. And it got a lot of national coverage.

DICK KNIGHT: There was overwhelming local endorsement for the homecoming propositions contained in the referendum.

BOB BRUCE: The referendum certainly bolstered the view of the council that Falmer was the right way to go.

STEVE BASSAM: I had watched, in my lifetime, a whole range of football club/local authority disasters where club and council just never got on, and that seemed to me to be ridiculous: OK, football clubs are a commercial entity, but actually they are about a sense of community and identity, and their sort of significance in an area is much larger than just being about a game of football, it really does carry people's hopes and aspirations. Local authorities really ought to work much more closely with football clubs; I believed that to be right then, I am absolutely convinced of that argument now.

I think for all the difficult phases the relationship went through, the fact that we rooted the club and the council together so clearly right at the beginning has made it much easier for them to resolve problems throughout; even over the last three or four years when the council has been of a Tory colour, there is some obligation left, politically, to carry the thing through and to their credit they have been supportive, even though they haven't been as enthusiastic.

I had to resign a couple of months after we won the referendum because Blair called me in to be a Home Office minister, so I wasn't able to finish off what I started really - but I carried on doing what I could do in government to make sure we got what we wanted.

TIM CARDER: The referendum was a fairly short, sharp campaign over about a month. This was the first massive, positive supporters' action with regards Falmer Stadium.

IAN MORLEY: This, to me, summarised what the club and supporters and their campaigning was about – one great entrepreneurial spirit; great PR and marketing that came about because of fantastic organisation from the group. And fantastic foot soldiers, where you click your fingers and 200 people turn up. The major political parties in Brighton couldn't command that, so as an operation it was just fantastic.

ADRIAN NEWNHAM: We got the referendum result on the Friday and our last game at Gillingham was on the Saturday.

11. THEM AND US
The new Board and the fans unite

PAUL CAMILLIN: In the Archer days we had two negative ions and all of a sudden it dovetailed. I think Dick harnessed that, used it to the club's advantage, because we didn't have the resources and those fans who'd waged war on the club, when Bellotti, Archer and Stanley were involved, were being used to good effect.

ROY CHUTER: I always admired Dick greatly because of what he'd done – he obviously hated Archer as much as the rest of us and was very keen to get rid of him, and my impression from speaking to him a couple of times was that basically he was one of us. He could go back to 1946 and he told me what his first Albion game was and we looked it up in the Tim Carder book and there it was. He knew what he was talking about.

IAN MORLEY: It was fascinating being one of the campaigners in the inner circle;you got a fascinating glimpse of how the football club worked. It wasn't the machine it is today where there is a better defined department and managerial club structure, a team of coaches and backroom staff, marketing department, etc.

Back in those days it was a shoestring existence. There was no money, even though Dick had put the money into the club, there was still a gap – a huge gap – versus operating costs.

ROY CHUTER: It wasn't like all the fans immediately got totally behind every member of the consortium. There was still a little bit of distrust and that dissipated over the next few years. I had a big run-in with Martin Perry because of the way the Board was set up: Archer had 49.5% of the shares, the consortium had 49.5% of the shares and Martin Perry had the other 1%, which meant Martin had the controlling influence. And we didn't know anything about him. He had just come in from McAlpine and had been building Huddersfield's ground and various things like that. So, I said, in a fanzine article I wrote, what happens if Archer manages to persuade McAlpine, or anybody else, that Martin Perry's been working for, to come in on his side, rather than the Dick Knight side. What happens then? We've lost control of the club again. Nick Rowe, who was the general manager at the time, rang me up and said: "Martin Perry is really upset about this, so what we can we do about it?" We had a little chat and eventually I ended up interviewing Martin for one of the fanzines and that, from my point of view, at least, helped me to understand. Me and Martin get on OK now… he loves my dog for a start… so I don't have a problem with Martin at all now.

ADRIAN NEWNHAM: I remember the togetherness at that point – you got directors going out together and doing stuff. You had Bob Pinnock offering to give out leaflets at Brighton station and he turned up at the Excelsior hotel an hour and a half later and he went; "Some man offered to bop me on the nose".

The fact that you got directors willing to put themselves on the line like that, you had Dick Knight out delivering leaflets, Martin Perry out delivering leaflets, Bob Pinnock out delivering leaflets and then there was Nick Rowe – he went out and spent an afternoon at Withdean Stadium, presenting the plans for the stadium, got absolutely ripped to shreds by the residents over some really irrational things. He couldn't possibly answer the question; "What would you do about the mating badgers in the nature reserve?" The guy's not a badger expert but, you know, he's left there being asked this question by someone who knows about badgers… What would you do? So he's left looking exposed but he was prepared to do that.

DAVE SWAFFIELD: They were fantastic – a lot of passion coming out. We let the representatives do our business for us because they were almost elected by us and they had the right to be doing what they were doing because people trusted them – they'd worked hard at it. So the Town Hall meetings were great because the passions were able to come out and you were able to talk and ask questions of Martin Perry, of Dick Knight – God, this all seems so long ago compared to where we are today!

PART TWO

Withdean

August 1999 – May 2011

12. THE OPENING OF WITHDEAN

Back where we belong

TIM HERBERT: 6-0 win? I remember thinking – what's happening? We've just scored six goals in our opening game, phenomenal, we're back in Brighton and we mean business! It was a party atmosphere. The sky was completely blue.

DAVE SWAFFIELD: The first game was absolutely amazing – a very emotional day for me.

TIM CARDER: It was a very hot sunny day and to see my team run out – and to hear Sussex By The Sea on the speakers, it was just fantastic to be back where we belonged – it was one of the best days.

SAM SWAFFIELD: You know when you go to the first game of the season and the pitch looks a perfect green? And we had the best football kit that we had had for 15 years and we had this new team and this great young manager and I just remember, regardless of the scoreline (which helped), it was just unbelievable. The atmosphere was like nothing I'd seen before. It was the happiest times for me because I'd never had the chance just to enjoy football really, not in a conventional sense.

GRAEME ROLF: One of my earliest memories of Withdean would have been in 1966 when the World Cup was on. I was in the cubs and there was a big jamboree or jubilee thing and I was chosen to go out onto what became the centre spot and shout 'Arkala, we will do out best!' I presented Lady Baden-Powell, with a basket of fruit… So 40 or whatever it is years later, there I am in a completely different guise as an Albion supporter.

TIM CARDER: I remember Withdean well from my childhood; it was very run down. I was absolutely amazed by the transformation that had taken place, how well it had been made into a usable football stadium. It may seem hard to believe, but that's the way I felt.

DICK KNIGHT: We spent, in the end, nearly £5m on Withdean, most of it funded by the shareholders; to even get into Withdean for the start of the next season, 1999/2000, cost us just under £3m to bring it up to Football League standards.

ADRIAN NEWNHAM: I was an absolute statto for what was going on at Withdean. Putting the floodlights up, excavating on the south side to put the temporary stands in, rebuilding on the North Stand, I was there twice a week to see what was going on.

DAVE SWAFFIELD: We used to go to the Sportsman pub next to the stadium and shout at the workmen: "Get that bloody stand built! Hurry up!" It was really quite exciting seeing the seats go in.

MARTIN PERRY: We were due to be given a safety certificate so we could open the stadium but the date and the time for the inspection kept on sliding and sliding and sliding… It wasn't until 5.34 on the day before the friendly against Nottingham Forest that they said OK, the game can go ahead.

ADRIAN NEWNHAM: I remember Ecovert were doing the catering at Withdean and I got an invite into the Sponsors Lounge – all of those who had worked on the referendum campaign and the Bring Home the Albion campaign had been given an invite. It actually only struck me what I'd done when the guy stood up and said: "On behalf of Ecovert I'd like to welcome you to Withdean Stadium, the temporary home of Brighton & Hove Albion." I felt, actually, this is it! This is what we were arguing about, and it was just tremendous.

MARTIN PERRY: As the team ran out Dick turned to me and he said: "We've done it, Martin, we've done it!"

PAUL SAMRAH: The euphoria of the first season back in Brighton! The clamour for seats was great.

MARTIN PERRY: The first season at Withdean was packed out. We had a capacity, at that time, of 6,000. The first league game was against Mansfield Town and I can remember us trying the new systems out for the first time, the park-and-rides, etc. and I remember a guy from the buses came back to us after the game and said: "Your fans are really friendly," and I said: "Well, winning 6-0 helps!"

SAM SWAFFIELD: Our generation, we were the sort of kids who were born around the time of the FA Cup Final in 1983, we'd seen nothing really until we got to Withdean. I think to some of the kids who will be in their early 20s now, or their late teens, Withdean was quite inspirational. When we moved back to Brighton there was a great feel about it, and they wanted to go to the football but because of the size of the stadium, because of the way you had to get tickets, because of the price of the tickets... so for a while Brighton & Hove Albion became sort of exclusive; and when you are looking at kids who are 15, 16, 17, if their dad's aren't going to take them how are they going to go? They're not going to queue up at the ticket office. It's not like the Goldstone where they just turn up.

ROY CHUTER: As far as I am concerned the first game at Withdean was everybody's first home game for two years. And certainly one that sticks in the mind, not just because it was 6-0, but the fact that coming back to Brighton after those two years was an extraordinary experience and, yes, there were a few tears shed that day. Withdean was a convenient stop-off point on the way between the Goldstone and Falmer; the fact that it took 14 years to get there is fairly disgusting, but that's the planning process for you.

13. FEELGOOD WITHDEAN
"The coolest club in the country"

SAM SWAFFIELD: I remember Brighton changing and getting a lot smarter and colourful. We went from *Gulls Eye* which was a traditional fanzine printed in black and white to something like *Scars & Stripes* – a glossy, colour, professionally produced fanzine with a sort of very positive spin. We obviously had Dick Knight at the helm, the guy behind the Wonderbra adverts. All of the output from the club was much brighter and smarter and engaging. We opened the first Seagull shop! During the Archer years, there was a bloody Man United superstore on Western Road, by the time Dick Knight arrived that had closed down. And we were sponsored by Skint Records.

MARTIN PERRY: We had some great years, three championships, and we were able to increase the capacity – I remember going to the council and saying we can get 9,000 in and they looked at us in absolute horror.

ATTILA: Once we got back to Withdean that first season I was made Poet in Residence. I published the *Goldstone Ghosts* book and the Kit Napier book of writing. I started doing some poetry at the games and sometimes people said "This is great" and sometimes I was almost threatened with physical violence.

SAM SWAFFIELD: My mate Stefan brought back a slipmat for turntables and it was a screen printed, BHA Skint Records slipmat! We were so excited! The club changed and we became like the coolest club in the country.

MARTIN PERRY: How many people in administration in football can have had four bus rides through the city!? I have! They were great years. And a great team spirit. And a number of those players who played in those teams are now working for the club – Paul Watson, Charlie Oatway, Dodge, Guy Butters etc.

IAN HART: I have always been a little bit perturbed at the amount of people who have slagged off the Withdean. I remember going there when the atmosphere has been electric – playing Palace in 2003 and we were murdering them 0-0 (I said to Derek Alan; "If the Albion score Derek how long will my ban be when I run on the pitch?"); the Cardiff game the year we went up, obviously the Chesterfield game; when we beat Watford the last home game of 2002/3 season – some great night games. How can you say Manchester City wasn't a good atmosphere? Swindon, how can you say Swindon wasn't a good atmosphere? It's the easy option to be a Withdean basher.

PAUL WHELCH: For 11 years I ran the litter patrols after every game in the Withdean area; I and one or two other people have gone round the streets, round the park and round the immediate area of Withdean picking up litter, whether it was left by the fans or not. It demonstrated not only the commitment of the fans but also the important point that this is the kind of club that keeps its promises.

TIM JOHNSON: We have had the local residents saying how good we have been. To start with they generally thought hooligans were going to wee in their gardens. I am sorry but I don't know any hooligans who want to do that, I sure they have got better things to do!

GRAEME ROLF: I didn't miss a single game at Withdean in any shape or form. I've attended every single game; cup games, league games, all the paint pot games. And, yes, I did do my sports days there as well, I went to Rudyard Kipling and we competed against other schools there.

PAUL WHELCH: We won three championships and got to a play-off final at Withdean – so it was the most successful period of time for the club; we never did that at the Goldstone. It says a lot about the reach, the chairmen and the managers we had.

One of the things that the success of Withdean demonstrated was that this isn't going to just go away; we aren't going to roll over and become Wycombe Wanderers or something – this is a big-city football club looking to find a home.

14. FALMER FOR ALL
Sounds better than Falmer Stadium Campaign

DEREK CHAPMAN: The new stadium is here because of the fans and nobody should forget that. Not directors or anybody else, they shouldn't forget that.

TIM CARDER: From 1997 to 1999 there were regular meetings between the Board and supporters' representatives: the Supporters' Club, Brighton Independent Supporters' Association, activists, the fanzine writers, and they would report back to supporters through the fanzines or the programme. All that developed into a campaign group for the referendum and that eventually morphed into what eventually became the Falmer For All campaign.

PAUL SAMRAH: We had our very first Falmer For All meeting the day after losing 4-3 to Rochdale in the torrential rain at Withdean.

TIM CARDER: Initially it was called the Falmer Stadium Campaign, 'For All' was Dick Knight's phrase because he felt the stadium should be for all people to use, a community stadium.

At the first meeting Martin Perry showed us the first draft of plans for the stadium. Obviously, they were drawings on pieces of paper and to the untrained eye it perhaps didn't have the wow factor that Martin was emphasising at the time, but it was obviously serious stuff and the Falmer For All campaign really started there.

PAUL SAMRAH: Main people were me, Tim Carder, Bill Swallow, John Cowen, Ed Bassford, Adrian Newnham, Liz Costa, Sarah Watts, Attila, who gave us the militant view…

LIZ COSTA: There were probably, in total, about 20 core people; we dropped a few off and picked a few up along the way, but the hardcore stayed the same.

BILL SWALLOW: It was like an ITV sitcom where the producer says: "We better have a punk rocker with a Chairman Mao hat and an accountant – no, let's have two, accountants – a teacher, we must have a teacher…" And Ed and Roz at the end of the table with fags on, just fabulous. They were all such huge personalities in their own way, brought together by the leadership of

Paul Samrah – his colossal energy was just unstoppable. There would be meetings in the evening and you would get the minutes coming through at three in the morning.

There was a common interest that drove everybody on and people worked in different ways and the fact that they all had different ideas and different approaches didn't matter at all, it just added to the mix.

TIM CARDER: Over the years we grew to trust each other I think, the Board knew they could trust us, we wouldn't be leaking information and we grew to trust the Board having completely and utterly lost trust in the previous regime. We were a little bit wary to start with, we were checking up on things we were told, but we learnt that yes this was a Board that we could, by and large, trust.

DICK KNIGHT: I loved working with Falmer For All. I didn't want to chair those meetings. Paul Samrah chaired them. We worked absolutely as a team all of us, it was never a question of them and us; it was simply, these are the issues, how best are we going to address them? We naturally allocated projects, he's going to do this, she's going to do that. We just worked as a team and Paul led it, it wasn't right for me to chair it. Martin and I were instrumental in what was being done, of course, but what a resource we had! It was absolutely brilliant! We all said, right, we are all underneath this huge rock and we have to work together to push it off us. I was never downcast in those meetings, I was always showing them huge enthusiasm saying, come on we are going to do this, and it didn't need much prompting.

ROZ SOUTH: Dick was genuinely democratic with the Falmer For All team, very much his own man but he accepted the fact that if you were working with a team then there was a purpose in having them and it wasn't just to tell them they were wrong… And he told you the most wonderful stories. I still remember him telling us that: "Paul Scally's Boardroom at Gillingham looks like a Chinese Bordello," and there was a pause, then Liz Costa said: "How do you know what a Chinese Bordello looks like?" and he said: "I'll save you the detail, Liz."

DAN TESTER: The great thing about the Albion was that they realised the fans were helping them. We – *Scars & Stripes* – had a brilliant relationship with the club, but still retained our independence.

PAUL SAMRAH: I was determined we weren't going to hold meetings that were formal minutiae bollocks… I mean I've got no time for that, you just want bloody people doing bloody action and that's it, keep it tight and finish within the reasonable time frame, two hours or whatever.

We agreed the whole campaign shouldn't be violent or aggressive, it had to be humorous and we'd keep it novel, and that was it.

LIZ COSTA: We were involved so we wanted to be involved in the next bit. Tell us what you want and we are here to do it.

SARAH WATTS: Paul Samrah has been absolutely brilliant leading everyone and to be honest there were times he can even sort out Martin Perry and Dick Knight! Politely. If things ran off he could bring the meeting to order.

ATTILA: I sometimes took a bit of a back seat because I was not right for specific campaigns: you needed the suit wearers like Paul Samrah and Adrian Newnham to deal with the Falmer nimbys on their own terms.

Paul Samrah was such a good front man and the sort of man you need to drill a campaign. Paul did the most incredible amount, more than you can imagine, the effort and putting his family and career and everything second.

PAUL SAMRAH: We worked well with the club and that was absolutely vital. They provided us with support but we weren't afraid of throwing difficult questions at them like: "How are you going to fund the stadium?" We were going to be on the radio defending the campaign so needed to find out what the bloody hell we were talking about.

I organised a Falmer For All workshop session in the council chamber in Hove Town Hall, addressing our strengths and weaknesses. I posed many questions to each group and they had to come up with answers. Put yourself in the opposition's shoes – what are they going to fire at you?

One of the strengths that came through was the community work. It was becoming a major factor. The opposition would say the stadium was going to ruin Falmer village life, but we could turn round and say: "But it's going to improve the life of thousands of people! Let's get it into perspective."

What I learnt throughout all of it was that you have to be totally and utterly prepared: if you're on a phone-in where you're up against the opposition, as long as you're prepared you'll rip them to shreds! I'm not bragging! But it was quite enjoyable.

TIM CARDER: While we were working together we recognised that the club had its job to do, which was to come up with a successful and professional planning application, while our job was to get supporters to turn out en masse when required, to write to the council, to write to the government to make sure the message was heard: that the supporters wanted the stadium and that people in Brighton and Hove and Sussex – and throughout the land – wanted the stadium.

BILL SWALLOW: Nothing ever, to the best of my knowledge, was referred back to the club for approval. We were very conscious of the fact that Falmer For All was not a club initiative. It would have been weaker if it had been. Dick and Martin were very valued members of the Falmer For All Committee. And members was what they were.

I have a memory of a Falmer For All meeting at Withdean. A senior member of the Albion team, who had just joined the club, was there for his first experience of how the club and its supporters related to each other. Attila came crashing in, chains clanking, and Martin then started talking about confidential stuff to do with the inner running of the stadium project and you could see the new member of the club thinking that Martin had gone completely berserk. After a while, of course, he realised this was how the Albion did business when people they trusted were in the room. I can't believe any league football club has ever related to supporters in quite the same way.

JOHN COWEN: At the time Dick and Martin looked like a seamless team; Martin had tremendous skills with what he was doing with the stadium and Dick had all his legendary skills anyway, plus he was able to pull lots of strings. So, it was like a great double act. It was a fantastic atmosphere at FFA meetings; there were never any serious fall-outs and rows, there were certainly enlivened debates, usually involving John Baine, obviously! "Well, I think we should be doing this," and Dick would say; "John, we can't have people setting fire to the pitch at Rochdale next week." Or whatever it was John was suggesting.

Or: "We can't invade the Boardroom at Bristol Rovers." There was this lovely contrast of personalities and instincts – but in the end it worked incredibly well.

PAUL CAMILLIN: I was working for the club but I've always been a fan. So you were doing a day's work in the office then coming to a meeting in the evening and getting involved if anything needed to go out press and PR wise, you'd be liaising on that. Towards the end it did get a bit intense and you sometimes had to switch off and walk away from it otherwise it takes over your life.

ROY CHUTER: As programme editor I was happily situated between the club and the Falmer For All team, being in the middle and finding out what was going on from all different angles and passing information from the club to the fans, and from the fans to the club; I always thought that was my job as one of the chief propagandists.

I don't think there was any real schism between the Board and the fans, there were times when the fans, quite understandably, didn't think it was moving on fast enough, but I think the Board felt that as well.

ED BASSFORD: Roz and I went along to our first Falmer For All meeting. It was an incredibly open access set up, it wasn't a clique of people, self-appointed individuals. And once you're in there you start doing things.

ROZ SOUTH: I became chairman of the moles, because it was quite obvious that if we didn't find out what other people were doing then we were going to weaken our case. Of course, the case was strong enough on it own, but you've got to be a bit covert, you've got to know what other people are doing, you've got to know what they're doing almost before they've decided. I knew people at Lewes District who helped who I can't name, but my main mole was John Cowen.

JOHN COWEN: My moling mainly involved going to The Swan at Falmer, drinking loads of beer and getting to know John Woodruff, the landlord. I volunteered because I hadn't been around very much and I didn't live in Brighton, so nobody would know me. I used to go to The Swan on my way back from FFA meetings. I introduced myself to Mr Woodruff as some sort of visiting sociology lecturer, who had a mate at the university. Mr Woodruff had anti-stadium and anti-Seagulls posters on his walls and I would sort of say: "This stadium? What's that all about then?"

He would always tell me what he thought and what was going on. I went down there loads of times, but he never twigged. It was an interesting place to be; just to sit in The Swan and think: "So this is the hub, the meeting place for so many people who are trying to object to what we are trying to do." John Woodruff was much maligned; OK, so he was a nutter but he was an eccentric British nutter – always ready to say or tell you anything. He would say things like: "It just ain't gonna happen is it?" It isn't going to happen for him, of course, because the poor guy died last year.

ROZ SOUTH: The nimbys' view of football supporters was that you went to football then you smashed a few places up on the way, you beat a few people up and you got horrendously drunk. They couldn't handle the idea that support for the glorious game could come from well, almost people like them.

15. NORTH STAND CHAT
A vital communication tool

IAN HINE: I actually do think NSC has been crucial. As we saw from Fans United in its embryonic days, what NSC does is it very quickly changes an idea into something concrete and meaningful.

TIM HERBERT: It's played an absolutely massive role. It's helped enormously. As computers have developed and people have had access to messageboards, rather than just speaking on emails, the word has got out really quickly.

ED BASSFORD: NSC is a great way of recruiting people to the campaign and making it accessible to everybody. For example, you were not chosen to take part in the National Falmer Day. People did brilliant things on that day having heard about it on NSC. And, of course, keeping in contact with other clubs and supporters through NSC, I think, was an important part of making it a national issue.

TIM HERBERT: The messages I've received from people on NSC and threads on NSC have been so valuable because they've told me what to write. There's been a letter on

NSC, just copy and paste it – Bang! Job done.

IAN HINE: For me, as a kind of an exile – we don't get *The Argus* or anything like that – you don't get that kind of day-to-day vibe that you get if you're in Brighton, so as the strength of the internet, and NSC in particular, grew you started to feel this real kind of momentum growing.

ED BASSFORD: The NSC-sponsored game when Lewes played Redbridge, that was one of the little bits of campaigning that was all part of a bigger thing. Through North Stand Chat you could say you need 40 people to give a tenner; it's not a huge commitment but it's joining in and you're actually giving money to a neighbouring football club, but it's all part of the bigger thing.

The Albion is the club that, if Wrexham are in trouble, they call upon us for a bit of support. If Plymouth are in trouble they call upon us for a bit of support, if anybody's in trouble it's natural that the Albion get involved and NSC is the first stopping point.

TIM HERBERT: Richie Morris did a badge 'Save the Racecourse' for Wrexham; we used NSC as a tool to communicate, it was brilliant in that respect. Then we met up outside Withdean with our box full of badges and handed them out, brilliant.

IAN HINE: For us people who didn't drive past Falmer every day you looked forward to Friday mornings when Jack Straw – aka Graeme Rolf – posted his pictures. A stupid little thing but important.

GRAEME ROLF: My office is the back of Stanmer Park and I used to drive by the site on the way home.

And low and behold when the work started, there were a few diggers excavating for things, a few relics, the old archaeology mob moved in first, and I went by and I took a few photos and then I saw something else happen and I thought 'Oh I'll take some

more photos' and then I thought 'I wonder whether people would like to see my photos?' and I started to put them on North Stand Chat. And, when things really got whizzing, early 2009, I started going every week, it was no trouble for me; just before work, pop round, park up, click click and dinner time I would put them on NSC.

As the weeks went by, I was getting more and more of a following and people actually expected them and were disappointed if they didn't appear. I became like the unofficial photographer of the build.

16. FANS OF THE EARTH
Campaign enters new fields

PAUL SAMRAH: We had in Henfield a few supporters who came up with the idea of 'Fans of the Earth' rather than 'Friends of the Earth' to address that we are actually quite nature-hugging; and so we did a sponsored walk raising funds for Sussex Wildlife Trust and Falmer For All, a sponsored walk right round the stadium site. Great organisation, it had a key charitable purpose and it also said 'We're not all football hooligans, we're on the ball'.

SARAH WATTS: I have got the T-shirt! Didn't go on the walk because I wasn't very agile at the time... but I helped raise funds and I think I sponsored a few people to make up for it.

TIM CARDER: Trevor Watson came up with Fans of the Earth. It wasn't a great player within the campaign but it was just enough to show that there are many football fans that care about the South Downs, the countryside, the environment – and I would put myself in that camp. I love the South Downs, I run over them, I walk over them, I cycle over them, they are my recreational area and I would hate anything detrimental to happen to the South Downs. But, I have always said that the Falmer site has to be seen in context of the built up area around it.

17. LETTER CAMPAIGNS
Write on our side

TIM HERBERT: I think I wrote pretty much every single letter but I cannot remember them, they were all so similar! It was just a case of get your numbers out. Support, support, support, support, support.

ADRIAN NEWNHAM: One of the problems that we had at Withdean was the terrible tannoy system, so when you wanted to get a message across to supporters we came up with the idea of putting adverts above the toilets, so that when you went for a pee the advert was right in front of you. You would see messages saying 'Our future is in your hands', toilet humour at its very

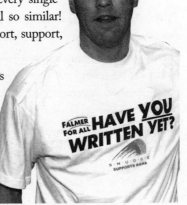

worst, but linked to the fact that underneath there was a message that people needed to write a letter.

BILL SWALLOW: At the time the Labour Party had what it called a 'Rebuttal Unit' – when anything critical appeared in a newspaper there would be someone to leap on it and set the record straight. We did the same thing. So, any time anything critical appeared in the Sussex press we would get a letter into that paper very quickly. We had a network of people all over, particularly in the Lewes area: it became particularly obvious very early on that Lewes was our problem. We would brief people on what we needed to get across and they would put it in their own way and get the letter off.

As a result, there would be letter after letter appearing in the *Sussex Express* and other papers, from people such as Percy Williams down in Seaford (who, with Mary Emery, is one of the oldest two Albion supporters, he started following the club over 80 years ago). There were people from all round Lewes and Seaford, Ringmer, who were getting these letters in and it worked very well. A lot of it was pre-email days so it wasn't always easy. New Labour would have been proud.

SARAH WATTS: There was a taxi driver who was responsible for something like a thousand letters being signed for one of the campaigns! In the end it's all about going out on the streets and getting people to sign.

18. PLANNING APPLICATION PROCESS
Eez complicated

ADRIAN NEWNHAM: This was a long drawn out process. Like most things at the Albion. If anybody saw democracy in action they would be appalled.

TIM CARDER: I was working for a printing firm and I had the pleasure (not sure that's quite the word) of printing the planning application so I got to see all the documents.

There were actually two planning applications being prepared; one was for Village Way North and the other for Village Way South. The University of Brighton and the club had not yet reached agreement, so the Albion, in what was quite a high risk strategy, put in two almost identical applications.

The Village Way North application had a stadium north of Village Way, where it is now, but the bus and coach park was not adjacent to the stadium as it is now, rather it was on the south side of Village Way. The Village Way South application had the stadium south of Village Way and the coach park adjacent to it on that piece of land.

Village Way itself is the boundary of the National Park and Brighton & Hove Council regarded that land south of Village Way as part of proper downland that should be preserved, and I tend to agree with them; the Albion were taking a risk asking for planning permission within the National Park.

The idea of having two applications was designed to force the hand of the University of Brighton to sign up to the agreement to Village Way North – with the alternative, the University of Brighton would lose out completely, with no control over the use of the stadium because it was not their land, it was purely council land.

Village Way North was Plan A, but unless the University of Brighton played ball, it wasn't going to happen because, to some extent, the university owned that land. Until quite recently, the land on which the university is built was public, when it was the old Brighton College of Education. When the polytechnic became a university independent of local education authorities, in that one move it became the owner of that land.

Dick and Martin were negotiating with the University of Brighton and that was the solution that they came up with which they felt was the best thing to do at the time.

So, two applications, loads of volumes and they had to be copied 15 times because there were 15 recipients. We took all these up to Derek Chapman's house, which was north of Falmer village and along a really rutted lane, and I nearly broke the company van. The applications were assembled in Derek Chapman's barn.

Martin and I submitted the application to Hove Town Hall, on October 8th 2001, on a wheelie trolley.

MARTIN PERRY: It took nearly two years to put that planning application together. We delivered the two applications together in 32 boxes to the City Council!

TIM CARDER: You get a summary of the applications, which is just about readable, but the rest of it is not the sort of thing you want to read on your sofa; it's all consultant reports into noise and transport and all that sort of thing. Some bits are interesting; there were bits on the archaeology and pre-history of the site which I found interesting.

Once the planning application was submitted the campaign could step up a gear because

we had something to express positive support for – both in terms of the letter writing campaign to Brighton & Hove Council, and also as a petition to the council.

We wanted people to write to Brighton & Hove City Council. We felt that letters from outside Brighton & Hove city boundaries would probably not necessarily be given the weight of ones from inside the city, so we encouraged all supporters living in the city to write to their councillors while we also encouraged people from Lewes district, for instance, to write to their council, and councillors, and the same for people in East Sussex and West Sussex.

The Falmer For All team were probably having weekly meetings now.

So, in November 2001, there was the official launch of the campaign for the planning application at Hove Town Hall.

The petition was distributed at home games, we had volunteers out and about at every game; some of them would be shaking buckets to get funds coming in for the various initiatives. Every petition form was numbered; when the petitions came back to me, I bundled them up, and sent them to a team of people I had all around the country who used to type in the postcodes against a number on the form; from that we were able to analyse where all the petition signatures were coming from – so many in this Brighton & Hove City Council ward, and so many in any town in Sussex you wanted to care to mention – or beyond! We had signatures from Germany, Australia and America, places all around the world – and there was only one mainland UK postcode area that wasn't represented!

It transpired that the most signatures in the whole of Brighton and Hove came from the Moulsecoomb and Bevendean ward, which was actually the ward in which the stadium was going to be situated in. It was a very close run thing with Withdean – maybe some residents signed it to get rid of the Albion! But, it was clear Moulsecoomb and Bevendean were welcoming the stadium so that was a nice little line we could use in our publicity. We handed in the petition, I think, at Brighton Town Hall, probably in May 2002, just before the committee meeting in June.

PAUL SAMRAH: The petition had around 61,000 signatures. I was a bit disappointed to be honest, we didn't really get signatures from other clubs, none of the Sussex-based clubs signed… 61,000 is still bloody good, it's the biggest petition ever handed in to the council – I thought we could've done a 100,000, but hey.

TIM CARDER: When we were applying to get to Withdean we had a small group – called SWEAT – of local residents opposing us; now the line-up to oppose the Falmer application included: Falmer Villagers, Falmer Parish Council, Lewes District Council, the Campaign to Protect Rural England, Society of Sussex Downsmen, Regency Society, Friends of the Earth, The Green Party – which was pretty serious opposition.

Negotiations with the council led to the Albion eventually withdrawing the Village Way South application; they also agreed to put the coach and bus park to where it currently is, adjacent to the stadium, north of Village Way. The City Council had said that they cannot build south of Village Way, that is sacrosanct and I agree with that – the Village Way has to be a barrier; I don't want to see anything built out on the Downs proper. But, placing the car and bus park north of Village Way, where it now is, complicated matters, as it's in Lewes District Council.

So the whole site was to be situated on land owned variously by the university, Brighton & Hove City Council, while from a planning perspective the site was governed by the city council and Lewes District Council!

Brighton Council said; "You can have the land for the stadium and the coach park as far as we're concerned, but you will need to negotiate still with the University of Brighton for the use of their land, and you will also need to put in a planning application for a coach park to Lewes District Council."

So, it got complicated.

The planning application went into Lewes District Council and they rejected it. The Albion had the right to appeal, but it never came to that, because the government stepped in…

19. PLANNING APPLICATION VOTE
11-1 home victory

BILL SWALLOW: There were quite a few villagers sitting in the public gallery for the planning meeting at the Town Hall and quite a lot of us, and we were conscious of the football supporter stereotype so our behaviour was preposterously immaculate.

In the end it was only these ladies with hat pins from Falmer who were being told off by the Chairman of the Committee for their mutterings…

TIM CARDER: It was very full of both supporters and opposition. Both sides were allowed to make small speeches for and against. I remember Councillor Les Hamilton Junior – there was some argument that the stadium would spoil the Downs, it would be lit up at night, that sort of thing. His argument was, what the hell are you doing up on the Downs at night?!

ADRIAN NEWNHAM: Councillor David Smith stood up and the first thing he said was he had previously been on the books of the Albion (I've never spoken to anyone who can come up with any proof on this), but he then said that the Albion were being deceitful and disingenuous to their supporters because the stadium wasn't going to be owned by the club. It was going to be owned by a stadium management company. He was telling us as if it was news.

Then the Albion supporters were given 15 minutes to present their support for the application and five of us had three minutes each. I'm sitting there next to the club's solicitor rewriting my speech because David Smith has just made this comment and somebody has to respond to it.

So, I ended up having to go up there and say; "Thank you for making that point. It is a well known secret that the 15,000 supporters of the club have been given a booklet by the club explaining how the application works, and will have read in there how the stadium will be owned by a stadium management company."

This was not some kind of devious, underhand trick. This was a known fact and it was actually done to protect the club, and its supporters, rather than it being an attempt to mislead them; another one of these surreal moments when you watch democracy in action. If I behaved like that in my job, if I turned up unprepared for a meeting and not having read the brief notes and not understanding what I am discussing, I would be sacked. Here you have councillors turning up, clearly haven't read the application and are able to say things in public that are clearly disingenuous.

MARTIN PERRY: It's a matter of record who voted against it; he's still a councillor!!

TIM CARDER: The councillors put their hands up in the air and it was 11-1, which was better even than the 10-2 being the vote for Withdean!

The one was David Smith. He claims that he used to be a player for the Albion in his youth. He represents Rottingdean Coastal ward and I think his agenda is to do with the traffic concerns of the residents of Rottingdean and Saltdean – their perceived concerns over traffic on the Falmer Road.

11-1 was not quite unanimous but a pretty good victory and, of course, at that point we were highly pleased to say the least, it had got through the council.

20. THE CLUB AND THE UNIVERSITY
More than just academic

TIM CARDER: There was an impasse between the club and the university over the stadium; looking at it objectively the university wanted to ensure that its campus was not adversely affected by the presence of a stadium and 22,500 football supporters on its doorstep, so I can see that aspect of it. But, I got the story from Martin and Dick.

DICK KNIGHT: The years of evaluating, preparing, addressing planning regulations and so on in themselves were bad enough, but we also had to embark on serious negotiations with the University of Brighton over land – which took more than 18 months – before we even submitted the Falmer planning application. From the beginning the UoB's stance was: "We are not going to put up with these hooligan football people." They looked down their academic noses at the very thought of the Albion intruding on the halls of academia… And Sir David Watson, who was the esteemed vice-chancellor of the university, a charming fellow, liked cricket but football was a step too far. He obviously envisioned these hooligans rampaging across their hallowed campus, which is hardly the quadrangles of Oxford or Cambridge…

TIM CARDER: I am sure Martin and Dick did their very, very best but they found, for whatever reason, that the University of Brighton were very obstinate in their demands and they would come back into Falmer For All meetings very, very angry.

DICK KNIGHT: We needed to make the stadium fit into this very tight area and so his demands to me as the club negotiator were preposterous… He asked for many millions for this small strip of land that we, as residents of Brighton, had given free to Brighton Polytechnic (as it was) some years before, when it wanted to become a university. We had given it (or the council had given it to them in our name) to this academic institution that was now trying to charge the club multi-millions – and I mean go past ten and keep going, double figures, millions. And, there were many buildings on their campus lined with asbestos because they were built in the 1960s, so they needed to rebuild their campus anyway. But, those negotiations stretched out over nearly two years before we finally reached an agreement with them that was acceptable to us.

TIM CARDER: Eventually, a long, long time later, in fact halfway through the first public inquiry, they still had not reached agreement with the University of Brighton which was absolutely crucial to the whole project. It's one of the main reasons why there was such a delay between the plans being prepared and the actual submission of the planning application.

21. PUBLIC INQUIRY CALLED
It was inevitable

BOB BRUCE: The planning application got 'called in' by the Secretary of State; basically, how that works is for certain types of applications, including land owned by the council itself, you have to refer to the Secretary of State where he or she decides if they want to make a decision because it's a big development, and if they do it is called 'called in'.

ROY CHUTER: I wasn't that surprised that they called in the plans, for the simple reason that the opposition in Falmer had influence at government level, and we knew they had they had influence in the press, a lot of the opposition were journalists. I didn't expect there to be too many problems about that at the time, but obviously that didn't prove to be the case.

MARTIN PERRY: We had been warned that the government might well call the application in, and, of course, disappointingly, in July we were told 'yes, they've called it in'. But, the council said they were minded to support us. So then we had to prepare all the evidence for the public inquiry and, of course, that is when we realised the level of opposition. You have a pre-inquiry meeting when everybody who has an interest is invited and Lewes District Council turned up with their barrister, we were there with ours; and then we had all these other groups: Falmer Parish Council and their legal adviser, the Society of Sussex Downsmen, the Council for Protection of Rural England, and a load of individuals, so we knew we had a battle on.

TIM CARDER: I didn't have any doubts about the suitability of the site itself. It could be seen from places on the Downs but it's got to be appreciated in context, being on the edge of the built-up area and the universities. It didn't concern me from a visual point of view. I was aware, however, that the site was in the 'Area of Outstanding Natural Beauty', which is a national designation by the government, so whatever I say about the context of the site, it is a sensitive area. The problem was that the designation was out of date, in my opinion. The Sussex Downs AONB was designated in 1966; even then we had the University of Sussex there and we had the small campus of the College of Education, I think, so that boundary of the AONB, by this time, was over 40 years out of date. And, it was blooming obviously out of date because you had all this development within it.

MARTIN PERRY: We were also conscious of the fact that Brighton & Hove City Council had in this period become a unitary authority (the municipal Borough of Brighton had joined up with Hove); prior to that Brighton had had a Local Plan, but now this combined unitary authority was going to have to draw up a combined plan. So we decided that it would be a good strategy in fighting the planning case, to try to get two public inquiries – because the local plan was a separate case – get the issues related to the stadium heard at the same time, and that proved to be a decisive decision that we got absolutely right. The difference in the process is the Local Plan Inspector reports to the local authority whereas the Call-in Inspector for a planning application reports directly to the Secretary of State to allow the that political figure to make the decision. It was a key decision and we were spot-on, because we then went through the process with two inspectors sitting at the front.

TIM HERBERT: I remember thinking "Oh for fuck's sake, another hurdle to climb over!" But, it was just a case of 'oh right then, let's do it' and we'll be all right. I just had this weird implicit faith that it was all going to work out, it's really bizarre. My mates thought I wore rose-tinted glasses. I went to Withdean and I'd say "It's OK, we're going to be all right" and my mates would say "I want a pair of what you're wearing".

But, at points it does test your patience and your mental strength. It was hard enough week in, week out, going to Withdean, and yet there was all this other stuff, it's not just a case of being a normal football supporter and going to football, having a couple of beers after and then going home, you've got to then think about the state of the club at the same time.

22. PUBLIC INQUIRY ONE
It's all bats

PAUL SAMRAH: I remember going through the doors into Hove Town Hall on the first day of the inquiry thinking 'gosh, this is where Albion celebrated promotion to Division One'; 'this is where we got approval for Withdean'. We'd also been here for the 11-1 vote for the planning application, but now here we were starting out on a road we didn't know how long it was going to take.

It was like going into a courtroom. You had the opponents in clusters whispering to each other, very much two sides going in to battle.

What struck me when you walked into the chamber was the volume of paperwork – I mean there were papers everywhere; research and documentation, bibles of information. It was just enormous, there were trolley loads.

TIM CARDER: The inquiry opened on February 18th 2003 and although it was fascinating it was often very tedious; I fell asleep during a debate about noise analysis.

Our barrister Jonathan Clay was very erudite, as you would expect, but also very friendly. He was very good on his brief; he knew exactly what he was talking about.

The public gallery is raised up above the council chamber where the inquiry was being conducted, and opponents and Albion supporters sat together. There were usually at least half a dozen Albion supporters, in their blue and white, with Falmer villagers. We got to know who they were. There was a little bit of talking between us, no real unpleasantness and the proceedings went along.

MARTIN PERRY: I was there every single day! And I sat next to Jonathan Clay every single day. Various people came in to give their evidence. Jonathan said to me; "I want you on first..." It's quite challenging to go on first and reluctantly I agreed to it. I was on nearly two days.

I had arranged for all of our witnesses to go through a training course on how to give evidence as an expert witness. You don't go through the evidence that you are giving, you're not allowed to, but you learn how to give evidence on how to appear as a witness. There are all sorts of traps that an experienced barrister can throw at you. One of the tricks is... The person you're trying to convince isn't the barrister questioning you, it's the inspector, so when you're being cross-examined you actually ignore the person who's

71

asking the question, the answer you give goes to the inspector, and that helps you when they're trying to trap you, and there were all sorts of things like that that we did.

PAUL SAMRAH: The inquiry ran like a trial, effectively; lunchtimes you went your separate ways and got into huddles again, back for the afternoon sessions, then it would be adjourned until the next day; I tried to get along for a fair few sessions. One day you'd think we'd won this point, the next you'd be down because you thought we'd lost that one. We knew what our Achilles' heels were – the transport strategy and the need for that size stadium.

I remember the Albion's QC Jonathan Clay, in response to the opposition saying "If you go to the top of the Downs you'll be able to see the stadium!" replying, with masterful timing, "With respect, if you go to the top of the Downs you can see the whole of Brighton and Hove," which, neatly, in a few words, summed up the whole issue.

BOB BRUCE: One of the things we had to do at the inquiry was say to the inspector what the position was on each of the sites. A lot of the sites were owned by the council, so yes we do own Sheepcote Valley but we don't think it is a very good site because of transport links, whatever it was. We said Falmer was our preferred option. That is basically how it worked.

BILL SWALLOW: We didn't go as much as some of the people. Ed Bassford went to take notes. We were involved in producing the programme then and we published Ed's reports of the meetings. Because there were so many words it was in the tiniest type. Every club programme you see has got big pictures of players, but we had 2,000-word articles, column after column of seven-point type, and people would get the programme just to read that. That said it all about our fans really.

TIM CARDER: I did help out a little bit in that I provided some statistics on attendances that the Albion had attracted down the years, and I think that was used in Dick Knight's evidence: he was pointing to the fact that we used to attract an average gate in the First Division of 25,000 and we peaked at 36,000 – making the argument why we might need a 22,000-seater stadium whereas we were only getting five or six thousand at Withdean.

DICK KNIGHT: I remember this QC for Lewes, he thought he was being clever this guy; he started off with this line of questioning: "So Mr Knight, the Goldstone – your father came back from World War II and took you, what was your first game?" And I said it was against Mansfield. He said: "You saw some great games… bla-bla-bla…,""Yes I was there in the highest crowd and when we won 6-0 against Watford to get…" He went on like this… He had done his homework and what it was leading to was – "The Goldstone holds lots of wonderful memories for you?" … He was going to say, "So why did you and your kin allow the ground to be sold if you had all these wonderful memories?" I said: "Yes, those memories I have stored them, but as far as spectator facilities were concerned, the ground was a disgrace. I said when the season opened in sunny August they used to put the sausage rolls in the kiosks around the ground and if they weren't sold they stayed there until the following March… and as far as the toilets were concerned, well don't even get me started on the toilets." The people in the audience started laughing. I said: "The Goldstone had its time and place and that's finished and it's over, and along with a lot of people here and throughout this county I have very fond memories of the Goldstone and that's it."

MARTIN PERRY: There was the moment when Des Lynam came; the absolute professional and we had briefed him. The opposition knew that they haven't got a hope in hell of winning against Des, so they decided that what they would do would be to filibuster on the evidence beforehand.

The witness prior to Des was our expert from English Nature, one of the country's leading experts in diversity, ecology and, in particular, he was an expert in bats! We had been very careful to do a large number of bat surveys and we put up this bat expert who simply sat on the stand and said: "We've done a series of surveys; there are no bats, this is not a problem." And Charlie Hopkins, who was representing Lewes, decided that he wasn't going to let this go, so he said: "What would happen if there were bats?" So our bat expert said that that wasn't applicable, there are no bats. So Charlie said: "How do you know there are no bats?" "Because we have carried out a survey, at various times of the day and night, and there are no bats." So Charlie said: "How did you carry out the survey?" And, of course, our supporters are sitting in the public gallery, as they did through every single day, under orders not to call out, not allowed to speak, no mobile phones, they had to sit quietly… And today they were sitting there with tears rolling down their cheeks, and just at this moment when this whole farce was going on, in walks Des, and a hush descended over the room as this charismatic character came in and he sat down beside me, and Charlie Hopkins kept on going: "Would you apply for a bat licence if there were bats?" "There are no bats." "But is it appropriate that there should be a bat licence?" "There are no bats." At which point the inspector said: "I think we've got the message, there are no bats." And Charlie sank into his seat defeated and Des turned to me and said; "I bet when you joined the football club you didn't think you'd be in a room discussing bats!" And then, of course, Des read out his statement and the inspector said would anyone like to ask Mr Lynam any questions, and there was silence. Classic. There were some good moments.

BOB BRUCE: With a long inquiry it is very hard, unless you are there all the time, to see how it's going. If I was able to hear Martin Perry's evidence, Dick Knight's, Des Lynam's, whoever's it was, I might think this is fantastic, that is because it is, it is fantastic and that is because the other side are having their bad bit. But I suspect Des wasn't asked any questions at all. Some people may think that it's good but actually it is just showbiz, it's publicity for the club but it didn't really add any weight to what had been happening.

ROY CHUTER: There were some funny moments, but not many. It dragged on and

73

on – absolutely terrible.

ANDERS SWAFFIELD: I was made to go and watch it in my holidays with my Dad. I remember wanting an ice cream but having to listen to old men speaking about something I had no interest in whatsoever.

ROZ SOUTH: It seemed really obvious to me, really early on, that the first planning inspector had no time for us whatsoever. He was very officious and was an appallingly bumptious character. He has to be impartial, obviously, that's the whole point of the planning process, that's why it's done by an independent inspector. But, he gave off very negative signals.

It was no surprise to me when we heard that that first report looked like it was going to go wrong. And, that was the point when I remember thinking 'We're stuffed, we're stuffed now because where are we going to go now?' If they just turn us down with a "no"' what's going to happen? It can't go anywhere else?'

23. FALMER POND
Whatever you do, don't feed the ducks!

ATTILA: There was this madness that Falmer, this idyllic village, would be spoilt by hooligans. I went to look at the pond, I'm into creepy crawlies – I'm really into wildlife. It was the middle of summer, the level of the water was very low. Some sad looking ducks, sitting on a half-built nest, in a dried up pond, with two crisp packets and a plastic bag, and best of all a sign: 'Don't feed the ducks, it encourages the rats'. On the spot I had to write a poem. I performed this poem in their hall in Falmer village. They didn't find it funny, I don't know why! I am sure we'll all get on fine in the future.

FALMER POND

Upon approach, the stench of foetid mud.
If, undeterred, you head towards this place
Mosquito clouds fly up into your face:
A vampire squadron, hungry for your blood.
And then you see the rats. Their gimlet eyes
Bore through you, as if sizing up their prey.
But they are full: they have a meal today.
A local dog has just met its demise.

It decomposes while they gnaw its flesh.
Diseased and dying ducks are all around
Choking on the used condoms that they've found
Their scab-encrusted feet caught in a mesh
Of rusting supermarket trolleys. Worse!
A host of bats (protected species, these)
Each carrying a different foul disease
Rises on stinking wings to spread a curse
Across the innocent East Sussex sky.
A chill runs down your spine, the message clear.
Abandon hope, all those who enter here:
This is a place where creatures come to die.
Then, from the shadows, awful shapes lurch forth.
Pale, hideous forms, by putrefaction scarred:
With querulous moans of 'Not In My Back Yard...'
The zombie hordes of Falmer Village North!

But, Mr Prescott, you are stout of heart.
You knocked that deadly Welsh egg thrower down
And didn't let the crap canoeist drown.
We knew your courage: you have played your part.
Outstanding Natural Beauty there will be
Next to that awful breeding place for flies.
You gave the word, and we will claim our prize:
A Stadium for the City by the Sea.

Attila The Stockbroker

24. DOWNING STREET
Surrounded by giggling girls

TIM CARDER: Once the inquiry had finished in the autumn of 2003, we did a little bit more campaigning: we gathered handwritten and typed letters to the Deputy Prime Minister asking for permission to build this stadium, and giving detailed reasons. We gathered folders of the petitions and took them up to Downing Street.

So there was Paul Samrah and his son, me, Mary Emery, Liz Costa, Des Lynam and Norman Cook in Westminster, gathered on the green that all the politicians do interviews on opposite the House of Commons, with our petition, and it said 'Falmer For All' on the front of these folders and we walked along to 10 Downing Street, and went through all the security process. I had been to Downing Street once before when I was about five and then you could just drive into Downing Street; this time you had to go through about ten minutes of security checks. Eventually, we walked along to number 10, posed outside the door there, knocked and went inside, met some official who took these folders with these letters from us and promised to give them to John Prescott, the Deputy Prime Minister and that was it; we adjourned for tea in the House of Commons.

JOHN COWEN: My memory is that I was standing next to Des Lynam and Norman Cook and these giggling, star-struck girls came up to ask if they could possibly approach Norman to get his autograph, as if I was some sort of minder or something.

SARAH WATTS: I made sure that both Desmond Lynam and Norman Cook were wearing their Bring Home the Albion ribbons. I found a photograph of me and Norman Cook on College Green that Roz took; I had just put the ribbon on his chest.

JAN SWALLOW: It was fun to be on a journey that had started for Bill and me in the 1950s at the Goldstone and now we were in Downing Street...

TIM CARDER: So, with that we largely put the whole campaigning to bed and we thought well, we can't do any more, we have done as much as we can, we thought the club presented a good case at the public inquiry; we sat back, didn't know when there would be a decision, but hoped for an early decision and just got on with watching football, nothing more we could do...

25. HOILE'S REPORT
A serious setback

PAUL CAMILLIN: Martin appeared ashen-faced in the office.

He said: "There's a problem with Falmer."

And I went: "Serious?"

And he said: "Yeah, serious."

"Oh shit."

PAUL SAMRAH: It all went tits up on February 4th 2004; not a good day.

BILL SWALLOW: It was an extraordinary surprise!

MARTIN PERRY: Charles Hoile, the Local Plan Inspector, wrote to the council and sent them his Local Plan inquiry report, and we were shocked that he had said: "You should not include the stadium at Village Way North because there are plenty of other sites." There had been no evidence given about other sites! None whatsoever! We were completely stunned that such a statement could be made with absolutely no evidence given at the inquiry to support it.

PAUL SAMRAH: The Hoile Report was released in advance of the result of the Public Inquiry but given that the two were going to marry up, it was fairly clear that if Hoile completely kyboshed Falmer, Collyer's Public Inquiry would also be a 'no' for Falmer.

The Hoile report completely overlooked the huge demand for the ground, that there would be community events held there not just football, that there is no other location, the report ignored everything the club had done – on traffic numbers, on demand, on building an aesthetically pleasing structure – everything was ignored. A complete waste of time and money because Hoile just turned round and said: "You're putting it on a field, we don't want you to."

ADRIAN NEWNHAM: I was absolutely shocked. You felt that our case had been so compelling. We could not believe what Hoile said and that anybody could find an alternative site. And that was the key in all this. We felt we had done the arguments over 'It's in the public interest'; we felt we had proved that there wasn't an alternative site and that the use of the land at Falmer was an exception because this was nationally important i.e. you weren't setting a precedent by it.

All these principles about building in an AONB we thought were answered. I think the wording actually was: 'The inspector feels that there are alternative sites that are more suitable'. 'Where?' It was just a complete bolt from the blue. We hadn't thought for one minute that was going to come out.

DICK KNIGHT: Hoile's arguments were not well validated, he got it wrong. He had misinterpreted what we were talking about, so it was fairly easy for us to pick off his arguments, but nevertheless we knew that it would be foolish to assume that the stadium inspector would come to a different conclusion because there they were sitting next to each other, chatting. They are all from the same breed and sure enough when that report – the official first stadium public inquiry report – came out, despite all the advice I'd been given, that first inspector, John Collyer, damned Falmer as well.

ROY CHUTER: What Hoile wrote was just bollocks basically. The only word to describe it. Although I didn't use that word in the programme.

TIM CARDER: My instant thought was 'Oh dear'. Probably a bit stronger.

This was a really severe setback. Charles Hoile, by the way, hardly said a word throughout the whole proceedings – he barely said more than about five sentences. He was the sort of the mystery man next to John Collyer, who came across as a fairly pleasant chap.

I wrote a letter of rebuttal rejecting the arguments that Hoile presented. I did it in a structured, forensic way, which was submitted to Prescott along with recommendations from the club and representations from other supporters.

The existing situation was that that piece of land could only be developed if either of the universities needed extra land, and that was the stance that Mr Hoile adopted; it is OK if the universities need it but if a football club needs it, no, no you can't build it. So this smacked to me of academic elitism; it's all right for academics, but it's not all right for the football hoi-polloi.

There were other aspects to his argument which, to me, didn't agree with what I heard as evidence at the public inquiry – but we were presented with his report as a fait accompli, and we assumed that Collyer's report would be saying the same sort of thing. This was a devastating blow because if that was the case and Prescott acted on Collyer's report then the stadium would not be allowed, and we all know what that would have meant. We were convinced Falmer was the only possible site that the stadium could be developed and we were sunk.

FALMER FOR ALL

PRESS RELEASE:

Despite an overwhelming show of public support a report by a planning inspector on the new Local Plan this week summarily dismissed the proposals. The final decision, however, now rests with the Deputy Prime Minister. We've had a huge response already, ten clubs came back to us within the first 90 minutes of being contacted, we're overwhelmed at the support we've received across the country. John Prescott should be in no doubt that this is a matter of national importance to the sporting community and beyond...

PAUL CAMILLIN: Dare I say it, we'd become a little bit complacent, or certainly I felt we had. During the planning inquiry, there wasn't much being done, it was sort of like a quiet period.

BILL SWALLOW: Perhaps we had been guilty of believing our own propaganda – we all felt the inquiry was going our way and it became apparent very late on that it wasn't.

PAUL WHELCH: In my view the club had not demonstrated some of the things they should have demonstrated clinically enough around the design of the stadium; around its visibility and around its environmental impact. That's my impression. The stadium was turned down on the evidence and not on the emotion.

PAUL SAMRAH: We didn't know when the Public Inquiry report was going to be issued, could've been issued any day after Hoile – and if that report said no to Falmer, there would've been no way back; you can only appeal on judicial grounds, but basically that would've been it… and that's why we said: 'We've got seven days to save the Albion.'

26. SEVEN DAYS TO SAVE THE ALBION
All hands on deck

ROZ SOUTH: It was all done to influence Prescott's brain.

BILL SWALLOW: If John Prescott went along with what we now knew his inspector was going to say to him – which is what politicians normally do – we were dead. The aim was to stop John Prescott rushing to the obvious decision.

TIM CARDER: When was Prescott going to make this decision? There was no indication as to when it was going to happen, we didn't know if Collyer's report was on his desk or what.

MARTIN PERRY: What the Local Plan Inspector's report did was to alert us to the fact that we had a big problem – the report that would be sitting on John Prescott's desk was going to say 'turn it down!' And that is the point where we turned back to the fans and said 'We need your help again, big time'. And the Falmer For All campaign, Paul Samrah and everyone, came back together, they were unified in what we were trying to achieve, they could turn that energy on in a very powerful way. And that's what did it…

ROZ SOUTH: When we first heard that these reports were going to come out I couldn't see where we could go from there. But actually we didn't have time to start thinking where we couldn't go – we've got to get to these people.

PAUL SAMRAH: Tim and I, we had 20 hour days, we just hit it, emails all over the country, supporters' clubs, media, press releases, anything.

TIM CARDER: The first action was getting the message out to other supporters. By now of course email was fairly common, hadn't been in the past, but we now had that on our side; so we asked supporters to absolutely bombard the office of the Deputy Prime Minister with messages saying: 'We ask you to approve the plans for the stadium at Falmer.' I am led to believe that we actually blocked the offices of the Deputy Prime Minister's email system for a couple of days – this was messages being passed on from all sorts of football fans elsewhere, the spirit of Fans United.

Wycombe

TIM CARDER: Three days after we'd known about the Hoile Report we had the Wycombe sit-in. I got in contact with Wycombe and they said yes you can have a sit-in after the game. It is not often that a football club which has nothing to do with the particular cause you have allowing a demonstration at its ground. I assured them it would be good-natured.

SAM SWAFFIELD: I remember the Wycombe game because I was going out with a girl who was a Wycombe fan at the time and I stood at the Wycombe end and watched the protest going on and I remember them singing 'We want Falmer, We want Falmer'.

BILL SWALLOW: 500 people bought tickets at the last moment when it was confirmed that our campaign was in serious trouble. The away end was absolutely packed with people holding posters and the players came out with banners after the game. On the way home we heard Peter Near speaking eloquently on 606. No one could have done more.

TIM CARDER: All the nationals were aware of it and we got publicity, 5 Live was there, Martin Perry was down on the touchline doing interviews, Kerry Mayo and other players paraded the banner after the game and it was great. It certainly got the message across that something was going on again.

SARAH WATTS: Our directors had a sit-in with the Wycombe directors! They weren't going to allow the players to get too close to us for some reason but they ended up getting completely involved; when you have got someone like Kerry Mayo, Brighton fan, Brighton boy, you are bound to want to get involved.

ROZ SOUTH: I'd designed a banner. One of the North Stand Chatters printed 5,000 leaflets about why people needed to write straight into the Secretary of State to forestall him. Ever so many people were happy to wave placards and make their own.

KERRY MAYO: All the players were aware of it and we all wore T-shirts for the warm-up to support the fans' campaign, so the players certainly knew about it. Any player that has come to the club, even in those bad times, commented on how good the fanbase is.

ROZ SOUTH: We did the Clock Tower protests that week as well, got signatures from that. Yes, we did collect umpteen signatures at various times, but that alone isn't going to get a stadium, it's not enough, because we're basically taking the campaign to people who are already on the same side. We had to take it to people who either haven't heard of it or might not be on the same side, we just need to know.

TIM CARDER: I'd set up Clubs in Crisis under the auspices of the Supporters' Club and really because we'd had so much help back in 1995 to 1997, especially Fans United, regarding our future, that I felt it was helpful if there was some central website for any club that was in crisis. Details of their particular crisis could be posted on there and supporters could go and see how they could help that particular club, if it meant signing a petition or whatever. I always had in my mind that this might be useful one day for our particular circumstances! And this was it! The message was on the site; sign our petitions, write letters to the Deputy Prime Minister, whatever it was. www.clubsincrisis.com!

Flowers

PAUL SAMRAH: I had this wonderful idea – where it came from, no idea – I was walking to work and I thought 'It's nearly Valentine's Day... bouquets of flowers... let's do Valentines bouquets for the Deputy Prime Minister... from all the football clubs... well, clubs aren't going to organise it themselves... so we'll organise it, print an individual message from each club on the cards, we've got the funds, and let's give the flowers to hospitals afterwards – get the charitable bit right!'

So I told Dodge (Paul Rodgers, ex Albion midfielder and now working for the club) and Tim and Bill said he'd design cards with the club crests, so he produced 91 cards from all the other clubs. I contacted the Football League, 4 o'clock Friday afternoon, I came back from work early, I asked them: "How do I get an email out to all the clubs?" They said they send out a bulletin on the Friday to all Football League clubs and they will add my message to that, telling clubs what we were organising and asking them for the words they would like on the cards.

In a matter of minutes after they sent the email, I got three calls, Bolton was one... and there were emails coming through from clubs with their words. I went to the local flower shop and gave her the bulk order: I said 91 bouquets, here's the money and I want you to drive them up, if you can, to Whitehall. She said: "For 91 bouquets I'll do whatever the hell you want." She drove them up on the Tuesday morning to the Deputy Prime Minister's office in Whitehall in her white little van, she was great, brilliant, she got a picture of herself outside the deputy PM's office.

PAUL CAMILLIN: There was this carpet of flowers in Whitehall outside his offices which was great!

MARTIN PERRY: We thought, actually, that we better phone up Prescott's protection officer – he is the Deputy Prime Minister – and tell them look, there are some flowers coming and labels... But the protection officer said: "I've been getting flowers, chocolates and cards all fucking morning!"

PAUL SAMRAH: Then Jim the Balloon Man, great bloke, came with me after we'd put out all the flowers and a banner, photographed everything, and we took all the cards off the bouquets, gave them to the concierge to the ODPM with a note, saying we've delivered the bouquets, however, now we are removing the bouquets and taking them to the hospitals and these are the messages. Then we shot off in a taxi with all these bouquets of flowers, went into the waiting room at St Thomas' Hospital and the Westminster Hospital and walked in at the Casualty and A & E area, Jim and I handed over these bouquets of flowers, saying: "We're here to deliver a bouquet of flowers from Brighton football club," it was unreal, we felt like Father Christmas.

JOHN COWEN: We distributed some of the bouquets to unsuspecting old ladies and tourists – and I remember the look of astonishment on their faces when these people in blue and white striped shirts handed them a bouquet. "What is this? Is it an English custom in Whitehall?"

ROY CHUTER: There were a lot more flowers than in a flower shop; there's a picture of me carrying flowers somewhere and there aren't many pictures of me carrying flowers for many reasons.

PAUL SAMRAH: It didn't really get national publicity. Local was brilliant – but, it was getting through to Prescott, it was on his doorstep, we were mounting the pressure.

TIM CARDER: Supporters were sending Valentine cards into John Prescott's office, but we also came up with the idea of delivering a giant Valentine Card to him in Hull. We were playing Grimsby at the weekend and it is not that far from Hull so we diverted to his constituency office. Working for the printers again I had a giant Valentine card made that was about five feet by three feet and it opened up and there was this message: 'Roses are red, Brighton are blue. Our club's future is all down to you'.

Valentine's Day

JOHN PRESCOTT: I came home and found a Valentine card, something like seven foot by seven foot from the Seagulls; I don't know how the Post Office delivered it – but it showed me how much the community wanted the stadium.

PAUL SAMRAH: Roz South came up with the wording. Prescott still talks about it to this day. When he came to visit the new stadium he mentioned it. The luck of it, we were playing Grimsby down the road! The chances are we could've been playing Swansea away but we weren't and it was just straight in our lap. It was staring us in the face, 14th February we were at Grimsby.

PAUL CAMILLIN: Bill and Jan, in their little Citroen van, drove this huge card up there (or rather, didn't - see below), then we all decamped to Grimsby, which I remember was

a very wet and miserable day and we got beat 2-1 but, thankfully, it didn't derail the play-off charge.

BILL SWALLOW: Hull was fun with the giant Valentine's card. We designed an enormous card to fit in the van we owned at the time. Tim got it printed and the day before we were due to set off for Grimsby, somebody drove into the back of the van. Bit of a problem. Somehow we got this giant Valentine's card on to the team coach. We rented a car and followed the coach up to Hull, then borrowed the Albion's kit van - I don't suppose we were insured - to take the poster to the Labour Party HQ at East Hull, John Prescott's constituency. The supporters' coach did a detour and came to Hull, just so there could be lots of blue and white stripy people, and we took a photo and the people of the Labour Party thought it was huge fun. They took the card round to John Prescott's house and he put it up in his kitchen. Loved it, apparently.

RICHIE MORRIS: The Valentine's card – I forget whose ideas it was, I am convinced it was mine but I may have dreamt that. The fact we were going to Grimsby and it was so near John Prescott's office it would have been criminal not to do something. I was at university there and didn't live far from his base so thought it would be a great idea to take the campaign to his doorstep and hammer it home just how serious we were. Also it was light-hearted and this really shone through in everything we did.

Anyhow, we got down there and it was a pokey little office in East Hull. This really sharp suited New Labour guy answered the door, apologised, and said John had been called away on really important business but that he had left his agent, who he had worked with for 40 years and was his right-hand man, to accept it on his behalf. So they wheeled this old guy out and I said to him it was a real shame Mr Prescott had been called away but that we understood he was a busy man and the old boy said: "He's not been called away. He is playing golf in Hessle." They took the card off and promised he would look at it and I know someone who was interviewing him a couple of months later about something completely different and I told him to ask John if he got the card and, to his credit, he remembered exactly what was on it and had obviously read it. He said they had it up in their offices, but I never trust a politician.

About half a dozen Hull City fans turned up to show their support. Living in Hull I saw first-hand the benefits their new stadium had on their community, so I think our cause resonated particularly well with them.

One of the frustrating things I found was when you felt like you could not do anything – you were just waiting on these faceless civil servants to make their decision. You didn't feel there was much you could do to influence it. That is why these sorts of things were important. It kept spirits and morale up and I think, if anything, that was equally, if not more, important than actually influencing the decision-makers. It might have given John Prescott a smile but most of us know the decision was not really made by him, but it gave people a sense they could do something; it gave fans a sense of ownership of the campaign.

MARTIN PERRY: Prescott came up to the site in the General Election and he was falling about laughing over it. The list of things that they got up to was absolutely brilliant... I can remember sitting at meetings rocking with laughter at some of the things they thought up! It was brilliant, absolutely outstanding!

Letter Writing

ROY CHUTER: There was endless letter writing...When I was working on the programme the thing I remember most is having to come up with new explanations for why we were writing this latest letter. Different letters to different people and every one of them was backed up by a piece in the programme, and on the websites, and people wrote in their hundreds and thousands – so, obviously we must have been successful.

National Falmer Day

SARAH WATTS: National Falmer Day – March 6th 2004. An awful lot of other Brighton fans led the way on that one and that was good. We didn't have a game that day, they went off – Albion fans at West Ham United and around the country, it was great the support they got. Liz and I went down to Bognor, took our support out to local football. You can't do everything and it is great when other people are happy to take it on. I was quite happy to take a back seat on that one.

TIM CARDER: The National Falmer Day was again an initiative of North Stand Chat that was taken up quite well. Such was the intense nature of this part of the campaign that I chose to leave the travelling and canvassing of other supporters, to my fellow fans. I stayed at home but I did get a load of leaflets printed and handed them out to the supporters that were going; it was a very worthwhile initiative.

PAUL SAMRAH: We sent fans around the country and got loads of people to sign postcards which we then sent off.

TIM CARDER: One of the things we had to show in these 'Seven Days to Save the Albion' – which actually turned into nearer seven months! – was to build within an Area of Outstanding Natural Beauty, essentially, you have to show that the development is in the national interest. That this isn't just a local thing, this is a thing that affects people in Oxford, Bristol, Birmingham, so we did that by getting people across the country to email and write letters and also going out to get them to do that on National Falmer Day… Some people went to Crystal Palace and they got a good welcome, Crystal Palace aren't all bad despite what some people think.

Early Day Motions

PAUL WHELCH: One of the clear ways it seemed to me to demonstrate that Falmer was an issue of national importance was to demonstrate it to Parliament. What I thought was we have got some of the best football campaigners and negotiators in the country sitting round this table, we can organise an Early Day Motion and we can lobby support to get it moving.

I knew a guy who was, at the time, a Member of Parliament for Burnley, Peter Pike. What we had to do, to get the thing signed and into parliament, was get the motion signed by an MP. Then they try and get six members of parliament to, effectively, support it before it can go into the… I think they call it the 'votes office'. So, I spent the afternoon phoning up MPs who I thought were helping and getting them to agree. We got David Lepper, MP from Brighton Pavilion, then MP for Kemp Town, Des Turner, the MP for Hastings and a couple of others. We got our six and it went in on the website, which was great, and the Labour Party got behind it as you might imagine, those who didn't were the Liberals… In the end we got 145 MPs to sign it.

TIM CARDER: In the end we got up to 145 MPs, which was pretty good, this put it in the top five or ten per cent of all the EDMs in the Commons. We did this through sheer hard work: fans approaching MPs, it might be fans living in other parts of the country, even non Albion fans approaching MP's and asking them to sign up.

I did a fair bit of work, sending off letters to any MP that hadn't signed up, but I'd also encourage other people to send letters too, but as part of this campaign. I did a postcard

– like the seaside postcards you get, not the fat lady type, but four views around Brighton and Hove. One picture of the Royal Pavilion opposite a night view of the stadium – iconic view and an iconic building that was proposed for development. I took a picture of Sheepcote Valley, because that was one of the main sites being touted by the opponents. I took a very nice downland picture; essentially it is a downland valley, and it's a very, very open access area, people love going for walks there in stark contrast to the field next to the University of Brighton! And the final shot I captured was the view from across the A27 of our field at Falmer. I got about three or four shots of it. I'm not a great photographer but I took a decent enough shot and in one of these, there was a lorry speeding by in it and it was a Focus DIY lorry! I thought 'how ironic is that'!

Anyway, I had these postcards printed, stuck a little sticker on saying please sign EDM 889, with reasons on the back why the MPs should sign this EDM. We asked people via the Clubs In Crisis website all over the country to give us their name. We looked up their MP and signed the name for them and put their postcode on.

And just to make it look a little bit authentic instead of it all coming from Brighton, I split them up into Lancashire and Yorkshire, wherever it was, and sent it off to someone in Lancashire or Yorkshire to put in the pillar boxes in that area too so they came with a reasonably authentic looking postmark. It was a little bit of a con I suppose because the people hadn't actually signed them, but they had in principle, and they had given us permission to sign for them.

We drove it up slowly but surely to 145 MPs and that to my mind was a major achievement of that part of the campaign. I'm sure Prescott must have seen it and thought "Blimey, we've got all these emails coming in, I've got letters coming in and I have got these Valentine's cards, I've got most of my MPs signing up to this EDM... this is something that is not just an ordinary planning thing where I just go along with what the inspector said, I've got to look at this carefully" – and to my mind it was this campaign what won us the stadium!

PAUL SAMRAH: It didn't matter if we got a letter from MPs saying they couldn't vote for it because we weren't in their constituency – at least it had registered, they might remember the interesting postcard we sent. It worked.

ROZ SOUTH: I think EDMs are OK, I think EDMs are better than no EDMs, but as an effective tool they're not particularly great. Some of the Falmer For All campaigners were very excited about EDMs and some of us were fairly unexcited about them.

Moles

PAUL SAMRAH: The network of people we had around! People in various departments that we shouldn't have known about but we did... I wouldn't say they had an effect on the campaign – but I have no doubt it was a huge help. Steve Bassam and Ivor Caplin were lobbying discreetly, because the planning inquiry had closed and you can't really submit new arguments or issues... but, I think Prescott was well aware. Steve Bassam had Prescott's ear; he was very close.

ROZ SOUTH: There are people high up, that I can't name, even now, so high up in terms of working in places like the Deputy Prime Minister's office... We had to get to Prescott... One of the things we did know was that John Prescott wanted to reform the planning system and some of us wondered whether he'd had some sort of run-in with the planning inspectorate, who I suspect he thought were patronising, and I think anyone who patronised John Prescott made a very big error. So, I think Prescott took the view that I'm the Secretary of State, I make decisions, you can make a recommendation but you don't tell me. If I think something's right I'm going to take notice of what you've said, but don't you be telling me what I'm gonna do.

A different Secretary of State, without Prescott's more complex personality and his own issues, might just have turned round and said 'Well I'm not a planning inspector, if they don't think it's in the right place, well who am I to say different'.

STEVE BASSAM: What I was able to do was to talk to some of the political advisors within government, in the department which was then the Office of the Deputy Prime Minister, so that we could work out the fallback strategy; and the fallback strategy, in essence, was to look again at that site, as opposed to other sites, and see which was the best possible site for the stadium.

One 'F' in Falmer

RICHIE MORRIS: We did a one-off fanzine with some of the people on NSC. It was called *One F in Falmer*. It was different people's stories put together. A couple of people went to the pub in Falmer and interviewed the anti-Albion landlord while holding a 'We Want Falmer' banner underneath him; someone else wrote about spending a day handing out flyers to people stuck in traffic jams; another about their memories of the Goldstone. It was not the best publication in the world. It was botched together in-between me doing my university newspaper and a degree. Roz South did a great job making the mess I came up with readable (and printable). It came out and we sold about 1,000 copies and the proceeds went to the fighting fund.

It was when there was a bit of a lull and it was something I came up with to keep us busy. Loads of people from NSC sent their articles in, others lent money towards the printing cost. It was nowhere near as good as the fanzines of years gone by, but I think it was a useful way of giving people an insight into what some of the other fans were doing. There was a lot of feeling powerless during the campaign and doing things like this was something which not only made you feel positive but also filled the time while we all waited for the cogs of democracy to turn.

JOHN COWEN: I had some ideas which weren't taken on board... like An Hour For The Albion; everyone, instead of just donating money into buckets, (and this is all very democratic and socially levelling), for one designated hour, regard that hour as being worked, not for ourselves, but for the Albion. However, it was suggested to me that people were already having a sort of Albion charity fatigue and would not wish to put their hands in their pockets anymore.

Cardiff (Thank you, Adam Virgo)

TIM CARDER: The play-off final – from the campaign point of view we couldn't have hoped for anything better.

PAUL SAMRAH: We're at Cardiff for the play-off final, we're on national TV! The luck we had was phenomenal! I remember walking to our city office the morning after the Swindon game, and thinking: "Everyone's going to be buying tickets, they were going on

sale on Saturday – we must be able to give them something, they're all on our side…" As I walked up from Farrington Station to our city office I'd worked out in my mind a 'Wish you were here' card, so I rang Bill Swallow and Bill said excellent, Tim said excellent. So that morning Bill did the artwork, agreed who'd we write it to, agreed the wording, absolutely fantastic, straight in. 'We're pleased to be here, but we wish we were here' with pictures of the Millennium Stadium and Falmer on it. We picked the printed postcards up from the printers, Tim and I, at about 9:30 that Friday night – 13 hours after the idea generated in my mind! Tim and I got back to Withdean the next morning at 6.30 am.

People queued up to get tickets and we put boxes of these on turnstiles and everyone who got a ticket got a card. We got 16,000 sent to the DPM's office! It was just staggeringly easy! And the best thing, it was such a simple idea; no committee, no nothing, we just bloody well did it.

BILL SWALLOW: The bit I liked best of the things we did was to do with the play-off final. Jan, me, Paul Samrah and Paul Camillin sat round our kitchen table for no more than an hour and came up with 15 different banners for the Bristol City game and within days they were distributed around the Millennium Stadium. I don't think any other organisation could have done that. Paul S had found out where people were sitting around the Millennium Stadium and the ones next to balconies were contacted and given banners. I remember handing one over to a woman in Coldean and she asked if I was Paul Samrah's father. Wounded me forever.

We handed out banners in Cardiff as people went into the ground and within an hour of the stadium opening they were all round the stadium. From the kitchen table to Cardiff in ten days. With Paul Samrah's drive and determination; no committees, nothing vetted, we just made up the messages, submitted them to no-one and up they went. That is how it was done. And just as we did that so other people were doing other things – we were certainly not exceptional. Having the showcase of the Millennium was a bit fortunate. Thank you Adam Virgo.

PAUL SAMRAH: Organising all the banners and flags I simply rang up Millennium Stadium and said: "Can you email me a complete stadium plan, I want to know all the banner places, can we put banners up?" "Yes." "That's all I needed, thank you very much." I needed people in each block. And I just made a list of all the blocks and put an appeal out on North Stand Chat, people would come and collect the banner with string and I turned up at the Millennium Stadium and the banners were up. Brilliant, just absolutely brilliant. That was just so uplifting.

BILL SWALLOW: When we started putting some banners up at the Millennium Stadium, stewards came up and said; "You are not allowed to do that because they are political messages – 'Listen to us, Mr Prescott'". But, Paul had previously got clearance for all the messages with the Chief Safety Officer at the Millennium Stadium, which was extremely clever. Our campaign sometimes looked anarchic but all the time Paul was quietly writing memos to make sure everything worked. Paul manufactured our own luck really.

KERRY MAYO: I remember all the Prescott banners, definitely, and to be fair, fair play to Prescott – it was him who granted us the stadium wasn't it? So the message must have got across.

STEFAN SWIFT: It's funny how newspaper coverage of the lower leagues has just diminished and diminished, and it takes you having to have the play-off finals to be able to publicise things like a stadium campaign. I was always shocked at the level of disinterest towards the Albion stadium campaign across the national newspapers.

DAVE SWAFFIELD: It was an absolute gift, the amount of support, and the banners at the Millennium. It was just very well run and you know every interview was saying look, we've got 30,000 here, we could fill that stadium at Falmer, don't worry about that.

ANDERS SWAFFIELD: I remember the banners being put up, I remember getting there and seeing all of them. I kind of got it then by that point, got what was going on.

PAUL SAMRAH: And how brilliant it was we won in 90 minutes because there still was 30 minutes left of television coverage and they were just showing our publicity for Falmer. More luck!

27. JOHN PRESCOTT FAN CLUB
"All around the world, people ask about the Albion"

PAUL SAMRAH: We had to influence John Prescott. We needed civil servants who advised him to pick up on what was happening and tell him there was a bloody big problem down in Brighton and if you turn it down you're going to get all the sports pages going at you – and that will seep into the front pages. The club has cleansed itself. It's going places and you will be seen as stifling a burgeoning community. Every bit of publicity had to be milked to get that message as close to him as possible. He needed to know what it meant locally, and what it meant nationally.

We still didn't know when the decision was going to come, could've come at any time.

John Prescott Fan Club (~~provisional~~)

After five months the word on the street was that he'd got the message, that he was trying to find any way around it – going beyond the planning inspector's report and appealing to what the mass public wanted; we had to demonstrate there was the demand and we were up against a handful of objectors – what hadn't come through at the first inquiry was the strength of support for what was being proposed – and that's what Seven Days to Save the Albion was all about. Now, broadsheets were writing articles, football fans around the country were supporting us. It was about the strength of support. We got that campaign right; I'd run it like that again.

PAUL CAMILLIN: For me, the fans' campaign moved Prescott's decision from a 'no' to a 'maybe'. The campaign was intense, Prescott said it himself, he had Brighton fans coming up to him all around the world; in Japan, Singapore and Australia and Hong Kong. "Nice to meet you John". "Yeah, it's great that I'm here for this trade conference…", "Bugger that, are you gonna say 'yes' to Falmer?"

JOHN PRESCOTT: It's amazing how many people want to be identified with the Seagulls; it's the only football club where I have gone round the world and someone has come up and said: "What are you going to do about the Seagulls?" I am half way round the world and someone comes up and identifies with the bloody Seagulls! The fans' campaign was absolutely remarkable! Anywhere I went in the world – I was doing climate negotiations in Kyoto and suddenly this guy came up and said to me; "What are you doing for the Seagulls?" They have fans all around the world. Even on trains, I was travelling on a train and someone came up and said; "Can you just give me a couple of minutes, I want to…" I said; "You don't want to talk to me about the bloody Seagulls do you?" "Yes". It's amazing. Of course, I had to say I couldn't give them a comment, I was the planning officer, and at the end of the day that is what secretary of states are there for, but eventually the decision came and that was the right decision and seeing that ground there are no more doubts in my mind at all, not that I ever had any.

BOB BRUCE: Prescott was bombarded by all the fans wasn't he? It was hilarious, they would turn up everywhere… so he had a sort of respect for the fans…

MARTIN PERRY: There's a wonderful story about when he was campaigning in the north-east, and he was outside a shopping centre and this little old lady saw his entourage, goes up to one of Prescott's aides and says; "Can I have a word with John Prescott?" So they say; "What about?" And she says; "Brighton. Brighton's new stadium." And he says; "Not another one…" On North Stand Chat later that day, there's a thread comes up 'Respect To My Mum'.

And it was because of the campaign that Prescott realised he had a problem, because he realised that he had, at that time, three Labour MPs in Brighton and he understood that this was a political decision. This was a big, big issue and he had to get it right. The key points that we needed to get through to him were, first of all, that there wasn't any other site; secondly, the big arguments with the social and economic benefits of the stadium. And, the argument hinged around the fact that the stadium site was in an area that was an Area of Outstanding Natural Beauty – but when it was designated an AONB that was 40 years ago and, of course, since then it had suffered severe environmental damage, but at that point it was still an AONB. But, there is case law in the Pembroke National Park where planning permission had been granted on the basis that there had to be a proven need – and nobody, nobody not even the opponents denied that we needed a new stadium – and secondly that that need could not be met in some other way, and that was about was there a better site? And the third key issue was the development would deliver social and economic benefits in the national interest and it was proving that they were in the 'national interest' that was the issue.

ROZ SOUTH: It had to get very political at that point and I think we were very fortunate in having John Prescott, because I thought that John Prescott saw himself as a bit of a maverick, he wasn't popular amongst the Blair coterie. I think he has a huge sense of pride John Prescott, in that he'd risen from what you might call old Labour ranks – working class – and I think actually he liked being a bit of a maverick, he wanted to listen. He thought the campaign was fantastic; he laughed, he said that everywhere he went he saw a Brighton fan and they all popped up and said; "Hello Mr Prescott, now what about the stadium." And he laughed, and he loved getting Valentine's cards, and he loved the attention. Now another Secretary of State might have been horrified by that.

It is unlike almost any other campaign to have been able to keep up that almost constant flood of creativity and wit and charm and to encourage thousands of fans to work to that kind of agenda. It got nasty later on.

Prescott enjoyed the postcards, his agent said: "Oh it's wonderful, he loves it, more stuff from Albion fans, oh good."

STEVE BASSAM: John says that it was one of the nicest campaigns that he ever had pitched at him.

ADRIAN NEWNHAM: You can't have a giant Valentine's card turn up at your constituency office on Valentine's Day and not be affected by it. You can't have 91 bunches of flowers turn up at your office and not be affected by it… and none of that could turn round and be accused of bribery. Norman Baker complained about the glass of water and the meat pie but actually nobody could claim that getting 91 bunches of flowers was in any way bribery, because it was all little symbolic things that kept dripping in at the government officers.

28. PRESCOTT'S (IN) DECISION
There's no other site

JOHN PRESCOTT: My choice was to say – were the alternatives better than the site that was being chosen and which the council preferred? The obvious one, Falmer, had the transport locations and I thought made sense.

I came and looked at the site and talked to a number of people involved with it, and saw where they were going to use the parking grounds on the college there, and there was a railway running, it was just a no brainer.

ROZ SOUTH: Simply, what he said was: there will be a stadium in Brighton and Hove; what we're going to do is make certain that there is nowhere else more suitable than Falmer.

PAUL CAMILLIN: On BBC radio they said; "It's 'No' to Falmer". That was the news. They'd got it wrong, and we very quickly rang them and said; "No, it's 'maybe', we've got another chance effectively."

STEFAN SWIFT: On the front page of *The Argus* was the Albion campaign team sipping champagne, on the third page of *The Argus* was the anti-Falmer group sipping champagne, and I couldn't quite work out what had happened, so I remember thinking: "I'm just going to just read the front page, because the third page was a bit depressing;" it was bizarre.

STEVE BASSAM: What John Prescott did was he re-opened the inquiry with a different inspector (I think the previous one was unavailable) and the remit given was to judge Falmer against other sites, using criteria.

A minister receives a report from a public inquiry and acts on the advice of officials, so his or her officials will read it, summarise and advise. On the Hoile report they advised that we need to have a further look because we need a resolution to this problem; so the suggestion of the advisers was 'what you might then do, Deputy Prime Minister, is judge Falmer against other options'.

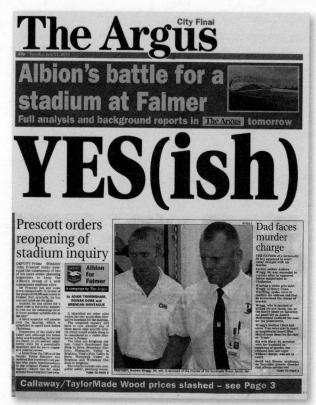

So, Prescott then decided that is what he would then do, which was very wise of him. It was the moment where the whole project was saved.

MARTIN PERRY: Prescott took the decision not to take a decision – but to re-open the inquiry, which although frustrating, was his only route out.

TIM CARDER: The inspector's report had said: 'I recommend against this proposal', and yet he hadn't gone with that recommendation. At that point, I was convinced that we were eventually going to get Falmer. For me, that was a high.

I think Paul Samrah called it an 'amber light' for Falmer: if we could show that the other sites were not feasible, and I was convinced that we would do that, then I could see that Prescott was going to give us the green light for Falmer.

I was interviewed by BBC South on that day, and I had to go to The Swan at Falmer to give my reaction, and the strange thing was that I was upbeat saying; "Bring on the second inquiry, we're going to show that the other sites don't work, Falmer is the only site for the stadium." But, just a few yards away from me were the Falmer villagers celebrating because they thought they'd defeated the proposal.

BILL SWALLOW: We were all thinking, 'oh gawd, are we misreading this?' The anti-Falmer brigade had the bubbly open and credit to them, their PR was pretty slick. One sometimes wonders about the BBC. They go to Falmer village pond, which is where most people had been persuaded the stadium was going to be built, to interview the villagers talking about victory when it wasn't a victory at all. All our campaigners had a moment of deep depression but then we thought, hold on… the fact that he hasn't made a decision is almost a decision in itself. Very quickly people began to think if we play it right now, we are almost there.

ADRIAN NEWNHAM: His legal advisers had done a great job. Prescott could have said 'no' on the information that he got; I think most people would agree the reason he didn't was political, although in law he has to be above it being a purely political decision. But, at the end of the day, politicians have to make decisions which are in the interests of the majority.

DICK KNIGHT: He found a reason to re-open the inquiry because he realised that the findings of this first inspector were flawed. Our campaign gave reasons why his report was flawed and they hadn't understood the issues properly, so by the time the stadium report was officially published, we had inundated Prescott with all the reasons why the recommendation of the first inspector was invalid.

He was touched by the wit, ingenuity and power of the campaign. He was strongly advised by other people in government that this was a big issue, a national issue. We had made our stadium a national issue and the media had made it a national issue. And Prescott was told he'd better listen, because you know there are ten million football fans around the country and most of them had voted for us...

So Prescott was minded to look at Falmer again, only due to the public pressure. He did listen to the fans.

In the public perception, John Prescott is seen as a bit of a buffoon, but as far as I am concerned in the dealings I had with him, he was on the ball, smart and very fair. He said; "Dick, there are two sides to every argument, but I never realised how much support you had for it."

ROZ SOUTH: It was quite obvious that all Prescott wanted to do was to say 'yes', but he was being advised very carefully to make sure that you don't give the opponents any loopholes, and that although you might want to say 'yes', it's not tactful just to overrule two planning inspectors, you've got to do something a little bit cleverer than that. Otherwise he might have ended up with a judicial review, which would have taken it way out of his hands. A judicial review is entirely to do with the fact that decisions have been made incorrectly; it would have been a slap in the face for Prescott if it'd gone to judicial review, because they'd have said 'well you're incompetent, you know nothing, the process is so flawed that you've presided over a flawed process and given your agreement to it'.

It was very depressing to think about all that expense that was going to have to be found, and all the work to be done, but it did seem to me to be a positive step, because the other step would have just been to have agreed with Hoile's report. We were still in the game.

ED BASSFORD: Where the club were very lucky was that Prescott's decision not only acknowledged the need for a new stadium in the Brighton area, it also said it needed to be a stadium that met the requirements of the football club, which was 22,500 people, and you can't build a 22,500 capacity stadium at Withdean, because the site isn't big enough. And, that's what won the argument at the end of the day, it was that little detail.

I think someone was being very clever in all of this process and that's partly why the campaigning was important, because it was focused on the fact that tens of thousands of people want to watch football in Brighton.

The critical factor in Charles Hoile's conclusion was that this application was not in the national interest. His judgment was that this was a small town football club; there wasn't the national interest at stake. Well, the national interest is a matter of judgment, it's not a factual thing you can demonstrate, it is a matter of opinion. And, my understanding of the law is, when you get into the area where an opinion becomes a relevant factor in a decision, you reach a point where it's fair to have the opinion; and if someone who is the decision maker has the opinion that this is in the national interest, you've satisfied the legal requirement that it's in the national interest… And, I think that's what happened, but it only happened because of the campaigning.

It's very rare in the planning process for a planning decision to be considered by the decision maker at the top, it's considered by the advisers and they say, 'this is it, this is the advice we give you, we've taken everything into account, rubber stamp the recommendations that's given'. This particular one clearly got to Prescott, got to a lot of other people in high places as well.

SARAH WATTS: We hadn't had the door slammed in our face – we still had a life-line. We just got on with it, it was just the next step. What do we do now was the next question, what next?

29. LABOUR CONFERENCE ONE
Operation Barry

TIM CARDER: There was a player for the Albion called Barry Bridges. So we called this Operation Barry.

The idea was to hang banners on all the bridges down the A23 and A27 so the delegates driving to conference could see all the signs: 'One 'F' in Falmer', 'Enjoy your conference, don't condemn us to ours', 'We still need a stadium' and so on. Paul and I went out at night to find the routes to all these bridges and see what mechanisms could be used for hanging banners on them.

PAUL SAMRAH: On the Saturday night, at midnight, everyone met at the Black Lion Hotel and I gave instructions out to the teams. Tim and I had numbered all the bridges, we had directions on how to get to the bridges, how to access the bridges because not all of them were road bridges, some were footbridges. We had 36 banners to put up.

BILL SWALLOW: All the cars headed off into the darkness, loaded with banners. The first one Paul, Jan and I do is on a farm flyover at Pyecombe. I have this memory of Paul dashing over the bridge giggling – you can always spot a chartered accountant – chased by the lights of a car. Later, we got a call through from Peter Near – who taught at Shoreham College – saying he was on the brink of getting arrested on the A27 by the Met. Paul somehow managed to persuade the police that it was all right.

JOHN COWEN: I was deputed to go with Liz Costa and Sarah Watts in a very small car. I remember one bridge we had to do, by Hollingbury; we were parked up, and we suddenly realised that there was a police car opposite, and I think Liz made us get back in the car and zoom off again. Goodness knows what the police thought – this elderly gentleman and these two buxom ladies... It must have looked pretty weird.

PAUL SAMRAH: There was a real concern about terrorism and the policing was heavy, there were police on basically every bloody bridge, which didn't help. We had to duck and dive.

BILL SWALLOW: On the Sunday morning, we thought we'd drive down to the Conference and bask in the glory of all these banners we had put up. Every single one had gone overnight.

JAN SWALLOW: And apparently that was the Met. It wasn't Sussex Police. They were involved because of the Prime Minister's security.

BILL SWALLOW: There may be a by-law involved but there was nothing really illegal about what we were doing.

JAN SWALLOW: We tied them very carefully with those plastic ties. We were very careful so that none of them could fall down into the traffic.

BILL SWALLOW: Very disappointing. Our greatest failure!

The First March

JOHN PRESCOTT: I remember the march. I think I was up in my room when they

marched past; they gave cheers and I thought that was nice but that was the reception I always got really from Seagulls fans and I thought it was very good; next day it was the fox hunters – I didn't get as good a response from them.

SARAH WATTS: For the march we came up with the idea of making huge sticks of rock – huge cardboard tubes, painted them pink and put the writing through the end.

It was noisy and joyful, it was again something easy for fans to do, they felt that they were doing something; we had to show up and walk and sing a few songs. It was visually and audibly a great wave of support and it got a lot of support, and Prescott loved it.

TIM CARDER: The club reported it as up to 10,000 people but I think the official consensus was about 4,000 which was, nevertheless, pretty good. We marched along the seafront from Volks railway station to the Brighton Centre. Lots of singing and chanting, it was led by Carnival Collective, a great happy noise, but there was a serious message behind it – there were plenty of placards, local celebrities were joining in, and local politicians – and Billy Bragg was there wearing an Albion shirt. It was friendly and it was asking the government to make a positive decision.

DAN TESTER: The first one was huge. That was brilliant. Most of the first-team squad were there. You had to be there to show your support to the cause. Everyone turned up straight from work, in their suits.

STEVE BASSAM: There were a few ex-managers on the march; they're a good bunch aren't they? They always come out for the Albion, it does say a lot actually about the affection for which the Albion is held really, I think it is brilliant.

TIM HERBERT: Really good for morale, incredible. The team and the manager were behind us. They all came out with us and they supported the supporters – Peter Ward turned up at one of them. Fantastic, just brilliant he got involved.

JOHN COWEN: I remember the crowd on the seafront and Prescott waving on the balcony… he never had so many fans, did he?

ROY CHUTER: I wheeled my mum along there in her wheelchair. She was an Albion fan, all my family are huge Albion fans. Mum sadly died 18 months ago and she was in a wheelchair for the last few years of her life. You've got to do these things. She was really keen to get involved and she'd written all the letters and things and she hadn't been able to go up to Mellor to protest against Archer or anything like that, but I could take her on the marches.

ROZ SOUTH: I designed a 'pledge card' which is a montage of John Prescott giving a 'thumbs up' gesture in front of supporters at the Millennium Stadium, Cardiff. He's carrying a report in his hand to which I then added the words 'It's Falmer For All'. On the back was a take-off of the original Labour Party pledge card from their election campaign in 2001, which the Falmer For All team altered to make it relevant to the stadium campaign, and was circulated to all delegates at the 2004 conference.

RICHIE MORRIS: I was doing my NCTJ in Brighton and I skipped lessons and spent the week handing out flyers to the delegates. One day it was pouring down and I was stood next to a socialist worker and some woman called Kitten, who had been on that year's *Big Brother*, handing out leaflets calling for the smashing of the state.

I felt obliged to do it more than anything. The camaraderie was good. That sense of community and togetherness has really shone through. Maybe because of the trouble we have been through there are fewer divisions in our support. As strange as it sounds it felt like a privilege to be one of the people who got to give out the flyers to MPs. Especially, having missed out on the campaigning at the end of the Goldstone years, it felt like I was paying my dues. I am still a million miles behind a lot of people in that respect, but a week of flyering is not exactly much to ask when you look at the big picture. Spending a week in the rain was the least I could do.

Media vs MPs

PAUL SAMRAH: We had the media football match – the MPs versus the media – and both in 2004 and 2005 it took place at Withdean, so, of course, it's a perfect opportunity... I'm on the PA and Martin said you can have freedom, you can do what you want and I just listed about 30 things while they were playing. Things like "Could players kindly stop shouting instructions across the pitch because we've had complaints from the neighbours that you're ruining their Sunday morning"; "We've had a report a Jag is blocking the entrance to Withdean... and we've had a report of another Jag blocking the entrance to Withdean so would the owner of two Jags kindly move their cars..." "Can we please have volunteers to take down the goalposts and replace the hammer net please". Tessa Jowell was there, Ed Balls and Ruth Kelly; fantastic, great fun.

TIM CARDER: The whole week of that Labour Party conference in 2004 I found quite uplifting because of the support we were getting from the delegates, they were asking questions like 'why did it have to be in an AONB' for instance, to which I explained the reasons, explained the context of that piece of land that was still in the outdated boundary of the AONB, and I found their backing to be uplifting – probably eight out of ten delegates that I spoke to were supportive, so hugely uplifting.

Also... I went to a fringe meeting at the Queens Hotel which was about football and football governance and I spoke up about the state of the local football club and its lack of ground and its history of bad ownership. I was reassured at the end of that meeting privately by... might be slightly improper... bearing in mind at this stage there was a second public inquiry to come... maybe for this book it's best to say: "I got positive vibes from a leading politician." I left the meeting feeling reassured.

PAUL SAMRAH: I had a meeting with Tony Blair, pure luck.

TIM CARDER: The Albion themselves were putting on a fringe meeting at, appropriately, the Royal Albion Hotel, and Paul Samrah and I went down into the room to arrange the chairs for the meeting, put leaflets and flyers and things on the chairs…

PAUL SAMRAH: And, as I came up the stairs having set up the room at about 7 o'clock in the hotel lobby area – and it was immediately apparent that something big was about to happen – there was secret service people around, there was a hush in the lobby and I immediately thought I know exactly what's happening here – obviously Tony Blair is due any minute! So I quickly went back downstairs and said to Tim "get some material"…

TIM CARDER: So, we nipped back upstairs and put ourselves in the line of dignitaries to greet the Prime Minister, and along came Tony with one or two minders, and Cherie following him, and I thrust out one of the postcards that we had been sending to MPs, I put it in the way of Tony who accepted it and said; "So what is this then?" And I said; "Please take a postcard from the seaside, Prime Minister." And he looked and I said; "It's about our new stadium at Falmer," at which point Cherie came in and said: "What's happening with the stadium?"…

PAUL SAMRAH: …And, I said: "It's with John Prescott at the moment"…

TIM CARDER: …To which Tony said; "Ah ministerial decision"…

PAUL SAMRAH: …And we shook hands and it was just a great moment. That sort of motivates you, thinking blimey we're getting around – we could not believe our luck.

TIM CARDER: It made us think we were on the agenda, so again very positive. I remember getting excited about it and rushing home and posting something on North Stand Chat, and in my excitement I got it slightly wrong, what Cherie had said, but Paul came on a bit calmer and corrected me.

SARAH WATTS: We got to the highest person in the land apart from the Queen; we didn't bother petitioning her.

30. 40 NOTES FUND/ALIVE & KICKING
Karaoke with Attila

ATTILA: By 2004 there was a lot of concern about financial stability at Withdean. The Alive & Kicking campaign was set up, Alan Wares's idea, to get people to pledge money to keep the club going and come up with inventive ideas to keep us in the public eye.

ALAN WARES: The idea, initially set up at a meeting in Ian Hart's front room, was to help the club – which was paying huge legal and planning fees; money which could and should have been used on improving the playing squad – by asking 2,500 people to donate £40 each to reach a fund of £100,000 in order to help the club acquire new players. I wasn't there in the beginning but I offered my time and effort. Things got gradually left more and more to Doug Clarke (fellow Albion fan) and me – which was fine. Once I found out he worked for The Who, it was good to get to know him.

We organised gigs at Hove Town Hall, the Concorde II (where a VERY drunk Attila was compering), a comedy night at the Komedia along with Stephen Grant, and a few quiz nights.

ATTILA: I did a sponsored gig on a Sunday night in November at the Evening Star: ten and a half hours with two piss breaks – I didn't drink a lot – and I did everything I'd ever written, lots of covers, all my Albion poetry and the funniest bit was where I asked people to sponsor me to do the most unspeakable songs imaginable… Paul Samrah offered 50 quid to do the Logical Song by Supertramp, Richard Hebberd offered 50 quid to do Mistletoe and Wine by Cliff Richard, I had to do Star Trekkin, D.I.S.C.O and Son of my Father, many of these accompanied by my wife Robina on piano. We raised over £2,000.

ALAN WARES: There were a few people who didn't like the idea of the 40 Notes Fund – they saw it as penny-pinching by the club, even though the club had nothing to do with the running of the fund. We got a bit of grief from some fans for that, but mostly people were happy to put a few quid in here and there.

We never made it as far as £100,000, I think we raised about £30,000 or so. For that, we got to help the Albion acquire Dave Beasant, Tony Rougier, Ben Roberts, Chris Iwelumo and Joe O'Cearuill.

31. SEAGULLS SKA
Top of the Pops

ROZ SOUTH: I don't think you could have put together a less talented group of vocalists to be perfectly honest with you.

ATTILA: It was Ipswich away, Ipswich scored then played Tom Hark and, as always, it pissed me off. So many clubs play it and it's OUR song. I moaned quite a lot.

Sometime towards the end of 2004, we were in the PA box at Withdean, as ever throwing around ideas about how to take the campaign forward, and suddenly it came to me – "We'll reclaim 'Tom Hark' and release it after Christmas when few records come out and have a hit!" I talked to our then sponsors Skint, a successful record label. They could give us the opportunity to get records in the shops when needed. So I re-wrote the lyrics and we went in the studio and recorded the new version of Tom Hark (to which I'd give about 6/10 now in retrospect), with the ska version of Sussex By The Sea – which Ian Hart describes as the Chas and Dave version. We had backing vocals from Samrah and all of the Falmer For All campaign team. The fourth track was Roll Up For The Donkey Derby which I had written about Palace's cup final appearance, I reckon that was the best of the four tracks.

JAN SWALLOW: It was quite fascinating. In Cowfold, round the back of a house, in this specially designed, adapted part of it, made into a studio and we rehearsed, but not much, and then off we went. It was really good fun.

ATTILA: I thought: "We've got a single, now we need a HIT!" I knew that if we wanted to get in the charts we'd have to sell a lot of records and because it would only be in a few local shops we had to get it on the internet sales systems – that's when North Stand Chat really came into play. I told people we had to get loads of pre-sales on Amazon and HMV – and we beat Elvis Presley in pre-sales, number one on Amazon. This was before the time when downloads counted for the charts – we had to sell as many pre-sales online and we had to get as many physical records in the shops as possible. I put the word out to my mates abroad and they ordered 200 – St Pauli still play it now!

PAUL SAMRAH: I hadn't listened to the top 40 in years, but that night we switched on and they played 40 to 30 and then 30 to 20, and I was thinking "Oh bloody hell, it was a great idea but we've missed the boat". Then the DJ says: "Coming up, we'll do the round up of 20 to 10 including a new hit from the Falmer For All group, new entry for Seagulls Ska!" I mean how high can it be… so he plays 20, 19, 18 and it's kind of bloody hell, then: "And now number 17, 'Seagulls Ska'!"

ATTILA: We got loads of publicity and it was in *The Times, Independent, Sunday Mirror,* we were on *Sunday Football Focus,* Radio 4 and 5, it was the most successful single bit of advertising for the whole campaign.

Skint were brilliant and everyone took it the right way: we made over £7,000 for the Alive & Kicking campaign. After that I started to play 'Sussex by the Sea' at Withdean when we won, which divided people, some people liked it and some people really didn't.

ANDERS SWAFFIELD: I remember it being played when we won, which at the time wasn't a lot of the time.

ATTILA: The really funny post-script is that it would have stayed in the chart but it was sold out in that first week. Plus, we got the word that we might have been on *Top of the Pops* but Busted split up and they did a big TOTP feature on that, so we were blown out.

The whole point of it was that it was a month before the second public inquiry, it was really good timing, the amount of publicity was amazing, *Front Row* on Radio 4! And there's a footnote to it – The Piranhas have got back together and started playing it again!!

The Seagulls Ska campaign was so full-on for me it was unbelievable; I dropped everything and did more than in the rest of the 13 years, it was so intense.

ROZ SOUTH: Hilarious, absolutely hilarious. Every now and again I rehear it and think "Oh god, I can hear myself in the background" – awful. But it was just very well done.

JOHN COWEN: I am second to none in my admiration for what the guy does – but what a shame a man like John should absolutely murder Sussex By The Sea like that for the B-side!

JAN SWALLOW: It was another of those moments when you said, all those years ago, watching the Albion from 1959 and it comes to this… singing on a top 20 hit record!

32. PUBLIC INQUIRY TWO
It's a no-brainer

ROZ SOUTH: The club had got a lot more savvy. I think the first inquiry was kind of like; "Well, surely you must realise that the cause is right!" – but that hadn't been enough.

BILL SWALLOW: The personalities in the inquiry started to become known to us. The barrister, Jonathan Clay – it was a bit like a television drama really, with his silky tones and being dry and sarcastic. The inquiry was a bit procedural, but great stuff in its own way. We'd sit next to people and you could tell who the supporters were on each side really, even if you didn't recognise them. There seemed to be a certain UKIP tendency about the opponents at that stage – a crazy mix of that and the hairy-toed liberals of Lewes. There'd be chaps looking like used car salesmen from the 1950s, with tweed jackets and cravats and things.

And, Ed Bassford there for the programme. It's what sets the Albion apart… I don't think many clubs could a) have supporters at a public inquiry day after day after day with one of them transcribing every important fact and then b) being prepared to have pages and pages of dense transcript in their matchday programmes. Every football club is unique but there are so many occasions during this adventure where the Albion somehow seemed more unique than any other.

ED BASSFORD: This inspector was not one to say: "We've heard enough about that subject, let's move on". So everybody got their say and there were lots of objectors and only one football club, so the detail was incredible… trying to whittle it down into a relatively short report for the website – you learn to pick out the highlights – show the goals, not the 25 minutes when nothing happened at the beginning of the second half.

Charlie Hopkins, the advocate representing Falmer Parish Council, was a fascinating guy. He and I got to know each other quite well because we were both smokers; and the great thing about being a smoker is you stand on doorsteps during breaks having conversations which start with a; "Have you got a cigarette lighter that works?" And six months later you're best mates. Charlie Hopkins, like me as a child, lived in Newport, South Wales, and we are both Newport County supporters. And Newport County went bust; if you want to know what would have happened to the Albion if we'd lost the Hereford game, the answer is Newport County.

Charlie Hopkins knew that and he'd been involved in the revival of Newport County, where a supporter-led movement got football started again in Newport. And Charlie was involved in all that, providing legal advice to the supporters' groups that were setting up Newport; he understood the passion of football supporters – and it was fascinating getting to know him, somebody who was being paid good money by Falmer Parish Council, to oppose what the Albion was doing.

MARTIN PERRY: Effectively, what we did was to produce what made up the large proportion of a planning application for every alternative site.

TIM CARDER: The second inquiry opened in February 2005 under a new inspector, David Brier, at Brighton Town Hall; I attended virtually every session. It would convene

on a Tuesday and run through to a Friday lunch time, which was frustrating; these inspectors go home on Friday afternoon and come back on a Monday.

The question being asked at the second inquiry was; would any alternative to Falmer be capable of development as a stadium?

There were various criteria in Prescott's decision which had to be followed: every site had to be considered for transport issues, the effect on the environment, the planning framework, the effect on the proposed South Downs National Park. Martin Perry was there every day, there were club solicitors from DMH, they were there every day ready to brief our counsel Jonathan Clay. The opponents, led by Lewes District Council, had similar officials. There were other parties there, the South Downs Society, the Regency Society represented by Hazel McKay, the CPRE were there and, of course, on our side we also had Brighton & Hove City Council, who were represented by Mary MacPherson who was also a barrister, very friendly to us, slightly fumbling with her files but on our side and very good at it.

In the grand scheme of things our consultants and experts stood up very well to the grilling and it was really a grilling that they received. Martin Perry was in the witness stand for about two days.

BOB BRUCE: The council, of course, had looked at all these other sites before, but not in the detail that Prescott now suggested for the second inquiry. Some of the sites weren't even available. There was even a suggestion that the club should have reclaimed land in Shoreham Harbour, so the opposition were getting desperate – Shoreham Airport was another one, playing football in the middle of the runway wasn't my idea of a safe ground. Withdean was on that list as well. The reason why it wasn't a runner was not just because of the capacity but also the tunnel and the surrounding access issues – and the fact that the council really did genuinely want it as an athletics stadium.

TIM CARDER: The closest site in terms of acceptability was Sheepcote Valley, just off the middle of Brighton, a wonderful spot, an area that's loved by many people. It contrasts quite starkly with the site at Falmer, which is one field, 35% already developed land – and that one field is next to the dual carriageway and the railway, and was farmed for a cereal crop, with no public access, no wild flowers and very little in the way of wildlife there. As an environmental and ecological site, Sheepcote Valley is way ahead of Falmer.

Falmer Parish Council, at one time, pushed for the cement works on the road from Shoreham to Upper Beeding (which in fact was Barry Lloyd's preferred site back in the 1990s when he was managing director of the Albion). Firstly, it's a hell of a long way from Brighton and Hove and actually getting there is pretty difficult when there is only one road that passed it. Getting 22,000 fans in and out of that stadium would be, our consultants showed, an impossibility.

Waterhall, for a long time a favourite of supporters, was right next to a trunk road and a railway line, but the practicalities of building a road junction there and also some sort of railway station on the London to Brighton main line in what is a cutting, were huge; it opened my eyes to the fact looking on a map to find a site is not enough. Waterhall in any case was a true downland site – it was certainly going to be part of the new national park.

Toad's Hole Valley – how do you get 22,000 people in and out? The nearest railway stations were Preston Park and Hove, which were a fair walk away, not impossible but nothing like as convenient as having a railway station a hundred yards away as in Falmer.

Sheepcote Valley – opponents were saying Moulsecoomb station is within two miles or whatever from Sheepcote Valley. Well, that is true if you draw a line on the map but there is a great big hill in the way.

Because of my local knowledge, I was asked by our side to draw up walking routes to Sheepcote and agree them with Lewes District Council. The inspector would then walk them. I deliberately used the straight-line route from Moulsecoomb and Lewes were happy with that. But I knew it went up a very long and steep set of steps known as Jacob's Ladder. The inspector came back and said; "I climbed that route" – and this was about the only comment he made during the inquiry – he added; "It was a killer"!

We all had a smile every time one of our witnesses said 'it's a no brainer'. There were bets on to get 'it's a no brainer' into their comments from the witness box; and every time this happened there was an increasing snigger from the room.

PAUL SAMRAH: What the new inquiry did was to force our opponents into coming up with a suitable site and it made them increasingly look like a bunch of nimbys. When they did eventually settle on Sheepcote Valley, it was utterly perverse, the Friends of Sheepcote Valley were indignant and quite rightly so.

ANDY SIMONS: Regarding Sheepcote Valley, anyone who knows Brighton would be like, you are kidding aren't you? The planning pretty much ignores money, so yes technically you could have carved out a space in all that old domestic landfill in Sheepcote and inserted a stadium but outside the site area that you potentially own – you carve this whole thing into multi-level car parks, lifts to get everybody up and into it… it would have cost a fortune.

ED BASSFORD: The more I got involved with the inquiry, the more it became obvious that we were going to win. Our arguments were sustainable and the opposition's arguments were all flawed. We'd demonstrated the need for a football stadium and we demonstrated that there was nowhere else it could go.

TIM CARDER: The inquiry actually became a little way of life and there was a group of regulars there. It was actually quite sad to see it finish because it was interesting.

To me the club had shown that none of the other sites had the possibility of gaining planning permission for a 22,000-seat stadium and therefore Prescott would give us permission to develop Falmer.

MARTIN PERRY: By the end we had spent the best part of £6,000,000 on fees, design fees, planning fees, barristers' fees.

33. THE COCA-COLA KID
Colin adds some fizz

AARON BERRY: I had just seen this advert on the Albion website and I don't think it had even been put on North Stand Chat in the early days. It was just; 'Vote for the Albion – the more entries you have, the more chances you have and the Albion will have of someone being drawn from the hat – and the club will have a quarter of a million pounds to spend in the transfer market.'

I think in the end 1.7 million people, over a period of 90 days, entered it. They had this league table as to which club had the most entries and I think we were in the top ten somewhere but I think clubs like Leeds and Southampton were right up the top.

Me, like millions of fans who entered, thought all I have got to do is log on at work every day, or at home, and vote. The competition ran for about 90 days, I think, and apart from five days when I was in the States on holiday, I literally did so every day.

Never in a million years did I expect something to come from it. I came back from that holiday the day before the competition ended, so I was actually quite jetlagged when the phone rang on, I think, May 27th and I just ignored it because frankly I thought work may want me in, so I let it go. But the phone rang again and this really nervous guy just asked me what my name was and did I remember entering a Coca-Cola competition to win a player? And I said; "Oh yeah I did it every day more or less," and he said; "I am pleased to announce you are the main prize winner. We are going to send someone from Coca-Cola's legal department round in the next couple of hours." And I had to sign half a dozen documents to say that I couldn't tell anybody about it at all for the next three days and I was going up to the Millennium Stadium in Cardiff where they would give me the cheque on the pitch – absolutely amazing!

I was told not to contact anybody, not to tell family, friends – obviously I told my family I was living with at the time, and we had to keep it very quiet and they said if you break the news before the Monday game, which was the play-off final between West Ham and Preston North End (the one where Zamora scored the one-goal winner for West Ham) if you tell anyone about it before half past two that day then you will forfeit, and the team that was drawn second will get the prize. So there was quite a lot of pressure not to tell anybody! When they drove us up to the Millennium Stadium in the morning for the play-off final, we went into one of the hotels in Cardiff and Dick Knight and Mark McGhee walked in and I got up to go over and sort of speak to them and the Coca-Cola representative who was looking after me said; "No, sit down they don't know yet either."

They took me to the Millennium Stadium and they gave me a corporate box with some other winners of other competitions and then at quarter past two, he said; "Right we are going downstairs now to the players' tunnel, at which point we are going to tell Mark

McGhee." Apparently Dick Knight got told sometime in the morning. So we went downstairs literally to the players' tunnel and the Coke representative said; "I can't go any further now, you have got to go over there and basically see Chris Kamara – he will sort you out because he was the patron for the competition."

So I went up and Chris said; "You must be Aaron Berry; great stuff congratulations." He actually said he was really glad a club like Brighton had won it and then Mark McGhee literally legged it up the tunnel to me and gave me a huge hug, he was more made up than I was, he was so chuffed, he said; "This is absolutely brilliant – we haven't been able to buy anybody for a couple of seasons, this will finally at least get us back in the transfer market."

I got onto the pitch and Dick Knight came out and he was all hugs and 'thank yous'.

My phone didn't stop ringing then for about two weeks. I was so chuffed.

That quarter of a million literally kept them going on the pitch for a bit. I know the player the money bought (Colin Kazim-Richards) didn't work out terrifically well as a player for the club in terms of success, but the sell-on clauses that Dick Knight negotiated ultimately meant that the win won us five hundred grand which, from what I'm told, significantly helped us sign Glenn Murray.

I was just so pleased that with all these other people that do these wonderful things – the Paul Samrahs and the Liz Costas of this world who put in so much time for their campaigns and everything to help the club – it was enough for me to just be able to look back and say to my grandchildren, you know, "Granddad was lucky enough to win this and it helped the club keep going on the pitch for a little while".

34. DRENCHING DES LYNAM
Another downpour at Withdean

JOHN COWEN: I had the idea that every ground on one particular day in our league would have an Albion fan, who would be stationed in the middle of one of the stands, terraces or whatever. He alone would be stationed under one of those old fashioned showers or something. Then loads of water

would be cascading down on him, sitting there in his Withdean poncho, to show how it really is for people who support Brighton. But we needed to make it more manageable – we wouldn't actually get 21 teams to agree to do all that. In the end we scaled it down to have just one famous person, Des Lynam, getting drenched at Withdean by an assortment of 'away fans'. I think it was Dick Knight who persuaded Des to do it. It made the media – which was the main point.

PAUL CAMILLIN: Des was a Brighton fan getting a soaking, and it was like us saying: "Sorry, we're here in the Championship, the fifth biggest league in Europe, and we can't offer you a bloody roof on the away end. But, if John Prescott and the government make the right decision, it won't be long before we can not only offer you a roof on the away end, we can offer you the most spectacular away end in the country."

PAUL SAMRAH: We wanted to get across the idea that Withdean was the most inhospitable place to come for visiting fans – it's unlucky to get a winter fixture. And Des kind of volunteered and we decided to focus all the publicity on Des, and so that's what we did. It didn't really get heaps of publicity; locally it did, but nationally it didn't, so yeah we took it, publicity and everything… very good.

ROZ SOUTH: Good old Des Lynam and Prescott was absolutely made up by it, apparently.

35. POSTCARD TO HULL
To Hull and back

TIM CARDER: We were playing Hull City and I think they were in their new stadium, because we presented a giant postcard which I think had a picture of Hull's new stadium on it and the message was that we would like one for Brighton and Hove too, you have seen what it can do for Hull as a city, give us  a stadium and let's see what it can do for Brighton and Hove. So we delivered that again to Prescott's constituency office before the match and they were very pleased to receive this giant postcard that, I think, once again I probably arranged to be printed. On the day it had to go off, Bill and Jan Swallow were staying near Hull and they were taking this giant postcard in their van and there was a problem finding a printer that could actually print this five or six foot wide postcard and we had a photo call with *The Argus* and the television at Village Way at Falmer at one o'clock. The postcard was being printed at about twelve o'clock and I was stressed out by the experience. A very helpful firm called One Digital in Hollingdean did it for me and I whizzed straight up Lewes Road with it somehow in the back of my little car and got to Village Way just in time.

I think Prescott said he appreciated our campaigns and I know he has mentioned the Valentine's card and the giant postcard; I would like to secure one or the other, or both, for the museum if he is willing to. I shall be making inquiries in due course.

36. LABOUR CONFERENCE TWO
"Falmer, or we'll vote Tory!"

TIM CARDER: Essentially it was more of the same for the second march, and when I say more, more fans turned out. We just wanted a decision. The day before the march Prescott said to the opening of his conference…

JOHN PRESCOTT: Once again, we're delighted to be in Labour controlled Brighton & Hove at our Conference. I know many in this city want a new football stadium. They'll be demonstrating tomorrow in their usual good-mannered way. Can I say to them, this announcement will be made by the end of this October.

TIM CARDER: …and the words to me implied that he was not going to upset many people in the city and therefore I took that as a positive.

BILL SWALLOW: I remember saying at an FFA meeting: "Look, I'm not sure about this march idea, it could be a damp squib." I was so wrong – thank heaven for positive people.

JAN SWALLOW: I remember giving out flyers and getting as much publicity as we could to come along and march along the seafront, but sometimes we thought; 'What if nobody turns up and there's not many people…?'

IAN HINE: I remember getting to the seafront and turning round the corner and seeing literally thousands of people lining up just to march 400 yards. Symbolic but so powerful… You think, bloody hell, there's Steve Coppell! What's he doing here? He doesn't have to do that!

JAN SWALLOW: It was so emotional. And we were so lucky at every march that we had good weather. And all the supporters were fine. With some other clubs you thought this could degenerate into a bit of a riot but there was never any hint of that at all.

BILL SWALLOW: I mean the disabled supporters' banner saying 'Without Falmer we won't have a leg to stand on'... You just felt so proud to be an Albion supporter.

ANDERS SWAFFIELD: I remember going to quite a few of the marches. I enjoyed it in a way. It was finding out what we were all about and what was going on.

DEREK CHAPMAN: I did the marches yes, a couple of marches with the family.

ADRIAN NEWNHAM: It was witty, eye catching but actually a really positive message to get across. We were there with Kieron and his son, who was in his pushchair at the time, and we were singing; 'What do we want? Falmer! When do we want it? Now!' And the boy turned round after a bit of this and said; "Daddy, I want, doesn't get."

ROZ SOUTH: That was really funny, the second march. We got opposite the ludicrous cordon, the ring of steel, we got sort of towards the Grand Hotel and Prescott put his head out of the window. And someone shouts: "We want Falmer, or we vote Tory." And Prescott's clapping.

Albion Almanac, the always factual record of Albion events, reported that fans of the following clubs were present: Arsenal, Aston Villa, Barnsley, Birmingham City, Cambridge United, Charlton Athletic, Chelsea, Cowdenbeath, Crystal Palace, Derby County, Leeds United, Manchester City, Manchester United, Middlesbrough, Oxford United, Plymouth Argyle, Portsmouth, Rochdale, Sheffield United, Southampton, Stevenage Borough, Stoke City, Sunderland, Watford, West Bromwich Albion, Wolverhampton Wanderers and Wycombe Wanderers.

37. PRESCOTT YES!
We thought we had scored...

JOHN PRESCOTT: The protests and the fans appealing to me, didn't affect the decision in any way. I wasn't entitled to talk to them, you have a responsibility to make the

right decision and you mustn't be influenced inside or outside. MPs come up and say things to you but you have got to be dead careful.

I don't think any other planning decision was affected by so much fans' support.

When you are making a planning decision you have to take into account what is good for Brighton, what is good for the sport itself – it is a national sport.

MARTIN PERRY: The morning came for the decision. We knew it was coming. And we knew it would go to our solicitors' office in Queens Road. We knew his post came at seven o'clock in the morning. We were pretty confident that we knew the decision, but we were still thinking: "Will he, won't he?"

So seven o'clock comes and we're sitting in the office – Dick, Paul Samrah and everyone sitting waiting…

Ten past seven comes, we phoned the solicitors and asked if their post had come. They said: "Yes." "Was it there?" "No." And then I got a call from the council: "Well done! You've done it!" So we said: "Have we? We haven't got the decision here…"

Turns out they had sent two copies to the University of Brighton and we, as the lead applicant, did not get one. So the council said they'd fax it to us… the decision was 72 pages, they started on page one and the decision is on page 72! And we're grabbing this thing off the fax machine and reading it as it's coming off!

TIM CARDER: The first I knew that it was a definite 'yes' was listening to the radio at 8 o'clock in the morning because I think Falmer Parish Council had had a letter. It was the high point for me! Utterly elated, after having fought for four years for the planning application! So I went down to the football club offices in North Road and there was Martin Perry, Dick Knight, Paul Samrah – you name them and they were there and it was a terrific day!

ANDERS SWAFFIELD: It was a school day, and I heard it on the radio. Brighton have got the stadium, got a 'yes'! And I ran out the shower, soaking wet and told my Dad: "We got the stadium!" I missed school that day. Obviously, we phoned in, said I was sick or something but I think all of them kind of knew, especially my Year 6 teacher at the time, she was a big Brighton fan, I think she didn't go to the school either that day. We went to the pub.

BOB BRUCE: We all went mad! We thought right this is good… and then I realised, right I have to do the land deal! Yes, we were all very excited about it.

STEVE BASSAM: What the report determined effectively was that Falmer was the least worst option, in fact the best possible option on all the others… which is really what we said at the outset, no site is perfect but this is really more perfect than most.

I remember being at that little celebration at Donatello's, thinking this is terrific and drinking some champagne and feeling very merry; I don't remember going into work that day!

ROZ SOUTH: It was 'Right, everyone get down to Donatello's now!'

TIM CARDER: We went down to Donatello's and there were bottles of champagne being uncorked, Norman Cook was there, *The Argus* got in on the act with the headlines saying 'Yes to Falmer!' or something – they were dishing out free newspapers for fans to hold up, there was a small collection of fans there and it was a terrific celebratory atmosphere. There was a press conference inside Donatello's, everyone was upbeat, Dick and Martin were there, I think, even Ken Bodfish was there, leader of the council, expressing his pleasure at the outcome, which was ironic considering what he said about Falmer a few years earlier. I asked Martin, at the press conference, how it felt for him to have this triumph for his home town, he was born in Brighton, and he said it was really fantastic and just a marvellous day.

ROY CHUTER: We went to Donatello's and I had to interview people for the programme but everybody was just dancing and grinning.

PAUL CAMILLIN: The news came on Friday. We were at home to Ipswich the next day so it was too late for the programme but the printers said we could get a wrap on the programme cover. It was a thin yellow bit down the side, with 'Yes!' and a bit of a copy inside.

BILL SWALLOW: Champagne at the Ipswich game for everybody! That was a classic Dick idea. Plastic cups of champagne. Who could imagine such a thing?!

DAVE SWAFFIELD: There was champagne the next day at the Ipswich game – fantastic, brilliant – I mean, it doesn't happen does it?

JOHN COWEN: Champagne at Withdean! And I thought: "Oh, we are there!"

SARAH WATTS: I remember people quaffing champagne before the Ipswich game, and, to be honest, I also remember the fact that Liz and I were inside the ground, we were very, very naughty and took in half a bottle of champagne, and Richard Hebberd came round looking because he'd heard that people were drinking champagne inside the ground, in sight of the pitch, and we admitted it was us...

LIZ COSTA: We went up to the site with a girl from *The Argus* to take pictures and we stood just two feet into the field and the farmer was up the top of the hill watching us, he had got his dog and he was crouching down pretending not to be seen while we were having our pictures taken in euphoria, then he came running down the hill. He was fuming; "Get off my land! You haven't got it yet!" So there was a kind of dampener put on it but we laughed, you know, stupid old fool...

ROZ SOUTH: I do remember very early on, maybe even that day, Tim saying: "There's a mistake in the letter, it's not in the built-up area." And we went: "Oh Tim, don't be so anal!" But, he was right. Two years later...

TIM CARDER: I read the letter and found a mistake in it – there was an issue over the built-up area boundary of Brighton. There was some confusion whether the site at Falmer was included within the built-up area of Brighton or not: it was within Brighton & Hove City Council boundary but there was this secondary boundary that determined a different area of Brighton and therefore different planning policies. During the inquiry, there had been some confusion that was eventually sorted out after lunch one day, very quickly, but perhaps the inspector didn't make the right notes on this issue; so it was presented in his report incorrectly, and that was taken up by the government incorrectly, which was reflected in Prescott's decision letter incorrectly, which said that the stadium was within the built-up area of Brighton, which I knew, having sat through the inquiry, it was not.

I emailed Martin and said; "Have you seen this error?" And he said; "Yes, we have but we don't think its critical." Of course, while I was doing that, Lewes District Council, Falmer Parish Council and all the opposition parties – they were also reading this letter.

DICK KNIGHT: The outcome of the second inquiry was positive – it addressed the issues that the previous inspector had got wrong, and Prescott then wrote this letter to us basically confirming to our lawyers that we could go ahead... Unfortunately, in that letter there was what amounted to little more than a clerical error, which is to do with where the actual stadium land was, and they said that some of it was in the area of Lewes District Council, which it isn't.

The approval letter, the 18-page letter, repeated this error three or four times and it just showed the incompetence of the civil servants advising Prescott. Do you think Prescott read all 18 pages of this letter? Of course he didn't – he was advised, just sign there. He was minded to approve it and was obviously satisfied with the evaluation process rejecting why the previous inspector had said Falmer wasn't right.

Lewes obviously had an eagle-eyed lawyer going through the letter (I had spotted it and thought, that isn't right, but didn't think, at the time, anything of it, or think the consequences would be taken up the way they were) but Lewes Council saw this as an opportunity to challenge it on the grounds that if that's wrong, something else in this 18-page approval letter could be wrong.

ROY CHUTER: It was one paragraph about two bus stops; that was really all it was.

ROZ SOUTH: Lewes leapt upon the error and were delighted with it, absolutely delighted. It wasn't an adequate defence to turn over a public inquiry, not really, it was a technical mistake, no more than a typo really. But, they were absolutely thrilled and it became obvious that they were going to mount a legal challenge. And they did so in a kind of gleeful, malicious manner that made it perfectly clear that they thought that actually that was going to be the end of the football club now as well. 'We're going to mount a legal challenge, they're never going to get this stadium and that'll be the end of them' sort of thing.

MARTIN PERRY: What he'd done he had left out two words; the letter said "because the site is in the built-up area of Brighton and Hove it adds weight to the fact that it is suitable for development"; if he'd said "part of" the site was in the built-up area we would have been fine, but it's not all in Brighton and Hove, part of it is in Lewes district…

ADRIAN NEWNHAM: When they picked up on it you thought – can't somebody just rewrite the letter and say; 'Actually, yes, it's an actual mistake of fact, but it wasn't a relevant part of our decision making.'

TIM CARDER: Within a month Lewes District Council had launched their legal challenge. From being ten out of ten, it went to 0 out of ten within a month. It was soul destroying. After all the effort we put into it. And I did know, that whatever we said, I knew Lewes had a case…

38. LEWES LEGAL CHALLENGE
Offside appeal

TIM JOHNSON: The depression after we knew about the appeal, made playing at Gillingham feel like a party. It's a difficult thing when all you want is something quite simple: to be entertained on a Saturday afternoon by footballers. But when you have red tape and politics, and people with their own agendas, to spoil your enjoyment and you know that they can put stipulations in your way to stop you from doing something, and they can go to court and say this is a restraining order to stop you doing this and that, and it's like a Kafka novel, at times you were in this spiral where you didn't know what was right or wrong, and whether you could get out of it.

I remember I was absolutely astounded that we could have a new public inquiry on just one sentence – just change the sentence you know?

I don't hate people or organisations, necessarily, but my absolute loathing for the people at Lewes District Council and what they have put us through for the sake of, how much was it? 600 square metres of their land, which was going to be a coach park anyway.

ED BASSFORD: This was the era of the leaked document, so we knew about the likelihood of a legal challenge. I was phoned up by a Lewes District councillor and told that work was being done on mounting a legal challenge to the decisions. I asked how he knew, and he said he'd seen the report, and I said; "Could I see the report?" And he said; "Of course not." Then the report appeared through my front door later that weekend and I was asked, when you've read it, could you return it please, so the following day it was returned. What happened between it falling through my door and being returned might or might not have involved an email to Martin Perry and the use of a scanner, but I wouldn't know.

STEVE BASSAM: I said publicly; "Look, we would all be better served rather than going through this tortuous process again, if Lewes just politely withdrew and talked to the club, talked to the council and secured whatever concessions or arrangements they felt they needed to protect their interests mutually, outside the courtroom, rather than having a re run of having to make the decision." But they decided to ignore that good advice and they proceeded with their attack on the decision.

PAUL CAMILLIN: I thought it was a huge own goal, I thought Lewes should have been a lot more magnanimous in defeat. It's a bit like being 10-0 down in an FA Cup tie that's abandoned after 80 minutes and then saying no we want to play it again, knowing full well that you're going to lose 10-0 again, that you've got no chance. It wasn't sporting in my opinion.

STEVE BASSAM: I think so much time was wasted, which was a great shame really, and I don't think it was a glorious moment in Lewes District Council's history. I think people like Norman Baker calculated that if it was delayed long enough it would cost so much that the club wouldn't be able to proceed. They were wrong because we were all determined to make it happen and the money was there.

ANDERS SWAFFIELD: I remember my Dad was very moody. I didn't get what happened, I was just kinda like, we've got a 'yes', why are they saying 'no'? I was just confused by it, very, very confused.

MARTIN PERRY: We got the message that Lewes had taken legal advice and thought they could be successful in an appeal. We went to our lawyers and they said it could go to court and you could lose... The quickest way out of this is to go to the High Court, get it quashed and get the Secretary of State to make the decision again – there's no need to back through the inquiry, what will happen is you will be asked for further evidence, further submissions, they will go back to the point where the inquiry was finished and they are considering the evidence, the decision has to be made again on the basis that the site is only partly in the built-up area of Brighton and Hove, they have to test that their decision still holds water.

BOB BRUCE: The error was debatable; it was all a matter of interpretation. But, the challenge was made and we had to move things forward and we agreed to accept a mistake had been made and we had to do it all over again! Incredibly frustrating.

What triggered the challenge to the decision was just a small bit of wording so, in a way, that is what we should concentrate on. But, on the other hand, if we didn't review what had been said before in the inquiries, refresh it and update it, we ran the risk of someone like Lewes updating it and you being caught cold – so what we had to do was effectively review everything that had been said before, update it and then deal with the point of law that had arisen in the argument.

DICK KNIGHT: The die was cast. We were into the infuriating Lewes saga, which was one step beyond. Most people in Lewes were against it, but the council pressed on. It took more than a year and another several hundred thousand pounds in legal fees. In the end they withdrew their objections at the last minute, just before we went to court, because they were founded on nothing of substance.

LIZ COSTA: It cost us an extra few hundred thousand quid and a bit more campaigning and a bit more innovation, but we weren't going to give up, come on! We had come that far we weren't going to stop there; we just had to keep going.

BILL SWALLOW: They just wanted to cause trouble and we felt their strategy was to keep protesting in the hope that the club would go bust.

JAN SWALLOW: It was a delaying tactic wasn't it?

BILL SWALLOW: ...delaying in the hope that the club could no longer afford to build the stadium. That was the perception of what they were trying to do and I cannot see any other conclusion to be drawn from it. It was clear that a planning application of this size would not be overturned effectively by a typo and yet they were fighting it and using their council taxpayers' money. It was a pretty brutal tactic. At that time the club was short of money.

ADRIAN NEWNHAM: Don't forget, we were going into a credit crunch. The bank I work for, by 2006, was warning of bad news from the US. I think people did fear that if Lewes dragged it out a bit longer the club would cease to exist.

39. CAMPAIGNS AGAINST LEWES
Build another bonfire

TIM CARDER: So, back into campaigning again – the last thing I wanted.

But… we launched into a week of action. Many residents of Lewes who were Albion supporters were absolutely furious at Lewes's decision and got in touch with their councillors, who, some thought, had been gagged by the District Council and were unable to comment on the matter.

PAUL SAMRAH: We thought let's go out on the streets of Lewes and let's target Lewes residents to get them to sign a petition saying enough is enough – and in one week we got over 5,000 Lewes residents to tell their council to cease any further action.

TIM CARDER: We spoke about how much money it was potentially going to cost council tax payers in the district. There was a full council meeting of Lewes District Council at which we tabled lots of questions.

BILL SWALLOW: I have to say it was very nice having a pantomime villain – Ann De Vecchi. We went to a meeting at Lewes District Council when they considered whether to pour more money into fighting the stadium. We sat in the Council Chamber and Tim was able to speak to the councillors as part of the democratic process and was treated very, very badly by them. They were ostentatiously ignoring him; speaking over him, that sort of thing. De Vecchi had a look of supercilious superiority throughout the whole thing. I had even less time for them after that.

TIM CARDER: What I was able to extract from Councillor Commin, who was opposed to the stadium but was very polite about the matter, was a commitment to ensure there was no undue delay getting our case into court, because one of our fears was that Lewes District Council were just trying to string it out in the hope that the Albion, who were in a bad financial position at the time, might actually go under in the process; I also challenged him over the amount of money that Lewes District Council were committing to this challenge. He gave me his commitment that if it went above that figure he would resign.

Over the next year or so, Ed and I would ask questions during public question times where we could show up some of the nonsense of the Lewes District Council campaign – the hypocrisy involved within their decisions and their representations at the public inquiry.

Some of the campaigners felt that the chief executive of Lewes District Council, John Crawford, was behind everything… and at one public questions I accused him of being behind the campaign. To accuse a council officer of something is taboo, council officers only go along with the decisions of the council, so you are not allowed to say that the council officer is driving the policy – so I had to withdraw, which I thought was probably best because I didn't really want to get sued by anybody. So I packed my bags and got out, I was rather pleased to get out; it really was a bit of a bear pit.

This was definitely the nastiest period of campaigning.

The government had agreed that the boundary issue was enough for them to concede the whole case on the planning permission and start again effectively, but Lewes District Council said they had a dozen or whatever other points. They said they wanted these to be contested in court because they wanted those issues to be decided. We felt this was purely and utterly delay tactics. The government had agreed to have the planning permission quashed, spinning it out by insisting this goes to court was a waste of money and a waste of time. Eventually, they took out some sort of order that required the case to be heard in October – and what do you know? The day before it was due to go to court, Lewes District Council backs down and says: "OK, we accept the government's decision to have the planning permission quashed on that one point. We don't concede the other points but we will not go to court on the matter." So, that process delayed everything by five or six months and cost both sides a huge amount of money.

BILL SWALLOW: Lewes was effectively forced into campaigning for Sheepcote Valley. And we were forced into rubbishing them.

PAUL SAMRAH: Lewes told us that Sheepcote Valley was easy for transport. They said it was only 25 minutes' walk from the centre of Brighton. So then I thought right, Derek's idea of a walk. I thought we'd have something visual, a clock that was visible and I thought of marathon races and you see these digital clocks. I went on the internet and this company supplied these clocks, and they'd put them onto any vehicle and Bill had a beautiful little white van. We had 35 walkers, we set off on the morning of a home game

from the Clock Tower… it took 58 minutes. We then produced a DVD of it, sent it to the Deputy Prime Minister, proving Lewes's lie of the land, it was brilliant.

TIM CARDER: I am a bit of a runner and I took on the challenge to actually run it and see if I could do it under 25 minutes and it took me 24 minutes and 12 seconds or something like that. It was just a bit of fun but it put into perspective what we felt was the standard of the nonsense churned out at times by Lewes District Council.

MARTIN PERRY: What Lewes's and Falmer Parish Council's advisers tried to do was to knock the social and economic arguments and that in fact was our strongest card… There are pockets of deprivation in the areas of Moulsecoomb, Bevendean, Coldean and Whitehawk which are some of the most income- and education-deprived areas in the country. The work of Albion in the Community in targeting those groups of people had completely changed the hearts and minds of the city council, which is why they gave us planning permission in the first place. At the first public inquiry they actually said the work of Albion in the Community was so important that if the football club were not to survive it would be a disaster because in terms of social and economic programmes AITC are their biggest delivery partners.

And, so when the opponents tried to knock the work of Albion in the Community there was no way they were going to get away with that. In fact, Jonathan Clay said the more I see of this evidence the stronger the case gets; and that's what we concentrated on, just went for the jugular: this is the work, this is what we do to deliver for the community, 750 equivalent full-time jobs and opportunities for education schools training, it will draw in £23 million, not only within the turnover within the football club, but also the indirect turnover of people who supply goods and services to the stadium, but also to the leisure industry with, overnight, visits from people coming to visit the stadium – the argument was absolutely overwhelming.

ATTILA: People said that the stadium would destroy the Downs, but it is right next to a big main road. The reassuring thing is that Lewes seem happy now, proves all the Outstanding Natural Beauty thing was nonsense.

BOB BRUCE: We did play the Brighton versus Lewes card quite a lot, both the Albion and the council. We were basically trying to say; look, this fantastic stadium is going to be as much good to Lewes as it was to Brighton because of the location. It's right on the gateway to Lewes isn't it? I said people in Lewes are going to come to the community facilities, they will benefit from all the Albion in the Community stuff and, as for the traffic management scheme, a little bit of hassle on some matchdays but nothing too horrendous. It would be probably worse if it was an IKEA!

Lewes are fine now, I think. Professionally, we have always got on well with the staff, the lawyers and everyone they use, they are good. Like us they were just doing their jobs.

If you want to stop something at all costs it is well known that litigation and planning laws are so expensive you can just eke it out; there was a line of thought that suggested the club would have gone under. So at the time it was a real threat; we were getting quite worried as a council about whether the deal could be done because we didn't know how the club were going to raise the money really.

ED BASSFORD: It was very nasty, there was a lot of hostility around, the quality of the language deteriorated slightly, but again the fundamental thing was that there were thousands of people in Lewes, as well as thousands of people in Brighton, who were disappointed by Lewes District Council's legal challenge. We had won the hearts and minds argument that people wanted a stadium and here was a council who was continuing to oppose it. LDC really, genuinely, did not realise the extent for which there was support for the stadium amongst the population in Lewes.

40. WANTED
Every campaign needs a poster girl

ROZ SOUTH: So, at the start of the campaign, we went out to collect signatures on a Christmas shopping night and in only a week over 5,000 people had signed this petition, in Lewes district.

And, for part of this campaign, I designed the famous 'Wanted' poster. It had a picture of Anne De Vecchi, in the style of an old fashioned Wild West wanted poster and said 'Wanted, for the attempted murder of Brighton & Hove Albion FC' and then it said, I can't remember the exact words, something about the leader and her nine cronies. And that was it. It came out as part of a mailshot – we were trying to collect signatures against Lewes District's proposal to mount a challenge, for people to say; 'I'm a Lewes voter, and I want the stadium.'

About a week after this I get this mysterious email from a police inspector in Lewes, that said: "I've had a complaint about a poster that you've done, if you'd just like to take that poster off the internet, no more will be done and we'll say no more about it, otherwise you could be in serious trouble." So I said; "Which poster's this then?" And she tells me and I said; "OK, what's the complaint?" And she says; "Oh, I can't tell you what that is, I can just say there's been a complaint and you could be prosecuted under the Prevention of Harassment Act." And I said; "Who's made the complaint?" And she said; "I can't tell you that, all you've got to do is to take the poster down."

Someone connected with the club recommended a criminal law solicitor and I phoned him up. He said; "I'd take it down if I were you and just say you're sorry." And I said; "Well, thanks." And I put the phone down and I said to Ed; "Well I'm not sorry. I'm not the slightest bit sorry."

I could only presume it was Anne De Vecchi but, if she's got a problem, why didn't she write to me? So I thought I'm not sorry, not the way you people have behaved, so I wrote a very polite email back and said; "I'm extremely sorry but since I'm not at all contrite and the poster is part of a legitimate political campaign, I'm afraid I'm not prepared to take it down." So the police inspector said; "Right, if you're not going to play nicely, you're going to be in real trouble now." So I went "Fine". I rang Bindmans, the civil rights lawyers, and they were great, they were like 'OK, that's fine, we'll come straight down as soon as they arrest you'.

Obviously there was publicity and it went on the telly and John Young came down from BBC South East and did an interview. The BBC checked with their libel lawyers before transmitting the poster and they said there's nothing libellous about this. So I just sort of quietly persisted, and the police said; "Well, you do know you're going to be arrested soon." I said; "I'll be fine, don't worry, you tell me when." And it went on and on for months and the irony was, as soon as this got onto NSC the poster went viral, it was on everybody's signature.

The other side of this was, I asked the police actually to give me more details of this complaint, you can't just say to me; 'I'm going to get in very big trouble' – who's made the complaint? Because Anne De Vecchi had been interviewed by the press and she said; "Oh, I didn't complain." But, if you're gonna be done under the Prevention of Harassment law, it's a crime against the person, so Anne De Vecchi would have had to have complained if I was going to be prosecuted under that law, because it would be Anne De Vecchi who was, in theory, claiming she was harassed.

So, anyway, this went on. Then they decided that actually, perhaps that wasn't enough to get me done, so they decided that they would get me done for allowing people to be rude about Anne De Vecchi on NSC, as a moderator; say that I hadn't taken down offensive postings. And I said; "I'm one of something like six moderators, and actually I wouldn't moderate something like that, if anybody wanted to moderate it, it wouldn't be a person who was directly involved, so make your minds up, what am I in trouble for?" "Just you wait and find out…" And eventually they had to admit that actually I wasn't going to be arrested for anything.

So I put a Freedom of Information request in and got the information back from Lewes. And it transpired that the chief executive, John Crawford, kicked all this off, I guess thinking it would take one of the troublemakers out, to put the frighteners on. And the police sent the case three times to the Crown Prosecution Service and each time the CPS said 'you've got no case to bring'. John Crawford was emailing around the District Council saying 'it's all right, we've asked the police to send it to a more senior person at the CPS so we'll get a result'. And the more senior person just said; "No, you haven't got a case." The police had to say; "Um, actually, you're not guilty of anything are you?" But it took months and months and it was all manipulated by John Crawford, which was just amazing. And you think for God's sake man, you must be running scared of something!

It was a comic fiasco but it was one that you could have been very upset by if you were worried about being harassed by the police; I can be a bit blasé about it now but there were times I was very worried about it, yeah.

It was a mean minded trick pulled by the chief executive. And, amazingly inappropriate because, as I say, that particular law was created to help people who were being stalked.

Brighton police were watching this pan out and they were just taking the mickey out of the incompetence of the Lewes police in being used by Lewes District Council; they said it would never have seen the light of day, something like that, the police in Brighton would have laughed it off and said; "Who do you people think you are? Get over yourselves."

But, that somebody in the police allowed themselves to be used by somebody in power at Lewes District Council… Several Brighton coppers shook my hand at matches and went "Well done Roz". But it's just classic; it's Lewes's small town politics run by small town politicians and officers, with sometimes the Keystone cops.

41. SEAGULLS PARTY
"What's your foreign policy?"

ROZ SOUTH: It was very obvious that what we were fighting was Lewes District and you needed to be fighting as equals politically, you need to be more than just fans fighting them. Because it really was high time that there was some sort of change, or at least some sort of change of attitude which was going to be brought about by the political process.

TIM CARDER: The situation was actually getting heated – Norman Baker was coming up with all these questions in the House of Commons ('Pie gate!'); there was the Ann De Vecchi business with Roz South – it was quite nasty and personal so we felt that it was the right time to actually take on, not Lewes District Council, I suppose, but the ruling elite of Lewes District Council, which was the Liberal Democrat Party, to make some sort of blow in the ballot box.

So we formed the Seagulls Party.

Paul Samrah was elected as leader, Roz was communications officer, Adrian was deputy leader. I volunteered as secretary because I felt that would keep me out of the spotlight to some extent and allow me to organise things in the background, Bill Swallow designed the logo and we were up and running. I think we had 400 members join pretty quickly, all paid a pound and usually wrote us a cheque for ten pounds saying keep the rest as a donation. Of course, being a political party we have to keep a record of donations…

DICK KNIGHT: The Seagulls Party was an interesting development, but what it mainly did was say that this football club's supporters are deadly serious, full of resourcefulness and inventiveness, and don't ever assume you can take them for granted.

PAUL SAMRAH: Inside eight weeks there was a snap election in Ringmer Ward on August 17th 2006 – and we'd only formed the party June 5th. We thought it's good practice for the local elections so let's do it.

TIM CARDER: Ed was up for being candidate at the by-election and Roz volunteered to be his agent. I got volunteers to drop our leaflet through every door in this ward, it was a good bit of fun, and most of the reaction we came across was pretty supportive.

LIZ COSTA: We knocked on an awful lot of doors (it wasn't just shoving things through letterboxes it was actually door knocking) – a terrifying experience because you don't know if someone's not going to come at you with a shotgun; but we did it and we were just curious what people actually thought and if they objected to it.

JAN SWALLOW: Someone at the count asked me what our foreign policy was!

124

TIM CARDER: For Ed to get the 22% he did, we felt was pretty reasonable; it made the statement that this is a serious issue, if nearly a quarter of the residents of this ward, unconnected to the stadium site in any way, see it as a major issue that they support.

ROZ SOUTH: It rattled the Liberal Democrats, to put it mildly, because they just thought Ed would be a joke candidate. The person who got in, Peter Gardener – who was a Lib Dem – later on in the campaign, was the person who put a stop to Lewes District Council's continued nonsense about opposing the stadium. And I think he was very influenced by what happens if you tangle with the Seagulls Party and the points of view that they have!

The May elections were wonderful. I fought Lewes Bridge ward because it's where I used to live in Lewes, and Ed fought Ouse Valley and Ringmer; we had Steve Williams, a decorator in Lewes Priory ward, and then Mark Jackson did Newhaven Denton & Meeching. And basically we had a fairly wonderful time because we had a huge amount of help again, from the fanbase generally; leaflets, I did my town centre leaflets – Ed brought a bus home from work, which we had as a kind of campaign bus, because these wards are huge, there's actually hundreds of houses. There was a point at which we thought 'we're gonna win, oh hell, we're gonna be on the council'.

PAUL CAMILLIN: It was a bit of fun but it kind of worked and helped us. I remember doing a little media briefing session with Paul, Adrian and a few of the others to say, they're going to interview you, this is what you can expect, and asking them about, what are you going to do about emptying bins and potholes in the road – and, of course, they hadn't even thought of this, they thought it was all going to be about the Albion and the stadium. They were pretty well prepared. Was there any danger of anyone being elected? You never know with the Albion do you? But realistically, probably not.

ROZ SOUTH: The Liberal Democrat standing against me in Bridge ward was an old boy called Jim Daly, who's been a mayor more times than I can remember, but he's on his last legs politically. He's what you might call Old Lewes, and during the campaign an Albion fan collared him on the doorstep who said; "Of course we couldn't vote for you, look at your policy on the stadium." To which Jim Daly replied; "Well, it's not me mate, it's Anne De Vecchi and we all hate her." So the Albion fan rang *The Argus* with this piece of information, they got back to me and I said; "Well, it does seem a slightly odd campaign tool, to run down your own council leader in the hopes of getting elected yourself."

TIM CARDER: Mark in Newhaven won about 30% of the potential vote, which was fantastic, and in Lewes it went down to 22% or something. Overall we had about 25% of the vote in those four seats that we contested. The idea was we wanted to have a pop at the Lib Dems, or any councillor, if you like, who was opposed to the stadium, so the highlight for me was David Neighbour losing his seat – he was the councillor in charge of planning and I had had a run in with him in the council chamber at Lewes and for him to lose his seat; sorry David, but it made my day!

ROZ SOUTH: There is no doubt whatsoever in my mind that two high profile councillors, Marina Pepper and David Neighbour, lost their seats because of the campaign and because of the Seagulls Party. They were key movers in disrupting the possibility of getting the stadium. And they had never ever expected to lose their seats.

It didn't matter that we didn't win a seat, what mattered was the effect we had on the District Council. And that was what was necessary, because I don't think they would have been able to make any sensible challenge to the final decision. But, it would have just been more months, and more money, and every time you're further away from a stadium.

ATTILA: If you've got popular support, and you've got the time to stand, then it's the best thing to do.

BILL SWALLOW: Some people in Lewes resented our very existence. On one occasion we took a stall in the high street by the bridge and asked people to sign a petition. A lot of people were extremely nice but a number took the view that we should not be in Lewes. One well-spoken chap told Paul Samrah to eff off. The thing is, there has always been a stand-off between the county town of Lewes and vulgar Brighton. Lewes sees itself as superior. Maybe it is, but the row is as old as the hills and the Albion just got caught in the cross fire. The stadium application confirmed Lewes Lib Dems' belief that the city of Brighton is a bully and so when we turned up with our little stall it wound some people up. Norman Baker walked past us with a sort of rictus smile. It clearly showed how they read the whole campaign.

42. NORMAN BAKER
An anchor for the antis

ROZ SOUTH: I do know Norman personally, which always came as a bit of a shock to people who thought that I ought to be putting ground-up glass in his tea. He is quite good on supporting the villages, he is quite good as a local MP at taking issues, especially from smaller areas, so it looked like he jumped onto the Falmer campaign: 'Ah, little village, threatened by great big city wanting to build nasty stadium. I think Norman realised that he backed the wrong political horse, but once he'd got a certain way down the road he couldn't really go backwards. So he carried on with an ever less convincing case against the stadium.

ADRIAN NEWNHAM: He is my absolute bete noir. You know that fuss when he was

Minister responsible for cycling safety and he refused to wear a helmet? I think the only reason he doesn't wear a cycle helmet is he has got to let the hot air out from somewhere. He talks out the top of his head.

Derek Chapman is a very successful local businessman. A big employer in the area before he retired. John Prescott was visiting the city in his role as Secretary of the Department of Transport and Regions. At the offices of Derek's company Adenstar, Prescott meets a series of people who are undergoing apprenticeships. Derek Chapman makes no comment to him. Derek has been told prior to Prescott's visit, by his solicitors, don't mention the Albion, your directorship or the planning application.

DEREK CHAPMAN: Baker implied that I bribed John Prescott didn't he? And that was out of order wasn't it?

ADRIAN NEWNHAM: Anybody would have known that that wasn't the case. Or could have found that that wasn't the case. But Baker's behaviour seemed to be 'Let's throw a bit more mud at this. Let's just put a bit more confusion in people's minds'. Derek is a good, honourable businessman who has contributed something to this community and he was besmirched by a professional politician. That can't be right.

DEREK CHAPMAN: You know that it got put in *The Guardian* when I called Baker a wanker? I spoke to a solicitor and he said; "Well, he's got to really prove that he is not now, or never has been... and he does wear glasses so..."

SARAH WATTS: I think he is a bit of a pompous arse. He probably truly believed what he believed and did what he wanted to do but he didn't seem to want to actually find out what it all entailed, what the benefits of the stadium could be.

ADRIAN NEWNHAM: We did get our revenge on Norman Baker when he agreed to go on a Southern Counties radio programme...

BILL SWALLOW: Obviously we had no contacts at the BBC local radio and it was just luck that we knew Norman Baker was going to be on. A number of us gathered in a room at Withdean and miraculously we were all chosen to ask a question on air...

ADRIAN NEWNHAM: I went on first and talked about his relationship with David

Bellotti and his inability to count numbers correctly. Then somebody else went on and asked him about his leaked report that showed that the Albion had been looking at a hotel at Sheepcote Valley, when actually the club were duty bound to look at Sheepcote Valley because that's what the public inquiry looked at – I felt he had been disingenuous because he only released six paragraphs of that report.

BILL SWALLOW: My question was: "In the unlikely event that the stadium was built at Sheepcote Valley, undoubtedly as MP for Lewes you would be invited to matches. How would you get there from Lewes?" He said he didn't know so I was able to tell him that he would drive to Falmer, go through the village and over the Downs and park on a specially built car park for 6,000 cars because there is no public transport – that's how you will get there. To which he replied; "Don't let's get personal about this."

ROZ SOUTH: We set out to make Norman look like an idiot and… he didn't come across very well.

TIM CARDER: As a result of that phone-in Dick Knight and Martin Perry invited Norman Baker to the club to see the sort of work that the club does with regards to the community scheme, and Norman Baker was impressed as anyone would be, because it is a massive operation and a very worthwhile one. I think they agreed to disagree on the planning case for the stadium but they issued a statement applauding the work of the club and it just helped relations. Norman Baker become more docile, I suppose, he was not on the prowl all the time. His attacks on Derek Chapman, it was all nonsense really, stirring for stirring's sake with no substance to it and perhaps he realised with talks to the club that he was wasting everyone's time.

ROZ SOUTH: Norman, incidentally, was the first person to say to Lewes District: "Enough, now just stop it. You're not doing it anymore; let's just have enough of this."

43. THE LIB DEM CONFERENCE
"If one Lib Dem council could ruin a football club..."

PAUL SAMRAH: The luck for the campaign continues because who comes to town for their conference? The Lib Dems! So we thought let's have a rally, we didn't want people to be tired of marching, we didn't want Falmer fatigue to set in.

We organised a meeting for senior Lib Dems to explain a few things, on the back of Bellotti and what he brought to the club, and on the back of Lewes District Council who weren't listening to their electorate and who are bringing Lib Dems down. We said we have formed a political party, we're not blackmailing you, we're just telling you the facts.

Adrian Newnham: "Welcome to your conference."
Liberal Democrat Leader Menzies Campbell: "Are you
security? I understand there are protesters due."
Paul Samrah: "We are the protesters."

Go and have a look at the site whilst you're in Brighton. Learn about it and find out why
people are objecting to your party's actions.

BILL SWALLOW: We produced a very sober leaflet for all the delegates explaining how
Lewes Lib Dems were trashing the party's reputation. It was quite spiky – we actually
accused them of being liars. As we had proof that they had told untruths there wasn't
much they could do about it. One of our strategies was to isolate Lewes Lib Dems from
the rest of the party and it was said that there was a stand-up row outside the Brighton
Centre between Brighton Lib Dems and their Lewes counterparts. I do hope it was true.

TIM CARDER: People were told to assemble outside the conference centre. In the end
there were 1,000 to 2,000 people, it wasn't a huge event.

ADRIAN NEWNHAM: I heard that Norman Baker said there were two hundred
people outside the conference and claimed he heard that from a policeman, but the only
policeman on duty was the Albion's liaison officer who gave the number as 1,500.

WHY WE ARE
DEMONSTRATING AT YOUR
CONFERENCE

Ordinary Sussex people hurt and upset by the
actions of a secretive group of local politicians

TIM CARDER: There were Liberal Democrats from
Brighton holding up 'Lib Dems for Falmer' banners. I
had come up with a leaflet to hand out to the delegates
explaining why we were demonstrating at their
conference. It ended with a version of the byline that
we had used all those years before; 'If one Lib Dem
council could ruin a football club what would they do
to the country?' They didn't like that – but I pointed out
to them, this is the effect you are having locally.

JOHN COWEN: An idea of mine that did see the
light of day was 'Ming and the Menu' – the fake menu
for the Lib Dem Gala Dinner.

ADRIAN NEWNHAM: We had the menu from
the Gala Dinner and Paul Samrah and I turned up in
dicky bows and were handing out the menus to the
people who were arriving and actually a lot of the Lib

UNAPPETISERS
Pate de Norman Baker
Lewes hand-raised Porkies
Oeufs sur le Visage a la High Court

MAINS
Locally Fried Brains
Canard de Lewes avec Nimby Sauce
Seagull Stew (warning - extremely hot)
Freshly caught Codswallop à la Conseil de Lewes lunatique
Baker's Head Rolls (crusty, stale)

JUST DESSERTS
Baker's Fruitcake Fool
Humble Pie (new to Lewes)
Hard Cheese, with De Vecchi Toast
Bellotti Career Bruleé (grilled, tossed and flipped)
Death by Electorate (sticky and brown, not for weak hearts)

The Banqueting room • Royal Pavilion • Brighton • 17 September 2006

Dems were very friendly and you had the odd one who came past and said; "We haven't got a clue what Lewes District Council are doing. They appear to be just off their…"

I remember Don Foster, the Lib Dem sports spokesman, said; "We can't work out what Lewes Council are doing."

JOHN COWEN: And then, moment of moments, the limo drew up and out came Sir Menzies and Lady Campbell, and they looked rather bemused as these men in their penguin suits approached and handed out their menus, straight-faced and bowing courteously.

ADRIAN NEWNHAM: Menzies Campbell turns up and there is literally no-one about. So I shook his hand and said; "Hello Menzies, welcome to your conference." And I hand him the dinner thing and he says; "Are you the security? I understand there are some protesters due!" And Paul went: "We are the protesters."

PAUL SAMRAH: The menu was just fantastic: 'Un-appetisers – Lewes hand raised porkies!' 'Mains – Canard de Lewes avec Nimby Sauce', 'Freshly caught codswallop' 'Just Desserts – Baker's Fruitcake Fool', 'Humble Pie (new to Lewes)'… It was just genius. That is a class act – what a way of getting your campaign over rather than in your face placards; genius.

JOHN COWEN: 'Seagulls Chateau Ver Bellotti', 'Lewes Cabinet So Very Wrong'; the one that I like, d'you remember Lewes Council leader Ann de Vecchi got into a lot of trouble for posting fake pictures of the view of the stadium from Ditchling Beacon in their council newsletter? Saying, this is how this stadium is going to spoil the landscape. So in the kids' menu I had; 'Aunty Ann's Fantastically Fishy Snaps.'

The point of that was, okay, it made us laugh, but the visiting Lib Dem delegates, apart from the ones from Sussex, had not a clue of what it was about anyway. But it still got the coverage.

44. CARDS TO RUTH KELLY
Sunny greetings from the seaside

MARTIN PERRY: We went through what is called a Rule 19 process, which is rule 19 of the Town and Country Planning Act whereby the decision is referred back to the Secretary of State – now we have a different Secretary of State, Ruth Kelly who was a completely different person to Prescott, a complete unknown. With John Prescott we knew him, we knew to make him laugh would work… We were very unsure with Ruth Kelly. So we decided what we would do is a campaign where we would play it straight, but with a hint of humour, and see what happened.

BILL SWALLOW: As we come from a seaside resort we thought we should send her a postcard. We printed 37,000 and people like Liz and Sarah and Jan did wonderful jobs getting people to sign them and post them off.

JOHN COWEN: I did the copywriting for the postcards to Ruth Kelly, including some for Withdean away fans – their postcard headline was 'Away with all of this' and a picture of bedraggled away supporters under their white and blue ponchos. We gave them out to away fans. We got good support from Sheffield Wednesday, Nottingham Forest and Bristol City fans, who took the postcards and filled them in.

ROZ SOUTH: I did the photographs for those. Bill Swallow and I went out in this pouring rain and we trudged round and I took pictures of the 'beautiful' university buildings and the A27 with lorries thundering along it. And also there was a serious side to it – photographs of three buses at the bus stop, all going to Brighton, pictures of Falmer station to show that this isn't a tiny little village with a duck pond, this is where the stadium's going to go. It was about 'let's give you a realistic picture of what Falmer looks like'.

MARTIN PERRY: These were pictures of the site but with a message to them that it's not an AONB – it used to be, but it isn't any more. Now Ruth Kelly has said that she is a Bolton Wanderers fan, so we felt we will use a football theme. So we had a picture of the site and the old broken down buildings at the back and the caption read 'AONB? You're

having a laugh'. Then there was a picture of the A27 with 'Falmer's country lanes'.

SARAH WATTS: We did anything to make it easy for supporters to send them off – we were standing handing them out at games, taking them back in, sending them off, writing them, whatever had to be done.

DAN TESTER: I put a message up on the Hibs message board – they're my second team – saying 'Would any of you be kind enough to send some postcards from Edinburgh'. I got 73 separate messages saying send us some here. One was from the bloke who played Spud in Trainspotting. I'd be on the phone to Tim requesting more and more postcards. I was really impressed with the Hibs fans – they really helped us.

TIM CARDER: We got feedback that there were sackfuls landing on Ruth Kelly's doorstep so the message got through. It was just keeping the issue up there as many of these sort of activities were.

45. PRIME MINISTER'S QUESTION TIME
Ambush in Church Street

BILL SWALLOW: Classic Paul this. There was an event at The Dome with the Prime Minister-elect being interviewed on stage. We were sitting with Paul at the back and there was a Q and A session at the end with microphones halfway down the aisles – you've got to have more balls than I've got but, of course, Paul has! He strode down and managed to get to the microphone ahead of somebody else – you can picture it.

PAUL SAMRAH: Bill had brilliantly worded a question – it had to be short, concise and absolutely on the money, bit of humour and Bill got it absolutely spot on. I approached a microphone and I was thinking 'oh blimey, here we go' and I said; "Are you aware that the city's football club, Brighton & Hove Albion, has been homeless since the very week you became Chancellor?" And I thought I could hear a few murmurs, couple of people nearby saying "Oh god – football." But, I thought, no, I'll continue; "As you will understand more than anyone that is a very long time! A sensible 'Yes' decision from Ruth Kelly in early July would welcome the Gordon Brown era with an instantly positive legacy for the people of Sussex…" And then this roar from the top of the building and everyone started applauding. I tell you it was a tingly moment because I really felt I got everyone in The Dome on our side.

BILL SWALLOW: Gordon Brown chose his words carefully but the gist of them was colossally supportive. Given the support Paul had grabbed out of thin air from a packed Dome he really didn't have much choice.

GORDON BROWN (from the stage): As a Raith Rovers fan myself, I know all about the struggle of a local football team to survive, and look forward to returning to Brighton… when the decision has been made.

PAUL SAMRAH: He'd been entertained by Steve Bassam that morning at his house and Steve had lobbied and been a very good supporter and the message had got home. Two thousand people cheering in The Dome, it was just phenomenal. And I just came away thinking luck again, it was just utter luck. It was just amazing really.

46. BLEARS'S DECISION
Sunny day for the battle-weary

TIM CARDER: In March 2007 we were informed that the decision would be made on or around July 9th – in fact Tony Blair resigned not long before that date, Gordon Brown took over and there was a government reshuffle again. Ruth Kelly was removed from responsibility and this time it was Hazel Blears. We didn't have time to do much campaigning, I think we sent a few postcards to Hazel Blears, not 37,000 or anything like that but enough to let her know that we were there…

MARTIN PERRY: On July 23rd 2007 we were told that the decision would be out the following morning. "Is it coming by post?" "Yes, it's coming by post." "Could you make sure we get a copy this time please?" And so we all go into the office at seven o'clock in the morning. Nothing. Ten past seven, we phone up the solicitors: "Has your post arrived yet?" "Yes." "Is the letter in there?" "No."

And this time it's the University of Brighton who phone up: "Hello Martin, well done!" Where had our letter gone this time? I don't think we ever got it, I think they just forgot to post it to us. And the council rang up: "Well done!" And we said could you fax it to us – but this time could you do it from the last page to the first. And that was it… We had got it! And shortly after that Lewes District Council said that that's enough.

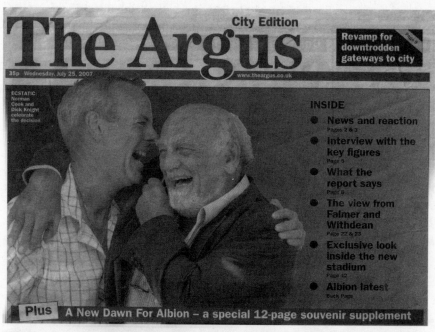

TIM CARDER: I was on holiday in Slovenia, which is an absolutely delightful country. I was in a tourist farm, which is like a bed and breakfast, but they grow all their own produce – and I was awoken by a mobile phone call from BBC Southern Counties and asked for my reaction. But, I didn't know what the result was; that's how I got to learn that the result was 'Yes'.

JOHN COWEN: I was in Toronto in my girlfriend's flat and a call came through from Paul Samrah saying; "It's a yes!" And I sort of danced around the room, and she wondered what I was doing.

DICK KNIGHT: So I got this letter in July 2007 from Hazel Blears, the final approval. 2007! Remember we started this exercise virtually from the time I took over in 1997! And we got the final letter and it felt completely anti-climactic, there was no euphoria… There had been an awful lot of disappointments along the way, too many battles had been fought unnecessarily, a waste of money – that was the thing that really got to me, the waste of time and the waste of money.

With all the planning application aspects, all those public inquiries, the total cost was £13,000,000; the total of all the legal costs, all the consultants, all the reports and everything you go through…

ED BASSFORD: I suppose it was a relief, but I can't remember, like one of those 'Can you remember where you were when…?' No, is the answer, I can't. I think we went down to Donatello's yet again for another celebration, all the usual suspects were there, Norman Cook, he always has to be there, Dick was saying the usual things: "I want to bring out the champagne!"

BOB BRUCE: There was a six-week period when appeals could happen and we were pretty confident, but you never know. I rang up Lewes and said: "I don't think there is anything you can challenge in this, what do you reckon?" And they said: "We haven't got the money even if we wanted to." Because they would have had trouble justifying the expense unless it was anything but a sort of 80% chance of winning, so I think they were resigned to the fact that it would happen.

LIZ COSTA: After Blears had said 'yes', a very reluctant 'yes', there was still that element of doubt because we had been caught out before, we didn't really want to go overboard celebrating. We all kind of said, 'yes', 'thank you' and all went out for a meal but it didn't quite feel the same because there had been so much time wasted and, of course, the recession had started to kick in and I think Martin and Dick were a tad worried where they were going to get the money from to be honest.

MARTIN PERRY: I remember it being a lovely day, the weather was great, the sun shone on Falmer, on the campaign and it was just… in a funny sort of way, I wouldn't say it was any sort of let down, because it was wonderful news, it was absolutely wonderful.

But you kind of almost got battle weary by then, so we'd actually had the joy, the thrill of, 'ah yes, we're gonna get it, thank goodness we're gonna get it'. But I think also because, I don't know, we knew it was gonna happen this time.

47. DEADLINE FOR APPEAL PASSES
The end of extra time

BILL SWALLOW: There was then a slightly worrying six weeks during which Lewes and Falmer councils – or anyone else for that matter – could have appealed.

TIM CARDER: Gradually all the parties came out and said they would not challenge, even Falmer Parish Council. If Lewes District Council was not going to lead the way I don't think there was any way that Falmer Parish Council could challenge the decision.

PAUL SAMRAH: Then six weeks passed… That was it. The stadium 'Yes', September 4th 2007, it was amazing.

ADRIAN NEWNHAM: Not so much dancing in the streets this time. I think it was more relief.

DAN TESTER: It was a weird feeling that I can't compare to anything else; we'd been let down so many times, it was so ingrained in our Albion-supporting psyche that something would go wrong – and it didn't. We sat in the Battle of Trafalgar and just had these weird nonplussed looks on our faces saying… 'Right, yeah, we've done it'. It was such an anti-climax.

RICHIE MORRIS: I think real football fans – not the plastic Premiership brigade – were delighted we got the go-ahead. That sense of footballing community is still there in the lower leagues. Although it may just have been because they wanted an away end in the same postcode as the pitch, with a roof…

DAVE SWAFFIELD: I think everyone felt they were just waiting for something round the corner to go wrong again – and you know there was stuff going on in the background – we heard rumours that actually the money wasn't there to build the stadium.

BOB BRUCE: When it was clear that that was singularly it, we then went hell for leather with all the property discussions and that took a long time… the University of Brighton, the council, the club and their lawyers were negotiating non-stop for several months, locked into quite acrimonious discussions at times.

The university's starting point seemed to be we don't really want this football club on our doorstep, let's be awkward about it. It became a lot easier once they realised it was going to happen with Tony's money and I think they got a bit more realistic then. The university are getting a good deal out of it; they are getting the basic buildings, money, landscape, better road, everything. For a certain type of student it is a great draw isn't it? In various areas, not just for the sport but for the sport science, probably architecture because of the building, catering stuff that is going on...

TONY BLOOM: The site at Falmer was no doubt the best location. I know that it has its issues, one being that a slight part of it could be in an Area of Natural Beauty but I think anyone unbiased can go along and look at that stadium and think the stadium has made Falmer a lot more beautiful. So, it is all a bit ridiculous but that's the laws of the land and these things need to happen, but something is wrong when it takes so long for an obvious decision; to cost the football club eight or nine years and the amount of money and all the work and the campaigns.

If it wasn't for the fans' campaigns we probably wouldn't have got it, so something is wrong in the planning process to do that, but we fans, as individuals and the football club, can only work with whatever the laws of the land give us... but it is a massive credit to so many people that we actually got there at the end.

48. THE END OF CAMPAIGNING
Time to sit back and enjoy the misery

TIM CARDER: From September 2007 there was still an awful lot of work to be done; there was another hurdle of a major planning application to bring the stadium up to date that had to go before the city council and get approval – we were writing letters in support of that.

But the main thrust of the Falmer For All campaign was over, we could get back to being ordinary fans at long last; sit back and watch the Albion lose every other week at Withdean as was the custom at that time – sit back and enjoy the misery. But we were miserable because of the team not because of the threat to the football club any more, the football club now had a future.

ROY CHUTER: I had this little nagging feeling that there was something missing, feeling slightly bereft that we are going back to being football fans again and not campaigners. I certainly haven't enjoyed parts of the last 15 or 16 years – I don't think anybody would say that – but it's been something that has been incredibly positive in different ways; especially the way we made friends – not just with other Brighton fans but with fans all over the country. That just didn't happen 30 or 40 years ago – a set of fans from Brighton would never have become friends with a set of fans from Doncaster.

LIZ COSTA: Falmer For all were the team that promised we were going to do everything in our power to deliver, and we did. The final hurdle? Well, we had no control over finding that hundred million quid. That wasn't part of our brief at all, the brief was to get the planning permission – and we delivered.

ADRIAN NEWNHAM: By then the credit crunch had started to kick in and OK, you have got permission – now how do you fund the thing?

PART THREE
Falmer
May 2011 -

49. GROUND-BREAKING
A real field of dreams

PAUL CAMILLIN: In December, Christmas 2008, we had the historic ground-breaking, and then it was sort of full steam ahead.

MARTIN PERRY: We decided that we ought to have a ground-breaking ceremony and we had the idea to create a goal from two excavators and that Dick and I would take penalties. So we invited a lot of people. There was great excitement although the site was just a muddy hole really.

ANDERS SWAFFIELD: I was in Year 7, I took the day off. We didn't have permission to go there, as many people did, we just turned up.

DAVE SWAFFIELD: I took Anders up there and we got the train out to Falmer and it was all timing it for the future reference – how long does it take from the pub to the station, from the station to the ground – and suddenly the famous Withdean stewards were upon us, and said; "What are you doing here?" And I said; "It's a public walkway and we're walking." And he didn't really know what to say, but he said; "There's something going on." And, I said; "Is there?" And he said; "You know there is." But fair play to the guy, he said; "I'll have a word with someone and see if I can get you in."

So we waited, feeling a bit stupid actually to be quite honest – but the guy came up and he said; "Yeah, come down." So we were there with the great and good – Brian Horton was there and Fatboy Slim, Micky Adams and Dick Knight and a few of the team members and it was brilliant.

ANDERS SWAFFIELD: It was a bit surreal the moment, how could a stadium go here? It was just a big field, what are they going to do to that?

MARTIN PERRY: Work had started on the widening of Village Way, but the site itself was just a muddy area and we cleared an area – actually in the position of the North Stand goal, and we set up a corner flag within the university. Now it's quite hard to imagine there were buildings all around. I remember Dick going up to take his penalty and missing; and I took mine and it went straight in. So I scored the first goal at Falmer! But I have to say if you were using the song 'How Wide Do You Want the Goal?' the gap between the buckets of the two diggers was quite a bit bigger than a normal goal!

DAN TESTER: Now, I love Dick and Martin for what they've done for the club but they can't play football, and they certainly can't have played football for the last 40 years. Dick's penalty was quite good actually!

SARAH WATTS: That was exciting, to actually see the ground semi-prepared and ready to go, that is when you knew it was finally happening.

DAVE SWAFFIELD: I've got a photograph of Anders by what is now the north-west corner flag, which was at that time in amongst some buildings on a pathway – brilliant! So that was a really good day – it all became real then.

BILL SWALLOW: It was at the ceremony on that day that the famous 'Stadium Yes' banner, the green one, was lost. Paul was terribly sad about it because it would have been great in the museum.

ED BASSFORD: When the work started on the stadium, it was the breakpoint in the whole thing, the end of the Falmer For All campaign and the beginning of something different.

PAUL CAMILLIN: I do remember the BBC around that time telling us we didn't have the money to do it, and Martin being furious with them.

PAUL SAMRAH: There was a feeling at the ground-breaking that it was all very well getting a tractor on site, and laying out the pitch where the centre circle is going to… but you've got to build it. Great, we've secured the land; great, we've got the lease on the site; great, that you've named the contractors – but there are still some people, as we were entering the recession, who were dubious, who thought it might be a half-finished job or not what we hoped it to be. Is anything actually going to rise from the ground?

We didn't know anything about Tony Bloom's money at this point, it hadn't been revealed. At least, we didn't know about it until May 2009.

50. TONY BLOOM TAKES OVER
'Tony Bloom, I think I love you'

ANDY NAYLOR: I think the question mark was always would Dick Knight be able to finance the dream?

ANDY SIMONS: I really thought; 'Does he have the financial stability to enter into a contract of this scale?'

TIM CARDER: There was lots of worries amongst supporters, the city council needed to be reassured that the funding was there because they didn't want a half-built stadium standing there on the edge of the Downs.

PAUL HAYWARD: I suppose my hopes overcame my doubts, but when I heard about these elaborate formulas for raising some money from the football trust and all these different areas – I couldn't see how it would make the enormous pot you would have to have to build that stadium.

PAUL WHELCH: The club touted around all the banks; they went to Lloyds and they went to all the others and my understanding is they almost all said; "It's a great idea but sorry we are not going to be investing anything." And they had no tangible offer of money.

DEREK CHAPMAN: It just didn't stack up and I can't believe how anybody believed it – oh we will get a few grants and forward sell a few of the tickets and hey, that will come to about 70 million and a mate of mine will lend us a few quid, and the council fell for it.

STEVE BASSAM: I didn't share any money worries that some people had actually. I have learned over the years that if Martin is confident about it, he sort of knows something that he hasn't revealed, and I suspected that he had a brilliant scheme up his sleeve.

MARTIN PERRY: I always said there would be two mountains to climb – the first one is to get planning permission, the second one, will be funding. Of course, that in itself is an astonishing story because the moment we got planning permission, Tony Bloom, who was supporting the club financially at that stage, called me in and he said I want you to run a series of numbers. And we looked at it in all kinds of scenarios – then he said: "I will support it."

And I went home and I said to my wife; "We've funded it, we've got it, the fans don't realise it yet, and they won't know for a while but we've done it – I cannot believe it!"

ANDY SIMONS: Martin phoned up and said: "We are off and running." I said; 'What are we going to take out?' He said; "We are not. We have got the funding, we are doing it all – press on, I have got the money!" But it was quite some time when I found out where, and from whom.

DICK KNIGHT: Tony's price for underwriting the stadium was to say, in May 2009, I want you to stand down, I want to be the chairman now. For my part, I felt that this stadium is my battle, I fought this battle, leading thousands of people to get it. But I also knew that with the global credit crunch looming, his way would get the stadium built sooner. I couldn't deny our magnificent supporters that, so I stood down.

I received a small amount of money for some of my Albion shares from Tony Bloom, but nowhere near the total sum I've put into the club over the years, and never taking a penny out, except for some expenses. I never took a salary, I wouldn't do that.

TONY BLOOM: I was six or seven years old when I started going to the Albion, since I knew what it was all about. I've long family connections with the club, my granddad, God bless him, was vice-chairman and he passed away in 1980, and my uncle Ray has been on the Board for the best part of 25 years. So yes, it goes back a long way. When I started watching, we were a very successful team, and ever since 1983 it's been pretty downhill! Albeit, we've had our moments.

DEREK CHAPMAN: I have known Tony for the last 11 years. He came back from Gibraltar and then gradually helped, because every couple of months, it was, "We have all got to chip in a bit more because we can't pay the wages", or something like that, and that happened all through the 2000s. I'd go home and tell the Mrs and she would say: "How much this month?" Another twenty grand… it was always sailing close to the wind.

If I had the money I would pay for it, as I'm sure a lot of people would, but not many people carry around £100 million in their back pocket do they? So we are very lucky, it's great.

Albion press release, 18th May 2009

Stadium Funding Secured

The club is delighted to announce full funding has been finalised for the new community stadium at Falmer. The full cost of the stadium project is £93m, the majority of which will be funded by Tony Bloom. Bloom will take over as Albion chairman, with Dick Knight taking on the role of life president, ending a very memorable 12 years at the club's helm.

Knight said, "This is the natural progression for the football club. Tony's investment will mean no need for external funding, which is absolutely superb news for the club and its fans.

"Being chairman of the Albion has been the most rewarding period of my life. To be able to give something back to the club I've supported since I was a boy has been a privilege. Helping to save it, building a forward-thinking reputation for the club, developing our youth system and encouraging Albion in the Community to spread its wings – I've enjoyed it immensely. And all of this while we fought the long and relentless battle to secure our new home against all the odds.

"Thanks to Tony's support, the club is now financially secure, the stadium is on its way, and the club now has the opportunity to reach its true potential. We have come a long way from what Bob Pinnock, Martin Perry and I inherited twelve years ago and I am proud of what we, the directors, staff, players and fans, have all achieved together."

Bloom said, "I would like to pay tribute to Dick. Nobody should be in any doubt that he saved the club from almost certain extinction at a time when no-one else was willing to come forward, and under his leadership we have had some very memorable times including our successful nine-year battle to secure the go-ahead for Falmer.

"I want to see the club build on the momentum under our newly appointed manager Russell Slade. I am determined to see us back in the Championship as soon as possible. I want to fulfil the dreams of so many of our great fans just as my grandfather Harry Bloom did in the glory days of the 1970s with Brian Clough, Peter Taylor and Alan Mullery."

TONY BLOOM: When Dick Knight took over, he had a very difficult job financially stay alive for the years at Withdean, you can have zero playing budget and still lose money at Withdean because of all the other costs involved. It's very low income there, and because of the costs of trying to get planning and so on, myself amongst other directors and shareholders, helped out financially to just stay alive.

came to a head to get the funding for Falmer, the Amex as it is now. Two things went against which is quite well known; one is the cost was a lot higher than we ever envisaged, in the ten years the inflation and all the other costs had gone up, and you can never get an exact number until you get planning permission.

And secondly, when it came to getting funding, we weren't looking to get funding for everything, I was always going to put a decent amount of money in to help build the stadium, but getting any money from the banks in the middle of the credit crisis was next to impossible. At the best of times the banks don't like loaning football clubs with the trouble football clubs have given over the years. So it got to a situation where I got to put in far more money than I anticipated, but I had no problem making the decision, the other option was not a very good option…

I am fortunate to be in the position to be able to do it, I had the money to do it, which obviously not many people did and also I had the will to do it.

There wasn't one moment where I thought, 'oh my God, I've got to put all the money in'. It was an ever evolving thing, gradually I thought I may need to put in more money, and then perhaps a bit later it was even more money, and then it was even more money. That is just the way it is sometimes but as I said, I have got the money and I am fortunate that I have had a successful career and this football club is in my blood and it's all worth it.

PAUL WHELCH: If you have got a sustained interest on a loan of 45 million or something, you are ending up paying something like £2m a year on interest; that amount of interest would have been the equivalent of 6,000 season ticket holders – the whole of Withdean paying the interest and everything was on top of that.

SAM SWAFFIELD: The money wasn't there to build the ground and if Tony Bloom wasn't there then that would have been really, really sad – so his role is invaluable.

ANDY NAYLOR: The thing was, you had this guy Tony who had obviously put a lot of money into the club and was quite content for a time just to be doing that and not paying a more significant role than that, but you always felt it was going to reach a point where he's going to want a real say in sort of driving the club forward.

I think there was probably quite a lot of bad feeling about the way it was done in the end. A shame it had to be like that but you can kind of see why it happened. On the one hand the chairman who had been there for all that time through all that – and I suspect this is the way Dick saw it – and then this guy just comes along and just sort of reaps the benefit if you like.

PAUL CAMILLIN: Tony Bloom has paid for the stadium. If he gets half his money back then brilliant, because it'll mean we've been successful and probably will be in the Premier League. If he gets all his money back then brilliant, because we'll probably be a Champions League club.

He said to me that it's the only business decision he's made in his life that takes into account emotion. Which I think is great because I think it's based 100% on his emotion and his love for the club.

IAN HART: Dick Knight was our Churchill, he won us the war and maybe in his own way Tony Bloom is our own Clement Attlee, he is the person who now carries it forward. Without Tony Bloom, Falmer would be a building site and we would be at the Withdean just bouncing along between League One and League Two.

In a podcast, I asked Martin Perry a direct question; "Where would we be without Tony Bloom?" And he said; "We would be in serious trouble." And that did grind with me, I have got a lot of time for Martin, but how many times did they come on the phone-in and say the finance was all in place and clearly it wasn't?

ED BASSFORD: Dick never had the money, Dick and his mates had the money to keep the club going. I don't believe the club was ever unrealistic, I think the circumstances were such that the international banking crisis made things very difficult and Tony Bloom had the money. Nobody saw that coming. Where did Tony Bloom get his money from, I don't know – he doesn't get it playing cards does he?

TONY BLOOM: I can see that it might have looked to fans as if I'd appeared out of the blue, how it looks too good to be true, but during the many years when I was helping out financially behind the scenes, I didn't want any publicity at all and I deliberately didn't want to be on the Board because I generally don't like the publicity.

If I could do the job with less publicity involved I would prefer it. I don't go out seeking it but I know there are responsibilities as chairman and an owner in terms of being a public figure and doing interviews and being slightly well known, but I am happy with how it has gone because I am well known in Brighton as chairman but certainly outside of Brighton and outside of Sussex no-one is going to recognise me as chairman of Brighton. It is good for me that it is not too much in the public eye.

ATTILA: When I realised that effectively Dick was chairman but Tony Bloom was providing the money, I'm thinking this is going to end in tears. Dick was there since the beginning, he never had lots of money in the modern football sense (though he was absolutely minted by most people's standards!) He gave his life and soul to this club. But if Tony Bloom hadn't been there to provide the money then maybe it could have all collapsed. I thought that Dick would stay chairman until the new stadium but it was obvious that Tony wanted to be chairman; Dick was really upset about it.

The reality that we had had so many years in a shit position but now we had someone who is a Brighton fan who is going to fund the new stadium, we couldn't really argue with that. In an ideal world we supporters should own the club, but this isn't an ideal world, far from it in my view, so I can only say hats off to Tony, it's very lucky for us he made all that money at just the right time and he's spending it on us! The whole new stadium will be a monument to Bloom's largesse.

ROZ SOUTH: I was very disappointed to see Dick go but I think he would probably admit that if he couldn't bring the ultimate prize, then none of the rest of it would have been worth it.

JOHN COWEN: We've got a billionaire chairman who is genuinely a fan, from a generation of fans, a dynasty of directors and the family is a dynasty!

PAUL WHELCH: What it meant was the old rule they had about nobody having overall control had to be thrown out of the window – but you know we are not throwing it out the window to an Icelandic multi-millionaire, we are doing it for someone whose grandfather was vice-chair of the club.

NIGEL SUMMERS: When Tony first came in and said he wanted complete control, I remember thinking we have had this once and we agreed that no one person would ever have complete control again and I wasn't entirely comfortable with it. But when you talk to the fellow and realise what he is doing then, of course, he wants the whole control and he is a proper Brighton fan with proper Brighton history.

LIZ COSTA: We saw him last year just after the chairman of Southampton dropped dead and we said; "God forbid that anything should happen to you Tony but is the money safe?" We don't want your family coming in and saying take it all out because that is what happened at Southampton and he said; "No, I can guarantee that it is ring-fenced and locked in, nobody can touch it."

KERRY MAYO: He is a great guy, wears his heart on his sleeve and is a Brighton fan as much as I am.

TIM JOHNSON: He is a genuine fan and you saw that at the Division One Championship parade. There was just this big Cheshire cat grin smile and it didn't go for the hour or so that we were watching.

TIM HERBERT: On the way back from Huddersfield last season I was on the train and there he was, sat there in economy hanging out with the rest of us having a beer. And he spent the whole journey chatting to the fans. Bless him, he was sat there completely cornered, he had no escape whatsoever.

STEFAN SWIFT: I was running for a train to go to Bristol – and I find I'm running alongside Tony Bloom – that was one of my proudest moments I think. He was with three of his mates and I said something like, "Tony Bloom, I think I love you", which didn't go down too well with his mates, but I think he got the idea of what I meant.

GRAEME ROLF: He is one of a rare breed of chairmen – he is a little bit Jack Walker-y isn't he? What Jack Walker did for Blackburn is like what Tony Bloom is doing for us.

PAUL CAMILLIN: He's like you and I, he's like any of the supporters in the book – the Albion is his team. At 4.45pm on a Saturday afternoon, if he isn't in the ground, which he invariably is, he'll probably be watching the game somewhere by satellite, but if he didn't, he'd be on the phone or on the internet or listening on the radio.

He's just an Albion fan, we're just lucky he's an Albion fan with a huge amount of money and enough to give the club £100m to build the stadium.

TIM CARDER: Lewes District Council could well have delayed it enough that the economic situation took a downturn and the banks weren't prepared to lend money to the club; it could have been that it would have added two or three more years before the economic situation improved before the club could gather the money to build the stadium. Planning permission might have expired and we might have had to go through the planning permission all again – just imagine that!

TONY BLOOM: It's ridiculous that building the stadium took so bloody long, we could have been there five or six years ago, we could have been in the Premiership. But who knows, my situation may have been quite different five years ago. On that side, they came to me at the right time for that amount of money: it's one thing five or ten million, but another thing for a hundred and three million, so perhaps, I haven't really thought about it, but perhaps… it may have helped us. It's something I have never really thought about – but if we got the permission six or seven years ago they wouldn't have been getting the help from me, there wasn't that sort of money in the old bank account.

PAUL CAMILLIN: Is it karma? The shit Brighton fans have been through since 1995, coming back to Withdean, the knockbacks, the blows, you feel that if any group of fans have earned it, or deserved it, it's Brighton & Hove Albion fans.

51. 'THERE'S ONLY ONE DICK KNIGHT'
A true hero to every Albion fan

TONY BLOOM: Who else would have done what Dick did and take all the risk on himself to get the thing going and the planning permission and to keep the football club alive at Withdean for so long?

ATTILA: As far as I'm concerned Dick Knight's a fucking hero, he's the resurrection of this club.

GRAEME ROLF: Dick Knight reminds me of my granddad; he is a really lovely bloke, very warm, sincere and again a proper Brighton supporter.

IAN MORLEY: Dick Knight is a fascinating character, like all self-made millionaires, there's something about them. And I don't think he'd mind me saying, there's a certain arrogance about him as well, but that comes with people of that type.

We'll remember him for his persistence. He's a retired guy, the history's well documented, he had a big advertising agency in London, sold his advertising agency, his wife died, young, and he threw his life into football, and into the club.

ANDY NAYLOR: I think the one thing you always felt you knew with Dick is that here was somebody whose heart was in the right place. Without the drive and determination of Dick, Brighton wouldn't be where they are would they? There is no argument about that.

NIGEL SUMMERS: The 'Knight in shining armour' is a dreadful cliché but I don't mind being the umpteenth person to say it; thank goodness for him, because we could have had all the ranting and raving and marches, but unless you have got someone who is prepared to sit in a room with Archer and take him on in a language that he could understand and let him in the door, that would have been that. That Hereford 1-1 game was absolutely gut-wrenching, but it would have meant nothing if Dick hadn't been there – if we'd won that game 6-0 and Dick hadn't been around we'd have been in massive trouble.

PAUL CAMILLIN: I think the one thing I'll always admire Dick Knight for is sitting in a room with Archer and going through the mediation, and having the patience and the stamina to sit there, with the man that had left his club on the brink of extinction.

KERRY MAYO: When Dick Knight came on board, he came into the dressing room before the game at Hereford and introduced himself and said; "Good luck boys, whatever happens today you have done us proud getting us into this position, and if you win there is a holiday on the table." I ended up going to Gran Canaria for a week and it was a nice touch.

IAN HART: Dick Knight is a PR man and he brought public relations back to the Albion because the Albion PR with Archer, Stanley and Bellotti was in the toilet. It was that bad at the Albion you could have had Gary Glitter as the chairman and it would have made things better... or maybe not.

ANDY NAYLOR: We had our ups and downs – he's a strong character, not a lot happened without Dick's imprint on it at the club, even what would be considered to be fairly mundane trivial things, in terms of press releases and stuff, he would always sign them off and go through them first and so on, so we had some fun and games along the way.

DEREK CHAPMAN: God, can he talk! I drive him to the away games a lot and he never stops talking. And he's always late. Dick's a great bloke isn't he? Martin had to talk to the councillors and the politicians because me and Dick get so frustrated with these people.

DAVE SWAFFIELD: And let's not forget as well, he brought in Martin Perry, which was an inspired move, absolutely.

LIZ COSTA: Dick was a bit like a boffin in a way, never really got rattled. He guided us perfectly; he never told us what to do.

There were the odd suggestions and he told us not to be so stupid and six months later used them as his, but we don't mind because we were a team.

DICK KNIGHT: I never felt that the job was ever going to break me, I wouldn't let it – not the apathy of Brighton Council, not the incompetence of the Football League, not the holier-than-thou legal manipulators of the planning system – because I was too bloody-minded.

I knew something they couldn't seem to comprehend. The fans make the club what it is. I wasn't going to let them down.

I would stand up at Football League meetings and say; "We don't respect the supporters enough in this business, the Football League needs to understand how valuable its supporters are, and what the clubs mean in their communities." Half of the club bosses were thinking; "What the hell's he talking like that for? Whose side is he on?"

Brian Mawhinney, who was the chairman of the Football League for quite a few years until recently, uses Brighton as an example of a well-run football club that works in its community properly and its principles are right – he uses our club as a model for everyone in the professional game, including the Premier League.

PAUL HAYWARD: There should be a Dick Knight statue on one of the concourses because to have held the club together really just through sheer chutzpah and charisma and his ability to keep talking… Amazing resilience and I think that the survival of the club really does reflect his spirit and his contribution to a large degree and we should all remember that.

STEVE BASSAM: I think Dick will forever regret that he wasn't there to see the final jigsaw piece in place as chairman, but being the pragmatist that he is, recognised that the project needed to be taken on to another level.

I just hope people don't forget just how critical he was for so long, keeping the club alive and making it happen and getting a lot of the decisions right really. Him and Martin particularly – you know Dick spotted some winners. Martin was the sort of person who made it happen and had a lot of the vision with him. A great combination really.

ADRIAN NEWNHAM: I would say Dick Knight is one of the most passionate and honourable people I have ever met.

I do feel genuinely sorry for him that he wasn't still chairman at the point where the stadium opened. But I am also sure that in his mind he knew it was the right time to change. Dick not only saved the club but he also got the club in the safe hands it is in now – by making it a club that people want to invest in and want to be a part of.

ED BASSFORD: Sometimes he's presented by some supporters as being some sort of megalomaniac who insisted on getting his own way, particularly over things like managerial appointments and the rest of it. I don't think that was ever the case, I think he was always somebody who would think over a problem and discuss and debate before a difficult decision was made. It was Dick's willingness to do that and open up the campaign to supporters by getting them involved in the arguments, rather than just resolving them at football club Board level, which more than anything has got this campaign to where it got to, which is building the stadium.

ANDY SIMONS: I wouldn't want, in any way, for Dick to be eclipsed by Tony; he and Martin were the team which had the drive to literally take this thing right the way through to the point of being; all those planning years, all those public inquiries, the indomitable spirit they embodied it.

Dick crossed it into the box, you could say, and Tony's knocked it in.

DICK KNIGHT: Brighton fans were important and I listened to them – I was one of them. We were on the same wavelength most of the time because I thought like a fan. That collective understanding kept the club going throughout the battle for Falmer, through all the Withdean years, and what we had was quite a lot of success despite everything.

And it set us up for the future.

52. BUILD A STADIUM
A genuine theatre of dreams

DICK KNIGHT: This stadium had a history already before a game had been played in it because of the huge, wonderful battle for it.

DEREK CHAPMAN: Even though I am there nearly every day, every time I drive the car past I get a lump in my throat. It's the bollocks isn't it?

PAUL HAYWARD: I think an older part of the town of Brighton has risen up and established itself with the stadium: it has been a very welcome spectacle because there has to be more to a town than stag weekends and expensive shops and boutique hotels; who wants to live in a town as superficial as that?

The Design

ADRIAN HOLDSTOCK: To design it – you obviously start off simply with a diagram of exactly how big a 22,500-seater stadium will be and will it sit on the site… We came up with a series of options; one of which was the arch roof and Martin always said: "That is the one I want."

Over the years, the concept has remained the same, the pitched angle of the roof is the same, the overall shape of the buildings is the same. But, from that period of time following on from the public inquiry, all the legislation relating to football stadia had changed, so we had to re-design significant chunks simply to conform to modern legislation, modern standards.

The landscape from the south-west corner to the north-east corner fell by about 16 metres; it was an old river bed that had dried up hundreds and hundreds of years ago and the landscape sort of rolled over. The fall was south-west to north-east and we picked up that undulation and just lifted it so it is a similar fall into the landscape that was under it.

All football stadia have the majority of the area within the West Stand because your backs are to the sun, so all the best seats in the house are in the West Stand and that is where you have to maximise your opportunities. It's the biggest stand, you can get more hospitality into it and you can get more facilities into it and it naturally followed the line from the landscape, so erecting a linear building with sharp angles really wasn't the right solution.

We worked closely with our structural engineers to try and get the arches to work properly, but just to have a normal arch didn't look right, so what we did was to lean the arches over as far as possible. I have got some original images in terms of actually how that arch looked with the grass bunds and this sort of butterfly-shaped arch, which unfortunately we had to change for the economics. We didn't appreciate all those years ago that the Chinese were going to have a massive investment programme in the construction industry and steel prices went through the roof, so those tubular butterfly arches would have doubled the cost of the roof, so we came up with the solution of the trusses as an alternative.

ANDY SIMONS: Why do the arches have to be like this? The point about the arches was, they are the flattest arches you can possibly do before they stop actually benefiting from being an arch and have all the elegance and structural efficiency of an arch – they become a beam, in which case they have to be a really big trunk, truss beam that are just curved enough to get the benefits of an arch but incredibly flat so you didn't break the skyline any more than you had to.

We took the arches and rather than just roll straight over like at Wembley, we'd laid them back so we had this arch form. Then we actually relaxed it backwards both sides and used the fact it was holding a roof and being propped up from collapsing any further and put the whole thing completely in balance so the whole stadium roof didn't actually work until it was finished. It is one of the lightest weight roofs to date in any stadium in terms of tonnage of steel per square metre.

So the construction guys cursed us because everything had to be propped up until everything was connected and then you could take the props away and it would just hang there; slam the beam in, hang all the bits of roof off it and slam the next beam in. It's got this complete tension wind beam holding it all together and once it is there it will resist all the forces of wind, it won't sag but it will just settle.

The engineers were just fantastic, they predicted the centre of the arch across this 180-metre arch would settle at 130 millimetres – once they took the props away it settled within about five millimetres of that…

ADRIAN HOLDSTOCK: From when we started, it was always the community stadium. It had never been anything else. The club do an enormous amount for the community with its outreach programmes and they do need to make this building work seven days a week, irrespective of whether there is a match on, so it has to be a building for the community and a building that people want to go to, want to use, not necessarily for a football match… it's all part of the original concept.

ANDY SIMONS: The quality of what Martin has allowed us to build is probably beyond what we thought. What happened was we designed it, and it was gorgeous, and we probably thought as architects that it would get pared down over time, that when we get down to what the club could actually afford it wouldn't look as good as this. But we knew something would happen because you are the only club for absolutely miles. The fanbase in Brighton alone is vast, it was quite vocal and quite obvious and existed and was keen to buy tickets in this new stadium if you could ever create it. So, 'build it and they would come'. We trusted that.

Construction

MARTIN PERRY: The period after we had got planning permission and we knew where the funding was coming from we had to put all the legal agreements in place, and so from July 2007 through to December 2008, that's all we were doing.

Derek Chapman, who had been running his own company Adenstar, was beginning to wind down and he then made himself available to take on the role of construction director and be directly involved in the handling of the contractor, which was a tremendous asset. He did a brilliant job pulling all the construction side together to get it built.

DEREK CHAPMAN: I retired and I gave my company to the guys who work for it, and I've become the project manager for the stadium. So I signed off all the payments, I supervised all the work for the club, and agree everything on site. I sat through the tender process, selected Buckingham, and then when we had meetings. I am the focal point. I am here every day… so I am project managing it, I don't ever get paid. I have done it for nothing. This is my legacy.

MARTIN PERRY: There was still an awful lot to do in terms of setting up the business to be able to cope with running a stadium – the business now is five times as big as it was when we were at Withdean – overnight! We had to recruit, in total, something like 900 people. There were huge contracts to let, including not only the building contract itself but the catering contracts and all the other contracts for services related to operating the stadium.

It wasn't just about building it – it was setting up the whole operation, which was completely different from running Withdean. All of that had to be done in that period, while we were actually building the stadium.

We decided that the right thing to do was to move out of the club offices and set ourselves up separately. So we set ourselves up with a project office at Withdean, which was the room that was used on a matchday for the directors' Boardroom guests. Every single match we had to clear everything away and set up as a hospitality suite, and after the game get it all out again – everything was on wheels! It was all very well when we started because there was actually just four of us; myself, Richard Hebberd, we took on a project assistant Laura Collins, and Derek Chapman. And it worked brilliantly. By the time we'd finished, there was 16 of us in there. So to pack all that lot up on a matchday was an absolute nightmare – especially if you've got a match on a Saturday and a Tuesday!

DEREK CHAPMAN: You go to a Board meeting and you say to Tony something about the padded seats, like: "You don't need them for the away fans and you don't need them for the North Stand, so we can save money." "No", Tony says; "I want the best stadium in the country, spend the money, I want it all padded; just make sure you get me the best price for it."

This is a different class. If you index link the cost of Southampton, Leicester City and Derby County to today's money, they cost £1,650 a seat; this one is £3,000 a seat. We have got the same seats as the Olympics – but their VIP seat is our standard. Wi-fi – the whole ground is covered in Wi-fi. They come up with great ideas; like Leeds are playing – we will get a few casks of Tetley's beer in and we will get local Balti pies... so they are going to get local food and drink for whoever – its fucking brilliant isn't it? If you treat them like human beings they will behave like them.

PAUL HAYWARD: Martin Perry said to me, they want away fans to look at the fixture list and say: "The Brighton game is in September, I am bloody well going to that because it's such a good day out."

DEREK CHAPMAN: I would have it all standing if I could but I am not allowed to. I think people should have a choice.

PAUL HAYWARD: This stadium completely inspires me architecturally, I just felt it was a landmark building and it was a kind of symbol of rebirth in so many ways.

DICK KNIGHT: I had already done one final, crucial deal for the stadium. In the summer of 2008 I persuaded the global top brass of American Express to spend millions taking the naming rights of the stadium, based solely on its community role. I had such a passion for this idea; it was why we had originally registered the name of our new home as the 'Community Stadium'.

DEREK CHAPMAN: Probably when you look at it – it is quite beautiful round here – how the fuck we ever got a football stadium out here I don't know!

53. LOOKING BACK
An incredible journey

TIM CARDER: Five parties in this stand out for me; Dick Knight and his leadership and his pure drive to see this project come to fruition.

Martin Perry, for his absolute expertise in his visualisation of how it could be built, including the financing of it in terms of bringing in educational establishments to the stadium. Working to find a site that would work within the framework, without having to have retail parks and all that around it, because the city council would not allow that.

Brighton & Hove Council, because they have always been supportive. Once the new Board was in place Martin and Dick wooed them and got the council on board and ever since then, whatever we may think of Mr Bodfish, the city council have basically been supportive; the likes of Steve Bassam and all the officers involved.

Tony Bloom, for coming along at the right time with the right amount of money; without Tony Bloom there wouldn't be a stadium up there now. The Albion Board members as well, I would include them along with Martin, Dick and Tony.

The fifth party, of course, is the supporters and it is the supporters throughout whose intention has been to get them to emphasise to the powers-that-be that this is a stadium that is necessary, it is wanted and it is in the interest of the nation.

PAUL SAMRAH: During the campaign I've been a politician, a pop star, a kind of saboteur – and I'm an accountant!

I think the club underestimated how clever we were at getting the message across, and I think we got the message across far better and quicker than the club. I recognise why, because the club has limited resources and Martin's trying to deal with many people, the council, the universities and everything and it's a bloody nightmare.

I've had a more interesting life, made great friends, developed new skills. I didn't know I had things in me, it was great fun!

Because of our history, because of what we have been through, we are probably the most educated football fans in the country. We know about balance sheets, and accounts and Articles of Association. We are now naturally inquisitive, nosey and we don't accept things on face value; we're cynical.

ANDY NAYLOR: I think what's interesting is how the fans just kept the momentum going. If you take it right back from the Goldstone and going to Gillingham... to be able to keep that momentum going all the way through what has been a decade, or whatever it is, and not being put off by all the setbacks along the way. It's just an amazing loyalty.

TONY BLOOM: I do think without the fans we may not have done it, but it's not just the fans, Martin and Dick, it took just so many people to make it happen because everything was stacked against us, ridiculously so, but it was. Steve Bassam, he was a great help – one of the good guys... again, probably one of those ones who likes to stay out of the limelight, but he deserves great credit.

SAM SWAFFIELD: Whenever I met someone and told them who I supported, they would say; "How's the stadium going?" They wouldn't have said "Congratulations on the play-off final" they wouldn't say "Congratulations on two championships on the trot", they would have said: "How's the stadium going?"

It's really important that we recognise the work of Knight and Perry and Bloom, but people should look at each other and applaud each other, and just say well done.

DAN TESTER: I've been to Whitehall with bunches of flowers, marched, sent postcards, written letters – a tiny amount compared to the main protagonists. Most Albion fans have done something to help. Thinking about the whole campaign makes me feel very proud to be an Albion fan.

LIZ COSTA: The passion that the Brighton fans have demonstrated over the last 15 years, I want to bottle it and sell it, because we've done it come hell or high water – we were going to win, it didn't matter, what, how we were going to do it – we were going to do it.

If we are all honest with ourselves, the man from Blackburn, he did us a favour. We wouldn't have been able to do an awful lot with the Goldstone because of all the various conditions that there were and I don't think we would have galvanised as much support from around the country, and even from our own fans...

We know what we have done and we know that without the efforts of this group of fans we wouldn't have got what we got – that is the bottom line. However much the present management would like to think they are going to move the club forward and sort of forget we are all there, without us they wouldn't have a club to be selling.

The fact that I had been banned from the ground, just wound me up even more, I thought I am going to beat this bastard if it is the last thing I am going to do, because he was so determined to screw us up by then. I wasn't going to give up. I thought we are going to win this fight, we are going to get ourselves a new stadium and you will not be a part of it.

BILL SWALLOW: Someone once asked where would we be without Tony Bloom, and the reply, quite properly, was in very serious trouble. And where would we be without

Dick Knight? The answer is that we probably wouldn't have been round long enough to have got into serious trouble.

JAN SWALLOW: I always thought we would do it and I never doubted it. There were so many people with so much imagination and so many different skills to call upon, I couldn't imagine it.

PAUL CAMILLIN: There was never any angst - it was done with a real style and a real flair. And that's why we were successful. We did it in numbers, but we did it with a great big smile on our face; we were desperate, as football fans we were desperate, we didn't want to see our club go, and yet they maintained a sort of stylish dignity. That was down to Falmer For All, and Dick and Martin as well.

Martin Perry – I still say he's the best signing Dick Knight ever made, and I stand by that. And maybe Bobby Zamora.

DICK KNIGHT: I think we taught English football something: it's possible for supporters to stand up for themselves. And fight for what they believe in for their club. I think it was a kind of a renaissance, it was actually bringing football back to the people in a 21st-century context, in a way that maybe most people wouldn't believe possible because of the glitz of Sky television and the money in the Premier League. But alongside that there was this new development in which fans were actually being important in the club.

What is it? 'Football, football will never be defeated'.

It's not that we won't be defeated, it's that we can't be. We had to make this happen. I'm proud to be Albion.

PAUL HAYWARD: The whole thing is just an object lesson in the art of the possible. Clubs who do have a near-death experience tend to be stronger because it makes their communities appreciate them more, and if you have to fight to defend something you understand its value more clearly. You can see that Brighton & Hove Albion, the regulars, the real hardcore supporters, they are the army, they are the people who have saved the club and the people who will always be with the club.

JOHN PRESCOTT: Congratulations for all those who have done it and the fans who stuck with you through difficult times. I kept watching how you were going up and down in the league and you were having some difficulties but, you know, you stuck there because you have got a good fanbase and I'm glad to see they have now got a great ground.

It's a symbol of community activity; it's Brighton, and you know when teams come to visit and they see the club, it tells you something about the character of the town doesn't it? And that is all embodied in that ground.

MARTIN PERRY: I think the key to the whole story was I never lost faith that, first of all, we could do it and secondly, that was the right site. People ask me now why did you think that was the right site? And I say, I never ever doubted when I looked at the arguments, when we looked at the other possible sites this one worked in every possible single respect.

IAN HART: I am not a violent person but the only thing that does give me a little bit of satisfaction is knowing that Greg Stanley and David Bellotti have had a life sentence now because they will look over their shoulder for the rest of their lives knowing that one day they could be in a situation where someone can have a pop at them and there is nothing they can do about it.

ATTILA: The story of the last 14 years was a group of the people, the FFA team, a group of diverse people, all with different skills and different talents, each popping up in different moments to take something on.

I've always said it was inspirational grassroots campaigning; I am really proud of what we did.

My still abiding memory of the last 14 years was lying in bed with my wife listening to Seagulls Ska on *Top of the Pops* at number 17, it was so funny.

ROZ SOUTH: Dick saved the club, the fans got the planning permission and Tony Bloom paid for it.

I can honestly say that I didn't go to a single Falmer For All meeting where there was ever a bitter dispute or an unpleasant argument, nobody fell out with anybody, ever, on the campaign, throughout the whole campaign, even if you had different ideas. What was actually amazing was the way in which the campaign engaged people politically, people who perhaps wouldn't normally have anything to do with politics, I think it broadened a lot of people's lives. I'm sure there are people now who probably vote because they've realised the importance of voting for things.

It was a wonderful thing to be involved in. But when you look back, how the hell did we achieve that?

IAN HINE: For me it's this kind of collective strength and power of will, if you like; we won't be defeated, the little throwaway lines and mantras that came out of the whole Fans United thing – they are absolutely spot on. We weren't divided, we worked together and as a club and as a collective band of supporters we made it happen. You need figureheads in any campaign, but the collective and the strength of the number of people you've got behind it is what carries it through. Never ever give up.

DAN TESTER: The Albion has prospered because they let people in. Most clubs don't. Fans can get involved. It's not all about winning trophies and making pots of money, it's about being a positive part of the community and helping people who didn't necessarily get dealt an even hand. Albion in the Community's work makes me incredibly proud to be part of the Brighton & Hove Albion family.

STEVE BASSAM: We were right from the outset and when you see the stadium now, right next to the railway line, and right next to the road network, you just know it is a really good place for it; and all of the things that will develop from the stadium, in jargon the synergies with the universities and the medical school and local schools and so on, I think it just works really, really well and we thought that then I think it now even more, I think it is brilliant.

I feel a great sense of involvement and I feel a bit of personal pride that I helped make it happen and there have been key times that I know an intervention I have made as a politician made a big difference to where the thing went and I feel a great sense of pride, one of the things I shall look back on my life and think, I helped make that happen and it was a good thing and I feel very proud about that.

ADRIAN HOLDSTOCK: The whole process has been an emotional rollercoaster; it was really, really good fun designing it, working with Martin, who is always upbeat and positive. It doesn't matter how beaten up he gets during the course of the process.

ANDY SIMONS: I think we know Martin pretty well now after 13 years and he has always been straight. They are all just thoroughly nice people that you want to work for. They have had tough times when they weren't able to pay us for a while, and we got asked if we could just bear with them, or wait until the end of the season because they are a bit tight. "We can pay you when we get our season ticket sales in May." But he has never not paid us.

ADRIAN NEWNHAM: I remember at the Goldstone getting into a debate with John Campbell, who was a former director, about whether I would rather watch a non-league football club under the control of supporters, than watch a league club under the control of Bill Archer. If the club had had to fold and start again, like AFC Wimbledon have now done, that would have been a better result than having a club still in the league and under the control of somebody who did not have its interests at heart.

SARAH WATTS: There was so much pain over what Archer and Bellotti did, so much anger and yet it was the catalyst of bringing us all together, the catalyst of making the club tighter with its fans and the community and we had so much fun out of it as well…

I will look at it in the eyes of my faith; sometimes you need the dark things in life to appreciate the good and you need things to happen to get to where you are, as I say a door shuts but a window opens.

I giggle like a school child as I go past Falmer every time.

ROY CHUTER: Campaigning for your football club is one thing but helping others with the knowledge you've gained by doing that is probably just as important. Doncaster is the obvious example and we are still friendly with them.

ED BASSFORD: There are people who think that the trouble is, this only dragged on because 'potless' Dick Knight didn't have the money, if he had the money we could have had this stadium built in 2003; utter rubbish. Tony Bloom couldn't have bought their way through the planning process and built this stadium any earlier than it's been built.

GRAEME ROLF: A poster I found when I was clearing out a drawer was one of the very first photographs of Dick Knight and Martin Perry. It was one of those really nice night shots of a muddy black background with the stadium there and 'Every big city needs a stadium' on it. Having seen Martin Perry and Dick Knight up close recently you realise – two real heroes, how old they have got since this started; a decade has gone since it all started off, it's just taken so long.

TIM JOHNSON: You can think what Bellotti and Archer and Stanley did was absolutely unforgivable, but the chain of events that has occurred since then… without it happening as it did we would not have this ground, with regard to Bloom making the money and things, we would not have it. Yes, we would have something different but we would not have this utter thing of beauty.

ROY CHUTER: The beauty of football isn't the 90 minutes you see, with 22 blokes kicking a ball about – it's the social side of it. It's your family, it's your friends, it's the people who have supported in the past and will support them in the future. Making sure you've got a club for those people to support in ten or 20 or 50 years, and that's what we were fighting for in the 1990s. As a football fan you don't have many rights and you don't have the right to expect success – but I think the right you do have is the people in charge of your club, should be the people who have the club's best interest at heart. We didn't have that in the 1990s – we've had it for the last 14 years.

54. MISSING WITHDEAN
"A Norwegian second division ground"

TIM HERBERT: It's been like a placenta, just there keeping us alive.

IAN MORLEY: I won't miss the rain, that's for sure. The cold and getting soaking wet. I'm looking forward to being dry at football matches.

ANDERS SWAFFIELD: I remember playing Millwall, at home, we got absolutely drenched, we might as well have just jumped into a pool, I mean we won, which made it better, but Jesus Christ. Everyone that came out looked like drowned rats. So I'll miss that I suppose.

STEFAN SWIFT: I still don't feel like it's a football ground. There were times early on when there was a bit of an atmosphere and, certainly, when we won the first three titles the place used to rock, but after we first experienced relegation there in the 2002/03 season, it went flat and it never really recovered from that.

TIM HERBERT: Ironically, I'll miss the fact that before you go to the game you've got to check the weather and make sure you've got waterproofs and you've got this and you've got that.

DEREK CHAPMAN: Gordon Strachan described it as a Norwegian second division ground.

SAM SWAFFIELD: They call it 'Fortress Withdean' but it's nothing to do with Withdean, it's to do with the quality of players we've got. That stadium has never helped us out when we were shit.

Because of where the TV camera is, every great goal that has been recorded in the stadium looks a little bit shit, every goal looks a little bit scrappy, like a Sunday league game, like it's come off someone's shin, because of where the microphones are, it always sounds like there are 150 people there.

IAN HINE: I will miss it because it was a kind of symbol of what we needed to escape from if you like. The Goldstone was a dump at the end but it was our dump and Withdean was a temporary home but it was our temporary home. There is a sense of a sort of amusement really you know; bouncing up and down at the Swindon game and feeling the stands vibrating and knowing we can't play any pre-season friendlies because they need the seats at the Open golf! All that kind of stuff added to the quirkiness of it, the park and ride and the athletics track.

LIZ COSTA: I'm glad to be out of Withdean, but it was the base for our campaigns; all the signatures, petitions, leaflets, the postcards... everything that we did was run from Withdean. Everybody knew who to talk to if they had a problem or if they had a suggestion and that was what we were aiming to do, to make sure everyone knew where the focal points were for collections, for signatures, for anything. That is what Withdean to me will always be – the place that we won.

ATTILA: I miss the camaraderie of the PA box.

PAUL SAMRAH: Without Withdean we wouldn't have got Falmer, never in a million years, no question at all. I think Withdean holds a very affectionate place in certain Albion supporters' minds and quite rightly so.

TIM HERBERT: I'll miss loads about it. I'll miss that little alley down from Preston Park station to the ground, flat and hilly on the way down. That whole dark, nasty little walk down to Withdean. I'm going to miss my seat. I've had the same seat since 1999 and it's on the halfway line, it's a fantastic view. Yeah, OK, we've got the running track and it can be difficult to create an atmosphere but I had a really good view and I've watched some fantastic football and I'm going to really, really miss that.

ANDERS SWAFFIELD: You feel it's a big family there, because everyone who goes to Withdean's actually a Brighton fan, no-one's going there just to watch a game of football, because you might get wet, it's going to be cold.

DICK KNIGHT: Withdean operated at a loss all the time we were there, but a containable loss. I got rid of the overriding debt but the losses were containable.

What we had was quite a lot of success despite everything.

MARTIN PERRY: I don't miss anything at all. What was there to miss? It was difficult in every respect; parking, ticketing, no roof, PA that didn't work… what was there to miss? We had 12 unbelievably successful years, it was never dull! It's an era in our history that won't ever be forgotten – very important years… But I don't miss it!

TONY BLOOM: To be fair given the difficulties we have had at Withdean, I think we've had big success the last 12 years; three trophies, play-off success, we have had two last games where we needed to get the result to stay up against Ipswich and Stockport and then, we had the game at Grimsby where we got close under Steve Coppell. I think that was a magnificent achievement to get that close given the resources and the start that we had. So good memories but we will be delighted to leave them behind.

PAUL SAMRAH: It's delivered some amazing football; Zamora made his name there, some great escapes, Virgo's last minute penalty, Manchester City, amazing memories there. It'll take a while to create that heritage at the Amex, it'll come, of course it'll come, but I don't think we should be too dismissive of Withdean.

55. BUILD IT AND THEY WILL COME
"An area of outstanding natural beauty"

TIM JOHNSON: I have to say the first time that I did come over the Rottingdean Hill with the wife and kids in the car, I had to pull over, with the kids going; "Oooh, what's that?" It's an utterly, utterly wonderfully designed stadium, and it's ours.

GRAEME ROLF: When you catch sight of our new stadium as you go in either direction along the A27, or especially travelling down Falmer Road from Woodingdean, it's just absolutely stunning.

SARAH WATTS: In September 2010 Martin took some of the Falmer team up to see the stadium. He took us up to the top tier and he said; "Right, you have got to come out and look down, you can't look out." We walked up these steps, roughly where the seagull is in the upper tier of the West Stand now; and he said; "Now open your eyes." And I looked down; I had to apologise to my uncle because I said; "Fucking hell!" And Martin said there is a lot of me in this stadium, and that sent Liz off – she started crying.

LIZ COSTA: When I bought my season ticket, I had tears streaming down my face, it was just the most emotional thing after everything we had been through, that I physically got something in my hand to say you have paid for it and you have bought a seat and it's exactly where we wanted to be.

CLAIRE BYRD: Our Teddy is only four. Fanatical, fanatical Albion nut who sleeps with his programmes, doesn't he? There is nothing more important to him as Brighton & Hove Albion in that stadium...

ADRIAN NEWNHAM ...Before we bought season tickets he told me where he wanted his tickets. He knew the orientation of the stadium before I did. He said; "This is the East Stand. This is the West Stand. The West Stand has got three levels. The North Stand's behind the goal. The South Stand's where the away fans are going."

He had taken it all in. He is so passionate about the Albion. I am so proud. Our seats are in the Family Stand. On the block nearest the middle of the stand about halfway up, by the stairwell and there's ten of us got tickets together.

PAUL SAMRAH: John (Attila) is sitting with us, which is a testament to a wonderful friendship that's endured, it's extraordinary that you'd hear John sitting in the West Stand.

ATTILA: We have decided to sit next to each other so I'm in the Lower West in the quite posh bits, not the 1901 bit! I think I might be a bit loud for the neighbours and we'll see how long it lasts. I'm a North Stander at heart.

ED BASSFORD: When God created football, he made it to be played backwards and forwards from where you're standing. We bought North Stand tickets and I've got a luxury seat, the same as they have in the West Stand. I do appreciate that, thank you Tony.

GRAEME ROLF: When you go past it on the A27, or you go over that hill from Woodingdean and you look at this cathedral of football hiding in the Downs. That is a proper stadium for a proper club in a proper city that is just wonderful.

ADRIAN NEWNHAM: I went out with my brother-in-law, bought tickets and then went to The Swan in Falmer village and had a couple of pints. There were all these residents saying; "Do you know what? It doesn't look half as bad as we thought it was going to." "There are only ten houses in this village who can actually see this stadium."

Which is what we had always said. A lot of them were not that fussed. So it has not proved to be the eyesore that they had all feared. In fact, it's an Area of Outstanding Natural Beauty.

56. JCLs
"We need to make them feel welcome"

NIGEL SUMMERS: The best thing, I think, about the new stadium is we have now got 17,000 season-ticket holders and a whole generation of people who have never been to the Albion regularly. I know dozens of people who are 'Johnny Come Lately'. I know one particular guy who used to be a season ticket holder at Tottenham and is sick to death of them mucking around with the kick-off time. He loved the look of the Amex and has gone and bought 1901 membership and is not going to be travelling to London but will come over the hill from Woodingdean – fantastic, the more the merrier.

TIM JOHNSON: We need the Johnny Come Latelies, you know? It's a horrible derogatory term and a little bit arrogant and it's an easy, catch-all title to lump people in with. We have missed out on a generation of fans who don't know anything about the club or maybe see the odd Brighton shirt around town. We need to include these people. We need to make them feel welcome.

ADRIAN NEWNHAM: If we are going to make a success of this football club we need people who were Arsenal fans, or West Ham fans, to turn up. And, if there are people who are not natural Brighton fans who are armchair fans for Premiership clubs who got up and bought a season ticket I don't mind if next year there are kids sitting there saying 'who's that number seven?' When does Wayne Rooney come on? Because, actually, they too will get the same bug as everybody else has because you cannot beat football live. No matter what you watch on television.

57. ALBION MOSAIC
A fitting mural to the fans

TIM HERBERT: The Albion Fan Mosaic was an idea that Warren Dudley and I came up with a few years ago. Warren had designed a giant flag for England fans to take to the 2006 World Cup out in Germany – it was the famous image of Bobby Moore holding the World Cup aloft in 1966, which he'd made from something like 5,000 photos football fans had sent in from across the country. I found out that Warren was an Albion fan, and we chatted about doing something similar to go in the new stadium.

We knew that, sadly, there would be lots of people who would never see Falmer become a reality, that's how long it had bloody taken. So we wanted to do something to commemorate the supporters who'd died during our exile in Gillingham and at Withdean. And the mosaic seemed like the best idea. But, we also wanted to celebrate Albion's supporters in general, because without the fans, there would be no club.

We put the idea to the club and they loved it, fortunately. We chose to base the mosaic on a picture of Peter Ward in his heyday, looking over the fields towards the new stadium, a nice mix of the old and the new. And the support from Brighton fans everywhere has been fantastic. We've had 3,000 photographs submitted, including pics from players, managers and celebs, so it's been brilliant. Peter and Jacqui Ward submitted a few pics, as did Bobby Zamora, and we've even had pictures and stories from the families of really old Albion legends, like Charlie Webb.

It's raised money for the Robert Eaton Memorial Fund, too, because Robert Eaton, who died on September 11th 2001, was one of the people we had in mind when we came up with the idea in the first place.

58. HOPES AND FEARS
"You aspire to win matches and get as high as you can, don't you?"

BILL SWALLOW: At the heart of anyone's affections for a football club are the intangibles. That's encouraging because it means the Albion can become a multi-million pound success story and yet still be our old Albion if we want it to be. And the signs are that the club understands it needs to build on the relationship the supporters have with it.

They realise that that is part of the brand of a successful football club – that it is close to its people. Brand awareness in a football club is quite different to brand awareness in a normal company and I just hope everyone connected with the club understands that. Football clubs aren't Coca-Cola.

DEREK CHAPMAN: Everything we have built out there is geared up to the Premiership. I will be amazed in four, three years if we are not in the Premiership. Europe will be two years after.

Tony has done it right, Tony is sorting out the infrastructure – it's the ground followed by the training ground, so in the years to come it's all set up isn't it?

TONY BLOOM: Our aim is to get promoted to the Premier League. I am not saying that it's going to be easy, I'm not saying we are going to do it, and football is football so you can never predict the year you will get promoted but I am confident we will get to the Premiership in the not too distant future; it could be one year if we have another amazing season, it could be five, even ten years but I am pretty confident we'll get there. That is our goal and I don't think you can have any other goal.

Once we get there obviously our immediate goal will be staying up every season. We as a club want to move forward in all directions, obviously we are looking to getting a new training ground, so all aspects of the club need progressing and moving on but we want to do things gradually, we don't want to rush ahead of ourselves and we want to make sure the club is always on a stable footing and run as well as it can be.

ANDY NAYLOR: When you look through Brighton's history, that period in the old First Division was unusual. They have traditionally been a lower division club but with the stadium in place there is no reason why they can't get back to the top flight again. Reading made it, Blackpool, Wigan. You look at clubs like that and you think why not Brighton?

LIZ COSTA: Let's not kid ourselves, we're not going to be a Chelsea – we're never going to have that sort of money, I don't think, and nor do I want it – spoilt brats driving big cars that they don't know how to control and no brains, basically, and no humanity – at least our players, at the moment, have a humility, which I like.

I'm doubtful as to whether I really want to go into the Premiership, because all the fans that we have from friends of clubs that are yo-yoing, which inevitably we would be doing, are always happy when they come back down – the players may not be and the Board probably isn't, but the fans love it when they come back down – this is the real life back in the Championship.

PAUL SAMRAH: I don't know if we want Premiership football. I don't want to watch football on a Sunday night in Manchester, I'd like to see Brighton play Manchester United on a Saturday afternoon at 3 o'clock. I'd like the stadium to be full and I think you can have full stadiums playing in the Championship.

SAM SWAFFIELD: I don't begrudge anybody wanting to play in the Premier League, but please, I would just love it if we just were a nice football playing upper-mid table Championship side, just for a few years, because I think that's our natural place.

IAN HART: What do you aspire to? You aspire to win matches and get as high as you can, don't you? So how can you say you don't want to be in the top flight...? Call the builders off and let's play at East Brighton Park if you don't want to go there. Absolutely ludicrous.

TIM JOHNSON: We have got to change our thinking as Albion fans from almost parochial underdogs to 'yes we are a bigger club'.

PAUL HAYWARD: I don't think it's necessary for a club to become corrupted by life in the Premier League, or become horribly corporate. You still go to Premier League clubs where there is a proper family spirit like West Bromwich Albion, Fulham, Norwich, so it is for clubs like Brighton to restate those values and take them into the Premier League.

You don't have to become a horrible, evil mini empire. It depends on the people running the club and the values of the club. Ours are pretty sound I think.

IAN MORLEY: I think we need to keep our feet on the ground. Obviously the club is structured in a very different way now; effectively it's owned by one person. It's an interesting dilemma isn't it? This is the guy that single-handedly, somehow, funded Falmer for us. What were the words that we were using back in 1998? "No one man will ever run our club again." So it's interesting, and a rich irony. I'm sure everything will be fine, but you learn with football that there are heroes who can quickly become villains.

DAVE SWAFFIELD: Archer learnt, De Vecchi learnt; never fuck with us. I'll say that to Tony Bloom – never fuck with us.

ROZ SOUTH: That campaigning spirit is still in the hearts of Albion fans; you only need another thing and everyone will go off and do it.

BILL SWALLOW: Inevitably the club is going from a business turning over X to one turning over Y. It is a different organisation but I haven't seen signs that the Albion wants to turn its back on supporters. Obviously, if you are making a ten million pound decision, you can't really chat about it with supporters and say; "What do you think boys?"

The whole point of the fans' struggle was to help give the people running the Albion time to turn it into the wonderfully successful club it looks like becoming. That's what we all wanted and no-one is going to complain that it's happening. We never did what we tried to do just so we could have cosy chats with Board members.

ROZ SOUTH: My genuine fear about the new stadium is that you won't have access to the chief executive in the same way. It doesn't work like that, and Falmer's not going to work like that. But, then on the other hand we've got a fantastic manager, we're in the Championship and we've got a beautiful stadium, I mean what's not to like? And some of us are back in the North Stand again. Ruffians!

PAUL SAMRAH: The club is moving into a different era, the number of employees engaged by the club is now into three figures, it's a huge operation, its turnover will have quadrupled, if not more, in a year and any business undergoing that sort of growth in that short period of time is going to have issues and problems.

Communication, as with everything, is vital and I hope they embrace the supporters who helped in a very positive way. The story of how we got to where we are is extraordinary.

STEFAN SWIFT: Falmer will be what we make of it really and it's our responsibility to step up and make it a home and make it not feel like a big club.

JOHN COWEN: I want the highest success, but not at any cost, not at any price and any loss of values. I want Brighton in the Premiership, but with the club's principles intact.

TIM CARDER: I think the relationship between the supporters and the club has grown a bit more distant. In a way you've got to think that the club will now be catering to 22,000 fans instead of six or seven thousand so you could look at it that the club is becoming more professional in terms of ticketing and marketing and sales.

I don't think the relationship between the fans and the Board was ever as close as it was in the late 1990s and early 2000s, and won't ever be the same again.

Obviously Tony Bloom, god bless him, has put a huge amount into the club and the stadium and he has every right to control the club at the moment – whether that's healthy or not in the long-term we'll have to wait and see – I sincerely hope it is.

STEVE BASSAM: The real worry must be that because a club becomes big and corporate it loses its sense of commitment to the local community and it loses a degree of involvement, but I think the club is alive to that.

It's got, for me, one of the smartest community education programmes in the country and it encourages participation and it encourages diversity, it has done a great deal in the city to encourage and promote those things. I really do see football as a force for good, it is much more than a game and politicians forget that at their peril.

BILL SWALLOW: The Albion is part of the local community that holds us together. What started the whole stadium struggle was seeing part of the local community being kicked away. It was like someone wanted to shut the pit. Right at the beginning, way back in the mid-nineties, Paul Samrah said "no-one is going to do this to us" and that was the prevailing emotion: "You are simply not going to do this to us."

ROY CHUTER: I would love to see a situation where every club in this country is run by, or partly by, the fans. There should be a law that every club should have at least one fan on the Board. Quite a lot of fans are on Boards around the country but that is something that needs to be stepped up, not just for the Albion but for everybody.

TIM CARDER: I would like to see a Supporters' Trust owning a small percentage of the football club. And perhaps increasing the percentage through fundraising each year, the money that the Supporters' Club would pay for shares would go into the club. The Supporters' Club in times past, for instance, raised significant sums in those terms compared to the turnover of the club. The Supporters' Club paid significantly for the old North Stand at the Goldstone in the early 1930s.

If an all-encompassing Supporters' Trust was there with one aim, which was to buy shares in the football club each year through supporters' fundraising initiatives, and year-on-year the Supporters' Trust increases its shareholding in the club, I would be very happy. I don't think you would ever get the situation where it would control the club, but if anything untoward should happen to the club it would be there, it would be ready to take over and it would also give supporters some sort of democratic voice within the football club.

PAUL SAMRAH: We mustn't forget our history and I hope future Board members will know our history and know how much a part the fans played; keep the lines of communication open, don't do it all corporate – have a laugh and be sociable.

ROY CHUTER: The great thing about Tony Bloom is that he is an old style chairman, his family have been involved with the Albion for decades and he's not somebody who's been parachuted in from Russia, or America, or the Middle East, or something like that. He's one of us. From that point of view, I've got no immediate worries at all but it is something we do need to keep an eye on.

IAN MORLEY: What is important, therefore, is not to forget what we've been though. That connection with fans that was so broken under the Bellotti and Archer era – that was reconnected with Dick and Martin – must never be lost. I have a slight feeling that it might have drifted a bit.

I am sure Tony will get this being a fan. The responsibility on club owners' shoulders is huge. They are the temporary custodians of our club who have it on leasehold from the true owners – the fans.

ED BASSFORD: The anticipation is enormous, what I'm genuinely concerned about is that there are people who haven't been to watch an Albion game since they were at Cardiff. I fear that they will not be there every game next season, they haven't bought a season ticket because they want to be at every game, many of the thousands of season tickets have been sold to people who won't come to every game, they will come to games they want to go to.

JOHN PRESCOTT: I hope the steak and kidney pie will be a bit hotter next time.

59. PERSONAL COST/GAIN
"We went into this as football fans..."

STEFAN SWIFT: The amount of people who have neglected their professional duties to put the time into the Albion… We all did our bit, but that was ten minutes a week, but there were people who devoted everything to it. You have to have nothing but respect for those people. I know every time I see those people I certainly give them a smile, probably a little salute and probably a free fanzine.

PAUL HAYWARD: If you think how many hours that burned up, how many lawyers, how many admin hours… I always used to look at Dick Knight and Martin Perry and wondered what it was doing to them inside you know? To have to be frustrated every day of your life; to have to keep picking yourself up and believing that it would be possible, when the system was saying 'no' to you day after day after day, making it harder for you.

IAN HART: I was lucky that the struggle catapulted me into the BBC and gave me 11 years that I really loved but I tell you what, I am going to enjoy the next 11 even more.

KERRY MAYO: To still be associated with the football club is amazing with regards to Falmer, when that opens I hope to be doing some sort of compering, or meeting and greeting or something, as long as I don't sit on a burger van where I could eat all their takings it would be all right.

Obviously and not only that, I would have been the only player who played at all four home grounds for the football club, and also as a fan as well, playing for your club at all home grounds would have been an honour, a self-achievement, like a dream... Nearly, but never mind – no regrets.

IAN MORLEY: If I had my time again I'd do it again. The only reference I make is to pay tribute to the people who've stuck it through from start to finish, the likes of Paul Samrah, Tim Carder, Liz Costa, Adrian Newnham and co. They're given a massive chunk of their life. It takes its toll in the couple of years I did it, it's effectively like having two jobs, it becomes all encompassing.

LIZ COSTA: I remember we were at a pre-season friendly at Worthing and it was bucketing down with rain and we were collecting signatures for whatever that time... Gary Hart came in and said; "Are we going to do it?" Sarah and I both said to him; "If we don't do it we will die trying... we are never ever going to give up."

I nearly lost my job because I was press officer for the Supporters' Club, anything that Paul sent out to the press people, and then it was me that they would end up ringing, and my boss got a bit hacked off with this.

ADRIAN NEWNHAM: We went into this as football fans and there was a point about two years ago when my enthusiasm for football was a bit iffy. We were watching some absolute rubbish being played at home and I have to say Teddy going to football has completely reinvigorated my Saturday afternoons. That is a fundamental difference when you start to view the football club through the innocent eyes of children, rather than having been battered and bruised by what football clubs do to you.

ANDERS SWAFFIELD: Everyone at school supported Arsenal and Man United and I kind of wanted to support them in a way. When I was about eight or nine, I asked for an Arsenal shirt, and that did not go down well. It was a look of disappointment, as an eight-year-old, disappointment in Dad's eyes, just looking at me, and I just remember thinking; "Oh God, what have I done?"

I never got that shirt. Instead of buying me an Arsenal shirt he bought me a Brighton shirt. At the time I was a bit annoyed, because it's that feeling of having a big club and wanting to get their shirt and playing football in their shirt and just feeling kind of special, as an eight-year-old, rather than being a relegated Brighton team, playing bad football.

I'm glad he did it because I wouldn't want to support Arsenal, I couldn't think of anything worse to be honest. I wouldn't swap supporting Brighton, not just because we're doing well at the moment. What's the point of supporting a Premiership team (well, I might do soon), but if you always win all the time, you don't appreciate it do you?

Funnily enough for Falmer, quite a lot of people from school have bought season tickets who have never been to a Brighton game before. I mean obviously its money, but it really, really annoys me, I mean a lot.

TIM CARDER: I have met the Prime Minister, been to 10 Downing Street, been to the Parliament, been to umpteen council meetings, public inquiries; I probably have a reasonable knowledge of how elections work, I was an electoral agent, I have a rudimentary understanding of planning issues, the requirements for major developments in areas of outstanding natural beauty... I never expected to be involved in any of this.

Would I have had it any other way? Absolutely! Something like 15 years of my life has been taken up with campaigning about the Albion. And the things I could have done with all that time I spent, none of it being paid, of course. I am sure that applies to many others: Paul Samrah, Liz Costa, Adrian Newnham, Ian Morley, loads of people – I pay tribute to them all but it was necessary, it was what we needed to do to ensure that the football club in Brighton and Hove survived, not just for this generation but the generations after us.

I had the feeling that I had enough probably around 2004 when we got the Hoile report... and I felt the same sort of way when Lewes launched their challenge in November 2005; I wanted it to end so I could get on with life but circumstances conspired against it. I hated it, I didn't want to do it, but things needed to be done, so I wasn't prepared to sacrifice the 40 years of support that I had devoted to my football club – 1965 to 2005 – and just let it possibly disappear, so there was no question of me backing out. I was just going to help how I could and use whatever skills I had to get things going and get involved with the campaign until it ended.

I did wonder occasionally what life would be like without the Albion – it would probably be so much better to be honest. Football support runs in my blood; my dad watched football, my brother watched football. In some ways I wish it hadn't been because life would be so much simpler without it, but I am what I am.

When I met my wife I originally told her that I was quite interested in the Albion... OK, it wasn't a lie but it was not the whole truth. I do remember her saying to me at one point; "Why do you spend so much time watching a bunch of mercenaries playing for a private limited company?" She has a cold logic sometimes that gets a bit close to the truth and it's a very, very good question. Why do I spend so much time and money on it?

I was born in Brighton in the old Sussex Maternity Hospital in Buckingham Road and Brighton has been my hometown all my life and for me, Brighton and Hove Albion is the embodiment of Brighton and Hove. I am proud of my city and I am proud of my football club... my passion is football, I love football. I want the Albion to succeed, when it does the whole town is given a lift and with the new stadium coming along, people talk about the stadium and how excited they are all the time. It's uplifting and everyone is buoyed a little bit more by what's happening.

As to whether I personally have any control over that situation, of course, is a different matter. I have very little control of the situation and having little control about something that is a big part of your life can be quite stressful – it is almost a definition of stress.

Losing the Goldstone Ground was obviously very stressful and having the planning decisions on the new ground not only out of my control, but out of the control of even the football club itself, other than presenting a good case to the authorities – that is very stressful. But, if I want my club to represent me and my fellow citizens and my town and city, I have to live with that stress, control that stress and perhaps use that stress to an advantage at times to help and do whatever I can to help my club succeed.

I wish it had been different. I always wanted to be just another ordinary football fan. Obviously, I have a love and interest in the history of the club so I would have hopefully taken that further but, of course, I could have spent a lot more time on that aspect of my passion than trying to oust the Board and gain planning permission – twice!

Has my life been enriched? Certainly I think the experiences we went through together made for a greater bond between supporters. When we were at our lowest ebb during the campaign to oust Archer, Bellotti and Stanley, or during early 2004 when Mr Hoile's report came out, we found enormous strength in the common goal; working together, not just with my fellow Brighton fans but also with fans around the country who saw what was happening to us and wanted to support us because we had right on our side and that was enormously uplifting at times when we needed it.

It has made the bonds between Albion fans very strong; I know an awful lot of people now who I wouldn't have known otherwise and it is great to see them at matches and it is great to talk about the Albion. We have all got the common interest of seeing our team do as well as it can and because of our efforts we have that team – we might not have had it had we not stood together alongside the new Board and fought for that common goal.

60. 'WE DID IT!'
Home at last

DEREK CHAPMAN: (Interviewed in Dick's Bar straight after the game)

Speechless... Speechless. It's my baby. I've been to lots of England games all round the world and that was up there with any World Cup game. Something special. Something special… Your last chapter should say 'WE-DID-IT!' There's your heading for your last chapter.

MARTIN PERRY: We had a whole phase of opening events. There was a club dinner, there was the Sussex Senior Cup Final – the first time we'd had a crowd of any size here; there was then the Tottenham game, the opening game and for that we decided we'd invite a whole load of guests who had been involved in the stadium through the planning process and building the stadium, something like 400 people. We built a marquee on the playing fields of the University of Brighton who graciously let us use their rugby pitch – it actually felt like we were organising a wedding on the same day we were opening the stadium! There were all these guests arriving and at the same time we had 17,000 supporters arriving at the stadium! But, it all went pretty smoothly… we tested the microphones the day before and everything was perfect but, of course, on the day the one thing that let us down was the handheld mics on the pitch – and all that was because they were being held in the wrong position. And we had a bit of fun with some of the software on the big screens which wasn't quite working. But, that was about getting the immensely complicated software to work and practise using it. Gradually those little wrinkles got sorted out.

It was actually a whole chain of events, which we started at the beginning of July, and we went into sort of automatic pilot where we went from one event to the next, to the next, to the next, which led us to August 6th…

AARON BERRY: That Doncaster game. Wow what an afternoon! Put simply, it came down to a couple of glorious moments that will forever live with me in my football annals. The uplifting tension and sheer emotion I felt during that last ten minutes of the build up to kick-off with all its big screen videos, music and memories – and all that joy, all those flags, all the singing, all the smiling… and feeling the tears welling up as my heart strings were pulling at me causing an overwhelming inability to get the 'Seagulls, Seagulls' chant out without getting choked up and crying my eyes out.

I looked down at my eight-year-old son Nathan next to me and seeing him wide-eyed and stunned at what he was experiencing was like a dream coming true for me. For so many years I had wanted him to witness this event, and here we were, side by side, living out my dream for real. He wasn't even born until 2003 and I'd barely started educating him on his club's history, yet he was so caught up in everything, and the happy look on his young face just made me feel so proud of what our fans had achieved. It was all done for these such children.

And what a cherry on the cake with the 98th-minute winner. Even just thinking about that goal now, the goosebumps rattle through me. At the time, after a few seconds of wild celebrating, I just opened my arms wide and let myself become immersed in the noise and the love. It just poured over me. Brighton were back, and then some!

ARGUS MATCH REPORT Brighton vs, Doncaster Rovers 6th August 2011

Buckley double makes it a party at The Amex

Million pound man Will Buckley was the hero for Albion as they opened life at The Amex with a famous victory today.

Buckley, the summer signing thrown on as substitute, scored two late goals as the Seagulls came from one down to beat Doncaster 2-1.

He fired between keeper Gary Woods and his near post in the 83rd minute to level after Rovers failed to properly clear a free-kick.

Then, with Doncaster reduced to ten men by injury, he raced away deep in added time to calmly side-foot the winner after Craig Noone had worked wonders to send him clear.

Albion were arguably worthy of their reward for an improved second-half performance but nerves were frayed at times on their long-awaited Championship kick-off amid a vibrant atmosphere at their new home.

Gus Poyet had already been sent to the stand for arguing when Doncaster went ahead in the 39th minute. The hosts played themselves into trouble in midfield and Ryan Mason launched a counter raid which ended in Billy Sharp squeezing in a shot off the inside of the post as Casper Ankergren and Inigo Calderon converged.

Sharp had earlier seen a shot saved by Ankergren in just the second minute and another fly just wide as Rovers made the more composed start.

Albion should have been ahead just before that when Ashley Barnes saw his close range effort blocked by Woods.

Craig Mackail-Smith headed just over when the ball was played back into the box.

Poyet was directed to the West Stand after his vehement protests when Kazenga LuaLua was booked for allegedly diving in the 29th minute.

The boss was watching, in more contemplative mood, from the press box when Craig Noone, sent on as a half-time replacement for LuaLua, wasted a glorious chance to level in the 59th minute.

Barnes flicked Matt Sparrow's pass into the winger's path as he broke into the box but Noone then spooned his shot well wide with just the keeper to beat.

Albion had another great opening in the 80th minute when Mackail-Smith's close-range shot was saved by Woods after Buckley pulled the ball back from the byline.

Buckley, though, was to have the final words on an afternoon most of a crowd of 20,291 will cherish for years to come.

GRAEME ROLF: I'd tried out my seat at the Spurs game a week before the first league game, but that was just an appetiser to what was to come. There was a full attendance from Albion fans, and Donny filled half of the away end.

The volume, quality and content from the PA system was awesome. The images of Albion's great moments on the giant screens made your spine tingle.

I looked around. It was approaching ten minutes to three. Flags had been left for each and every fan. Each and every fan was waving them. The sea of fluttering flags formed huge blue and white stripes around three sides of our stadium.

All the Goldstone war era footage and other memories started to appear in my mind. Walking out, sitting in, breaking in, writing in, marching, singing, leafleting, balloon hanging. The drive to Gillingham every other week. The soaking at Withdean every other week. I was 40-years-old when it all started to go wrong with the three stooges. I'm now 55. I never wavered in my belief that one day we would reach the promised land.

I was back in the room. The singing from joyous fans was deafening. I've never seen so many flags, so many happy faces, so much blue and white. This is exactly how it was meant to happen. The players emerged from the tunnel. The roar was ear shattering.

What happened next? It happened to me at Newcastle in 1978. It happened to me at Hereford in 1997. It has now happened to me at the Amex in 2011. I was overcome with emotion and unashamedly cried with joy.

Again, we had done it.

IAN HINE: Due to holiday commitments, my first 'proper' visit to Falmer was going to be the first league game. I was pleased about this. I wanted my first trip to be special, in a 'this really means something' kind of way.

I was woken up early (too early, but who cares) by my son Fraser who was almost beside himself with excitement. We live in Southampton and to be finally going to watch the Albion in a proper stadium was an amazing feeling. The past 14 years were now finally going to be put to rest, although what had gone on would never be forgotten. Football really was coming home that day.

On the train to Brighton the numbers of Albion shirts began to rise and I was reminded of the days in the late 1970s when I used to travel from my home in Bognor to watch Wardy and Mark Lawrenson tear defences apart. As a 50-year-old I was hoping to keep my emotions in check (some hope!!) but to see the look of wonder on Fraser's face as we pulled into a Brighton station literally awash with blue and white stripes was worth everything to me.

On the short train trip to Falmer the conversation was almost non-existent, as if people didn't really believe this day had finally come. We poured off the train and up the steps, not really daring to look over to what, for the past two years, had been a building site, viewed through a webcam perched in a corner amongst scaffolding and concrete. When we turned the corner at the top of the steps, it was as if the whole thing had been choreographed by a West End theatre director. As one, literally hundreds of people brought cameras out of their bags and stood for a few seconds, drinking in the view of the promised land. No-one minded that the queues were building up, it was all OK.

The build-up to the game was unbelievable, with flags and raucous singing making for a brilliant atmosphere. Doncaster threatened to spoil the party but they had been here before – they did their part in the last game at the Goldstone, surely they would stick to the script this time?

Sure enough they did, but only just. I will never, ever forget the sublime through ball from Craig Noone that fell at the feet of Will Buckley in the seventh minute of injury time. The whole stadium fell quiet as he surged into the penalty area and…

You know the rest, of course.

The Albion finally, finally came home that day and it was a magnificent, unforgettable experience that Fraser and I will treasure for the rest of our lives.

Oh by the way, I did cry.

A lot.

RICHIE MORRIS: I went to the Eastbourne Borough game. I knew I shouldn't have. I always said I wouldn't. But then my dad got me a ticket and how could I say no to the man who had a) introduced me to football all those years ago, and b) was ridiculously excited about seeing the first match at the stadium. But, if dad (Ian Morris, by the way – thanks for paying for me to get in all those times dad) had been like a child in a sweetshop, I was more akin to the kid who got an early glimpse of his Christmas presents and ruined the big day. Or so I thought.

Everyone remembers the first time they climbed the steps at a proper ground only for their jaw to drop at the sight of the crowd and their body break out in a sweat as the football bug took hold. For most people that happened in their youth. A single detail from that first-ever game you still remember long after childhood has faded. For a generation of fans though, that moment came all at once on a sunny and long-awaited afternoon in Falmer. I was 29. I felt like I was eight again. Falling in love with football all over again. The fact that, like the first time round, I was stood next to my dad made it all the more magical. This was a moment so precious that to be able to experience it twice seemed somehow extravagant. I even pitied my friends who support other clubs and would never get a second bite of the cherry. My jaw dropped. And with it fell away all the seasons of sitting in the rain, watching the Albion get turned over by some mediocre team or another and wishing, hoping against hope that one day we would have a stadium to call our own. Or, at the very least, a roof.

Nothing will ever detract from the look on my dad's face when we walked into the packed Amex for that first league game. For such a communal experience, it was paradoxically so personal. We didn't speak. We didn't need to. I just gave him a hug that said it all.

Dad had had heart problems a few years earlier. An operation went fine but didn't rid me of the nagging concern that I would be seeing in the era alone.

When the day comes and the old man checks out to the subs' bench in the sky that will be how I remember him. Smiling, content and home.

STEFAN SWIFT: The sun was shining, Brighton was buzzing and the dreamlike Albionites travelling towards Falmer glistened in a happy state of delirium. Everyone was smiling – it was like nothing I had seen before. I, and countless others, arrived in Falmer at stupid o'clock to savour that moment, that time, that place we had all imagined for so long. And here it was. The whole day felt about as realistic as signing a Spanish superstar and having a millionaire chairman. In fact, it's all quite dreamlike supporting the Albion right now.

Selling fanzines gave me the opportunity of being in the finest vantage point at the top of the ramp leading up to the stadium from the train station. Amongst hugs, kisses and tears I was regularly taking photographs of those posing in front of Falmer for the first time. I would like to see all of those photos one day – rarely, do you in life, witness sheer happiness etched across almost 20,000 faces in the same place at the same moment. Writing this now brings tears of joy, tears of pain, tears of fully-fledged emotion built into my consciousness over years of pain, delight, anguish and – finally – joy. Pure joy.

The game itself was largely irrelevant (well, that's what we were just coming round to thinking as we entered the final ten minutes in a losing position). But, the equaliser and that injury-time winner just added to that sense of unbridled emotion. When the final whistle blew, I was shattered, shattered from it all. But still smiling. And as for the beers behind the North Stand afterwards – we didn't leave until we were forced to do so. The best thing – that sense of emotion still cripples my senses for five minutes or so every time I visit Falmer. I suspect it always will. It's probably something to do with wanting something for so long but if you don't know where you've come from, how on earth do you know where you're going?

JOHN COWEN: Although I had desperately wanted this to be my first-ever visit to the Amex, I had been there the previous week for the Tottenham friendly, with the other FFA team members, as guests of the club.

But, brilliant as that day out had been, it was only a warm-up. And I'd not sat in my proper seat. So there was still something very special in prospect: joining with 20,000 other supporters in an extraordinary, shared rite of passage into this new era for the Albion. An incredible moment in our lives for everyone lucky enough to be there.

Looking all the way around that fantastic stadium, there was an unshakeable feeling of:

"This can't really be ours, can it?" I told Bill Swallow it felt to me like we were somehow still playing away, still using someone else's ground, possibly Reading's? This place just looked too clean, too neat, too perfect... Definitely not for us. It probably took two more games for that feeling to morph first, into a sense of genuine entitlement, and then unashamed, chest-puffing pride.

To be honest, that Doncaster game, and even its final score, was never, for me, going to be the main event on such a day. Of course, like everyone else, I was swept away by the excitement and tension of the match – and especially its totally unexpected and heroic finale.

But, even if we had lost that opening game, there still would have been one, overwhelmingly happy ending, writ large in those fantastic, living stripes of blue-and-white, that cascaded down from each of the three home stands as kick-off approached. A single, glorious and unassailable truth: that we, the Albion and the fans, had all – finally – made it home.

JOHN HEWITT: At last the day we had all been dreaming about, all those years of campaigning, not forgotten, but put to the back of my mind. The first-ever league game at our bright shinny new home the Amex.

After an hour and 20-minute drive down from Slough, navigating the dreaded M25, although my mind wasn't on the road really, I arrived at Mithras House Park and Ride early. After all, I had left extremely early – there was no way I would be late. After jumping on the first bus, and a short drive up the Lewes Road, there it rose out of the Downs, the hair stood up on the back of my neck. It was early but still a large number of fans decked out in anything from home shirts from seasons past, to brand new home strips recently bought from our bright Aladdin's cave that is the new club superstore.

My seat is in the West Stand lower, but first it was a quick interview with the radio in the press box. Already I had tears in my eyes as I looked across at the East Stand. Nothing could have prepared me for what was to come as kick-off approached and the crescendo of sound rose and the sea of blue and white flags proudly waved in the air all around the stadium.

The game itself seemed to be a bit of a blur. It had everything. How dare Doncaster spoil the party and score first. Was this very special day to end on a sad note? Up stepped instant hero, sub Will Buckley hit a low drive from outside the area and we were level, then, after what had seemed an hour of stoppage time, he struck home the winner. The joy of that moment will live with me forever but it was that very special day that I will never forget. HOME AT LAST.

LIZ COSTA: Having been to the stadium for both the Sussex Senior Cup (cried when we heard Paul Samrah's voice over the tannoy for the first time! I cried when Gary Hart was (a) picked for the team as a gesture of goodwill by the club and (b) scored!) and for the Tottenham match, albeit as a guest of the club and therefore not sitting in my own seat, it was with heart in mouth as I mounted the stairs of Gate C to enter the stadium for the first time for the new Championship era! Had to pinch myself to see the players warming up on the pitch, the flags already waving in the blue and white stripes and the noise! Coming from soulless Withdean, this was like nirvana and my personal feeling was simple: I wanted to hug every single soul in the place and say 'thank you' for helping us to get this wonderful structure, which already felt like home, although for some bizarre reason it still feels like it is an away ground! Unlike any other group of supporters who have moved into their new ground, we have well and truly earned the best stadium in the country and I think we thoroughly deserve it.

Long may our success on and off the pitch remain. We wanted Falmer and WE got it!

PAUL WHELCH: It was the end of the game that will live most in my memory. The two goals that made our pride swell as much as did the Donny netting. The sea of blue and white, the sheer noise of it all.

And afterwards, in Dick's Bar – the so aptly named bar that is inclusive to all football fans. It was heaving. I said to Attila; "Peter Ward's coming in." I was given a disbelieving riposte; "Who told you that?" Somehow I was thought to be in fairyland. "I have just seen him coming up the stairs," I exclaimed. Such fripperies were easily dismissed – the very thought – the legend right here right now!

John turned away. Then the chant went up 'He shot, he scored…' and I swear I saw a tear in the eye of our esteemed punk poet.

So there I was, standing with Dick Knight and Peter Ward in the longed-for supporters' bar in a stadium we had all given years of toil to fight for, celebrating an improbable victory, with the sun streaming through the window on a bright summer's evening, listening to Tom Hark being performed live on stage by The Piranhas, and thinking: "Does it get any better that this?"

Now all of football can hear our message of thanks and our warning to them all. Brighton are back!

ALAN WARES: My recollection of the Doncaster Rovers game began, in all honesty, ten days before. A group of us had gone to see Brighton 'Til I Die at the Theatre Royal a couple of days before the official opening of the stadium – the game against Spurs.

It was a brilliant, brilliant evening – Mark Brailsford singing Seagulls Over The Rainbow was very moving. However, the final sequence where, over a blasting of Praise You by Fatboy Slim, the cast acted out a résumé of the previous 14 years' trials and tribulations, rounded off with the time lapse of the ground being built – I'd be amazed if there were any dry eyes in the house at the end.

The show had brought into focus everything that we had been through, with a sense of incredulity that it really was 14 years. Archer, Bellotti, Stanley, Hereford, Gillingham, John Prescott, Falmer Nimbys, public inquiries, planning applications, letters, Valentine's cards,

Lewes District Council – all these things that had no business being part of Brighton & Hove Albion's history – just gone. It's like I've woken up from it all and – whoosh! – 14 years have passed by like a four-minute song.

I don't remember too much about what happened when I got to the stadium on the 6th. My abiding memory of the occasion was the flags. The club played its intro music and it finished a bit early. Or there was a delay. Whatever, it followed that there was the most heart-tugging, tear-inducing, throat-choking exhibition of spontaneous singing and flag-waving by thousands of fellow supporters.

When Will Buckley equalised for us the place went mental. I got hugged and jumped on and clumped all in the same second. The bloke in front of me – a big fella – somehow ended up upside down three rows in front of where he started. It was quite funny watching so many people going about the task of setting him the right way up again.

Seven minutes into injury time, Craig Noone, with his magic feet, evaded two Donny players, and chipped a through ball to an onrushing forward with the outside of his left boot. Will Buckley won the race for the ball, and from that moment everyone stood up, all 19,000 home fans – and time stood still.

It's an image I will take with me forever. He composed himself, looked up, shaped his body, looked up again and the calmest man in the stadium coolly knocked it past the oncoming goalkeeper into the empty net.

In that one moment, that simple act of passing the ball into the back of the net, 14 years of anguish, anger, fear, frustration, nervous anticipation, unexpected and unnecessary disappointment all on the back of Archer, Bellotti, Stanley, Hereford, Gillingham, John Prescott, Falmer Nimbys, public inquiries, planning applications, letters, Valentine's cards, Lewes District Council, just… disappeared.

It felt like the emotional raincloud had moved away, and the sun had come out, and Praise You blasted out again. The goals were scored in the 83rd and 97th minutes of the match; 83 and 97 – such appropriate times for the Albion.

First, last and always, I am and shall forever remain – Brighton 'Til I Die.

DAVE SWAFFIELD: There was much discussion in the months leading up to the game. Do you attend familiarisation days, the friendlies? Would it spoil the 'real' day? I felt that wouldn't be the case. The options were just tasters, so I went to the West Stand Upper familiarisation and the Spurs game.

Jaw drop number one

OK, stupid time. I was touching the walls on the way up. Just to believe this was really ours. Each beautiful step.

Jaw drop number two

The concourse. What an amazing sight. The smell, the view out of the windows. The hundreds of smiles. So many smiles. We walked into the stand.

Jaw drop number three

Just 'Wow'. Didn't want to leave. I could have stayed there all night. Martin Perry was there. What do you say to him? Can you actually speak?

The Spurs game

I listened to the Albion Roar breakfast special. Tension, tension.

I drove down to Hove Park for the unveiling of the plaque. Looking over the road at possibly the ugliest buildings in Sussex, the memories came back. But these memories were mainly of the protests. Making fires in the middle of Old Shoreham Road, fireworks, whistles, walk-outs and Fans United. Dear old Goldstone.

I hugged Paul Samrah, we welled up. I think we both said "Yeah, I know, I know".

Tim Carder said a few words. Dick made a speech, Attila just about read Goldstone Ghosts. Silence then applause.

The Day

I don't think I had felt this way for a long time. That anticipation of the forthcoming game. The pacing, the continual looking at the watch. A group of us had hired an open-top Southdown bus for a tour of the town and the seafront then to the Amex.

I had always said my dream was to walk from the station to the ground with my boys, Sam and Anders. It didn't quite work like that. The boys were going to sell TSLR outside. I went up Dick's Bar. In there, again, a sea of smiling faces. I looked out of the window, a pint of Harvey's in my hand. The crowds descending on the ground was amazing. And there were my boys, amongst it all, selling the fanzine. The whole scene was surreal. When we got upstairs to the WSU, it was incredible. The noise, the heat... The smiles.

Anders and I were quite envious of Sam. He was an Amex virgin!! He had the walk into the stand to come.

Sam initiated it. He grabbed our hands and into 'G' we went. I honestly don't think I can put into words, my feelings. We walked into this cauldron of noise, colour and high emotion. You could taste it. By the time we reached our seats, we were in tears. We stood there arms around each other, and tried to take it all in.

14 years

I was trying to sing, but I couldn't get my breath.

Going to the preliminary matches made no difference. This was the real thing. Honestly, the result was insignificant (I can say that now!!). To be there, with my 'bleed blue and white' boys, on this day, was one of the highlights of my life.

Thank you, Tony Bloom. Thank you, Martin Perry. Thank you, Dick Knight.

But my biggest thanks go to those who wouldn't let our club die. Us. The fans.

BILL SWALLOW: I suppose I never thought it would happen. I didn't think we'd have an actual three-dimensional full-size stadium. I thought we were campaigning for planning permission and perhaps a small model with foam rubber trees.

For more than two years we had to go to Falmer two or three times a week to check. Jan and I would walk up and down Village Way. Drive to Lewes just so we could come back along the A27, staring at it with small round mouths.

I couldn't grasp the wonderful reality then and, walking from park & ride past the foam rubber trees on that Doncaster match day, I still couldn't. We wandered round the West Stand Lower concourse, trying to understand that very soon this would be a home from home. And out into the bowl, that familiar feeling you get when entering any new away ground.

But this wasn't away, it was home, with familiar faces dotted here and there like family furniture in a house you've just moved into, dear friends, most of whom known only because of this wonderful old football club. Jan and me standing in our fourth Albion ground. We just wished the children were with us, although they soon will be. Our grandson Jack is now the same age as they were when they first kicked cans around the Chicken Run in the 70s.

Sussex By The Sea brought a tear and that was it really. Can't remember a thing about the match.

MARTIN PERRY: The night before the Doncaster game we had got everything ready, checked the stadium was ready, we didn't finish until late and we stayed in Brighton that night, so we went to a restaurant for a meal and then to bed. We were staying at Jury's Inn and when I got back there, in my room was a bottle of champagne from the manager of Jury's just saying 'Good Luck'. And I have to say that was the moment when the emotion hit me, and I just burst into tears… in the words of the hymn: 'The strife was o'er, the battle won'; it was over – we'd done it!

I suppose by then we'd had the two games, we'd learned a lot about the operation of the stadium from those two games. A decision was taken by Ken and our shop manager that we would put flags on every seat. So the night before the game a huge team of people went and put out the 20,000 flags. And I suppose my memory of that game will be walking out of the Boardroom, and going down to my seat and seeing 20,000 blue and white flags waving. I think it's an image that will live with me for ever. The stadium looked absolutely incredible, the sound was just unbelievable – we'd done quite a lot of work on the acoustics and thinking about how we could maximise the atmosphere in the stadium, but never quite know whether it's going to work. 20,000 people in the stadium, the pre-match build up, the images on the big screens, the music – just took my breath away and I think it took the breath away of almost everybody I met – who possibly can ever forget that day? And that moment.

And for the very first time the team walked out – there was a delay while Sean O'Driscoll, realising that the atmosphere was going to be absolutely like a cauldron in the stadium thought he'd try and delay Doncaster Rovers coming out, so there was a bit of a pause – but then they came out to this rapturous welcome on to the pitch: Brighton & Hove Albion against Doncaster Rovers… Was it 14 years since they had met at the Goldstone? What a difference! And the whole game was amazing – Gus getting sent off! And the winning goal in extra time! Fabulous! And such a fitting start to a whole new era for the club. Completely and utterly unforgettable!

The game kicked off and we had a lot of guests, the Boardroom was full and it holds about 100 people. There was a tap on my shoulder from the hospitality manager, and he said; "We have a bit of a problem…" And my heart sank. You'll never guess what's happened now… He said; "There is water pouring through the Boardroom; a drain got blocked in the upper concourse and it's overflowed…" So I rushed into the Boardroom, to find the ceiling down and a team of maintenance people desperately mopping up water; they said they could probably get it clear by half-time. At half-time we headed back in… and it was if nothing had happened! All this sort of thing goes on behind the scenes which nobody knows about. Just another little crisis averted! You thought at that moment, what else is going to happen?! But, it was fine and it's been fine ever since…

TIM CARDER: For me, the Doncaster Rovers match was always the 'big one'. The first league game at our long-awaited new stadium was THE moment when the club finally shook off its homeless tag, when the normal pattern of football life resumed after a gap of 16 years since the sale of the Goldstone Ground.

The previous Saturday we had unveiled the Goldstone heritage board in Hove Park, and for the first time I had looked the retail park in the face. The anger was now gone – although the history will never be forgotten. So, to mark this occasion, I walked six miles from the heritage board, via Withdean, to the Amex, along with a number of fellow supporters. We kicked a football all the way to our new home – how symbolic was that?!

I had already reccyed the route so I knew what to expect, but, coming over the hill at Hollingbury, the first sight of the new stadium framed by the South Downs is always glorious. Seeing the emotion well up in my companions at that point was suitable reward for planning the route.

After more photos at the new railway bridge, I made my way to the West Upper. On the TV screens I saw the flag-waving inside the arena and immediately went out to join in the fun. It was awesome in the literal sense – the scene that greeted me inspired awe. I can only compare it to the 1983 FA Cup Final as not even the 2004 play-off final lived up to it for effect. Thank you Ian Green (Albion merchandise manager) for an inspirational episode in Albion history.

For me, the occasion was everything, and to some extent the result didn't matter too much. I would still have had a wonderful day even if we'd lost, but to win the game in such dramatic fashion was the icing on a very thick and tasty cake.

I've experienced some momentous occasions in my Albion-supporting life. Brighton & Hove Albion v Doncaster Rovers, Saturday 6th August 2011, was the most important day in the history of our club, and the spectacle did not let the occasion down.

To my fellow Albion fans: it was such a perfect day, I'm glad I spent it with you.

PAUL SAMRAH: After the Spurs friendly, I was very upset at the debacle with my microphone failing on me as I was introducing the legends (especially my hero Chris Cattlin). I didn't really watch the game and almost walked out in the second half. I was therefore determined that nothing was going to ruin the Doncaster experience! So I arrived very early, the last time I'd got to an Albion game at 11am was the first game in Division One at the Goldstone against Arsenal in August 1979! Slowly, familiar faces started arriving, I popped into the club offices and together with loyal stalwart and staff member at the Goldstone and now the Amex, Sally Townsend, we began to see the hordes of supporters, bedecked in blue and white, walking across the railway bridge and down onto the concourse. It was an amazingly emotional sight. We had arrived. Brighton was back.

My wife Belinda was attending her very first football match. In the build up to kick off, I wanted to hug so many people. Attila, Bill and Jan Swallow, Belinda, my sons Sebastian and Toby – we were all seated together in the West Stand Lower. I looked at Sebastian and Toby – I thought yes, this was going to be their 'home' for their lifetime, long after I pass away – I had such a huge sense of building something vastly tangible for them. The flags, the singing – we had achieved (against the odds?). We had proved everyone wrong. I was (and always will be) so proud. Yes, a goal down, but it didn't matter. We could lose the match – we weren't going to lose our stadium! Yes, that had happened in 1997, but we were much stronger now – both on and off the pitch. And so it proved, Will Buckley's first goal meant that the winner was inevitable. The force was with us.

And walking around the concourses after the match was something so very special. We had united a city, we had built a home, we had made thousands of people so happy – I was so proud of the Falmer For All campaign team and for the thousands of supporters that had written letters, postcards, signed petitions, walked, marched, lobbied, voted and, above all, never ever gave up and stayed united. Sunday morning I woke up – and yes it was real. Boy was it real!

61. WE GOT FALMER

TIM CARDER: Whether the club itself allows me and my fellow supporters to get involved as much as we have done in the past I would rather doubt. Perhaps the need is not there in the future for us to get involved. It took supporters' campaigns to assist with the change of the Board – to assist with gaining planning permission for Withdean and for Falmer – and that may not be the case in the future. Therefore, the club becomes a little bit more distant. That is the state of play at most clubs, I would like to think our club is forward thinking.

You look at 18,000 season tickets being sold for the Amex stadium, hospitality sold out, the whole thing is on the up and none of this would be possible if it hadn't had been for the efforts of supporters from the 1990s through to the 2000s and, of course, having the right board in place, supporting that Board and working with that Board until the end result.

We got Falmer.

The Falmer campaign timeline

In eight pages of tiny type, a potted summary of league football's scariest saga.
September 1997 to August 2011. Courtesy of *Albion Almanac*.

1997

SEPTEMBER

2   The consortium takeover, end of period covered by *Build a Bonfire*.

OCTOBER

4   Demos against Ken Richardson at Doncaster led by Albion fans.

17   Board looks to move Albion from Gillingham to Woking.

22   The Argus reveals Albion planning application for Waterhall (a requirement of the Football
       League to sanction the Gillingham ground share). The resulting outcry convinces the Albion
       board that a two-stage solution to the stadium problem is required.

NOVEMBER

5   All-time low attendance for Albion game at Priestfield: 1,025, in 3-0 defeat to Barnet.

8   Albion organise double-decker bus to Gillingham for £4.50. Previously, only transport from
       Brighton was Supporters' Club coach for £6. Bus breaks down and gets back around 9.30pm.

11   Dick Knight calls for temporary stadium site.

19   The Argus phone-poll results in small majority against Withdean.

20   Albion slash season-ticket prices for remaining games and commit to running regular buses to
       Gillingham.

26   Tony Ford of Supporters' Club launches 'Buy a Player' appeal.

DECEMBER

1   Adrian Newnham of Supporters' Club launches 'Bring Home the Albion Campaign' (BHA).

6   BHA campaign decorates statues, lampposts etc with blue and white ribbons. Visits to businesses
       and shops to elicit support. The Argus includes BHA poster.

9   Supporters' Club invites Withdean residents to meet them at Sportsman but only one turns up.

11   Supporters' Club hands ribbons to councillors at Brighton & Hove Council meeting at Brighton
       Town Hall – most happy to take and wear them. Withdean group against Albion hold public
       meeting at Westdene School.

15   Albion hold public meeting at Hove Town Hall.

1998

JANUARY

10   Brighton Independent Supporters' Association (BISA) press release declares Feb 14th v
       Doncaster Rovers 'Fans United 2, the Heart of Football'.

11   Sponsored walk from Hove Lagoon to Palace Pier and back for 'Buy a Player' fund.

23   Exhibition of Albion history in Eastbourne by Tony Hylands opens – helps Tim Carder conceive
       Brighton & Hove Albion Collectors' and Historians' Society. The Argus launches Supporter Packs
       with Bring Home the Albion banner, hat, sticker and ribbon.

FEBRUARY

7   Dick Knight appeals to fans to write to Brighton & Hove councillors re Withdean.

9   The Argus begins publishing daily photos of workers in Bring Home the Albion hats and holding posters.

14   Fans United 2 at Gillingham v Doncaster. The Argus 'Love Buses' transport 500 fans. Gate is 6,399. Mobile shop makes its debut.

19   Steve Bassam, council leader, advises B&H Council that Withdean is only option for temporary home.

25   Steve Gritt, hero of last season, is sacked.

MARCH

4   The Argus reveals shortlist of permanent sites is Falmer, Waterhall, Greyhound Stadium, Shoreham Harbour.

7   'Magnificent Seven' cycle from Goldstone to Gillingham to raise over £2,000 for Buy a Player fund.

10   First statement from Save Withdean Environment Action Team (SWEAT).

11   Adrian Newnham from BHA campaign welcomes formation of SWEAT.

12   Albion submit planning application for Withdean.

19   Full-page The Argus ad from BHAFC and BHA campaign re Withdean.

21   Roy Chuter (BISA) appeals for fans to write to him with requirements for new stadium. BHA campaign launches petition.

28   SWEAT distribute six-page leaflet around Withdean advising residents to object to plans.

APRIL

8   B&H Council reveal 850 letters of objection, only 129 for Withdean.

11   BHA campaign issues 'You are Killing the Albion' leaflets to supporters, urging them to write.

13   Above leaflet handed out on turnstiles at Gillingham.

14   BHA campaign holds public meeting at Sallis Benney Theatre.

17   Advertising hoardings give message Albion would use Withdean for 1% of the year.

25   Pre-printed letters to B&H Council distributed at Gillingham, plus postcards from BHA campaign appealing for help from BHA campaign.

28   Withdean Invites the Seagulls Home (WISH) holds first meeting.

MAY

2   BHA campaign hands out over 4,000 pre-stamped letters at Lincoln for Albion supporters to send to B&H Council.

9   BHA campaign collects 2,500 petition signatures in central Brighton in four hours.

14   BHA campaign hands in 32,355 signatures at Brighton Town Hall.

16   SWEAT rally at Withdean attended by around 300. Petition of 6,000 names presented to Lord Bassam.

27   WISH meeting. Tim Carder presents analysis of petition.

JUNE

2   Planning committee votes 10-2 for Withdean.

3   Two more council meetings approve use of Withdean re safety certificate and landlord approval (9-4) of Albion use.

11   Government allows B&H Council to make final decision on use of Withdean.

12   Final committee approval of Withdean.

15   Albion announce Withdean expected to be ready by end of September.

19   SWEAT to take fight further if they can.

JULY

9   SWEAT advise B&H Council of intention to seek judicial review.

16   Archer resigns as director because of ill-health.

30   SWEAT file papers at High Court.

AUGUST
1   Albion announce free buses for season-ticket holders to Gillingham.
26   SWEAT withdraw legal action.

OCTOBER
     Letter number 1: supporters are asked to write to the Local Plan team urging them to
     include a stadium.

1999

MARCH-MAY
     'Yes Yes' referendum campaign. Yes to a stadium and Yes to a stadium in Falmer. Web
     site launched, posters placed around the city; every household is leafleted twice;
     promotional video tour of the city in the video van; team members tour the city with
     loudhailers in open top bus. 5,000 green 'Yes Yes' balloons are tied to lampposts overnight on
     May 5th.

MAY
7   Referendum comes out overwhelmingly in favour of a stadium 84% and a stadium at Falmer 68%.

AUGUST
7   First league game at Withdean (Albion 6-0 Mansfield)

DECEMBER
11   The first Falmer For All meeting takes place.

2000

FEBRUARY
28   Public meeting in Lewes to explain the proposals.

OCTOBER
     Letter 2. The Local Plan has come out in favour of a stadium at Falmer; supporters write letters in
     support of it.
     Fans of the Earth sponsored walk for Falmer For All and Sussex Wildlife Trust through Stanmer
     Park.

2001

JULY
     More letters and lobbying of councillors following University of Brighton/Ken Bodfish 'hiccup'.

OCTOBER
8   Stadium-related planning applications submitted to Brighton & Hove City Council.
     Letter 4. Fans send letters in support of planning application.

NOVEMBER
> Letter 5. Fans send letters to individual councillors asking for their support.
> Letter 6. Supporters' letters go to Countryside Agency regarding the boundaries for the proposed South Downs National Park.

26   Official launch at Hove Town Hall of the campaign to win Council support for the Falmer plans.

2002

JANUARY
> Further posters appear in support of Falmer on the city hoardings – plus car stickers.

MARCH
> A motion condemning the Falmer scheme put forward by Falmer Parish Council and the Green Party is defeated in open debate at the University of Sussex.

MAY
> A petition in favour of the plans, containing 61,452 names and collected over several months is delivered to Brighton & Hove City Council.

JUNE
12   The council planning committee comes out in favour of the Falmer proposals by 11 votes to 1.

AUGUST
9   The government call in the plans. A public inquiry will be needed.

2003

FEBRUARY
> Letter 7. Supporters send letters regarding the National Park boundaries.

18   The Public Inquiry opens, closes again within weeks, and resumes on October 14th.

NOVEMBER
> Letter 8. Supporters send letters supporting the University of Brighton's plans for redevelopment, which are linked to the stadium scheme.

DECEMBER
1   Letter 9. 6,200 letters in support of stadium are delivered to Downing Street.

2004

FEBRUARY
4   Charles Hoile's public inquiry report is released. Against all the democratic support for the stadium plans, Mr Hoile comes out strongly against them.

6   Launch of the Clubs in Crisis website.

7   Fans stage a sit-in protesting at the Hoile report, after the match at Wycombe Wanderers.

10   91 bouquets of flowers, representing all the other clubs in the league, are delivered by hand to the Office of the Deputy Prime Minister in Whitehall by fans en route to an evening match in Luton. At the same time, fans of clubs all over the country send messages of support for the Albion to the DPM – this causes his email address to temporarily close due to the sheer weight of messages.

14   Fans take a detour en route to a match at Grimsby to deliver a giant Valentine's card to John Prescott's constituency office in Hull.

FEBRUARY AND MARCH
Letter 10: Supporters send letters to local and national newspapers in support of the stadium proposals, and call radio phone-in shows. Meanwhile, more posters are placed on billboards around Brighton and Hove. (Over the course of the campaign, the plight of the Albion attracted huge national coverage.)

FEBRUARY
Letter 11. Pro-forma letters are prepared for fans to send directly to the DPM.

MARCH
6   National Falmer Day.

MARCH TO OCTOBER
A Parliamentary Early Day Motion gets 145 signatures – the biggest number of MPs to support a sports-based EDM.

MAY
A wish-we-were-here postcard is sent to MPs.
As Albion prepares to play at the Millennium Stadium in the play-off final, John Prescott is sent a postcard of it proclaiming Wish We Were Here. At the game itself, supporters sport banners in support of our stadium, which show up well on TV. At the previous day's play-off final, a Crystal Palace supporter displayed a banner calling for the stadium to go ahead.

JULY
26   DPM announces that the Public Inquiry will be re-opened, with a view to establishing whether there is a better alternative site in the area.

SEPTEMBER
24   First March: The Labour Party holds its conference at the Brighton Centre. Many thousands of Albion fans march peacefully in support of the stadium scheme. At the same time, lobbying continues at the MPs' football match, and via pledge cards in hotels and restaurants, banners on bridges, and on sticks of rock. Falmer For All campaigners Tim Carder and Paul Samrah personally hand pledge cards to Tony and Cherie Blair, fittingly at the Royal Albion Hotel.

OCTOBER
33 MPs sign up to the second EDM.

2005

JANUARY
Seagulls Ska achieve the most unlikely Top Twenty single of all time when Tom Hark (We Want Falmer) reaches 17 in the charts.

FEBRUARY
2   The Public Inquiry reconvenes under a different inspector.

MAY
80 MPs sign a third EDM.

AUGUST

4   Albion fan Des Lynam gets a well-publicised soaking in a good cause.

20   Back to Hull again delivering a giant postcard to John Prescott's constituency office.

SEPTEMBER

17   BODS (Brighton Official Disabled Supporters) undertake wheelchair push from Falmer to Withdean in 'Push for Falmer'.

25   Second march. An even bigger crowd than in 2004 – estimated this time at 10,000 – marches on the Labour conference. John Prescott promises a response to the Public Inquiry on or before October 31st as lobbying continues at conference.

OCTOBER

28   Prescott yes decision.

29   Champagne served at Withdean against Ipswich Town.

NOVEMBER

24   Lewes mount legal challenge to the decision.

27   Falmer For All launches a week of action aimed at LDC. Posters appear in Lewes including 'Wanted' poster for Ann De Vecchi. Petition begins.

29   Mailshot to 1,500 supporters in Lewes District Council with posters and petitions.

30   LDC responds to criticism with FAQs on website.

DECEMBER

1-3 Petition signature collecting in Lewes, Newhaven, Peacehaven and Seaford.

7   Petition of 5,165 names presented to LDC. Supporters ask questions of LDC at meeting. Ed Bassford makes five-minute speech. Tim Carder extracts commitment to seek early court hearing and resignation of relevant councillor should expenditure exceed limit.

16   John Prescott attends Albion versus Hull City game.

2006

JANUARY

11   Tim Carder and Ed Bassford ask questions at LDC cabinet meeting. Ed presents petition again and makes speech.

23   EDM 1151 condemning LDC action receives 50th signature in House of Commons.

26   LDC Scrutiny Committee rejects request from Ed Bassford to review the decision to challenge.

MARCH

2   The Argus reports that Roz South is facing prosecution under harassment laws re Ann De Vecchi posters.

APRIL

     Treasury solicitor offers to concede planning permission on boundary mistake. (LDC later refuse to accept this one point and insist on full hearing on all their points.)

MAY

5   Responsibility for planning moves from Prescott to Ruth Kelly in government reshuffle.

10   Tim Carder asks more questions at LDC.

19   FFA campaigner Peter Near challenges LDC over misleading photographs in its *District Link* magazine.

JUNE
5 Seagulls Party launched.
6 Seagulls Party calls for Ann De Vecchi to resign as cabinet votes to continue with challenge.
9 De Vecchi accuses "these people" of coercion, intimidation and harassment, welcoming the formation of the Seagulls Party.

JULY
12 Tim Carder asks more questions at LDC meeting.
12 The Argus says Roz South will not be charged.
31 Norman Baker insinuates improper conduct by Prescott/Derek Chapman in *The Times*.

AUGUST
17 Seagulls Party's Ed Bassford takes 22% of the vote in the Ouse Valley & Ringmer ward by-election.
26 Seagulls Party appeals for candidates to fight LDC wards in May.

SEPTEMBER
17 Rally outside Lib-Dem conference, 1,000 supporters. FFA meets Lord Kirkwood, leader's adviser. FFA hand spoof menus to guests at Lib-Dem dinner.
21 Martin Perry slams LDC for delaying tactics.
23 Meridian TV broadcasts about 'secret hotel' report at Falmer.

OCTOBER
3 LDC agree to sign government consent order allowing quashing of planning permission – the day before the issue is to be heard in court.
14 Norman Baker is challenged by FFA campaigners on SCR phone-in.

NOVEMBER
6 Brighton & Hove Albion and Norman Baker issue clear-the-air statement.
21 Interested parties receive invitation to make submissions on various aspects of planning case, especially Sheepcote Valley.

2007

FEBRUARY
3 A series of ten different picture postcards addressed to new Secretary of State, Ruth Kelly are handed to supporters at Withdean. Programme carries unusual cover.
8 EDM 882 tabled in Commons in support of Falmer stadium at request of FFA.
14 10 Downing Street website petition closes with 3,175 names.
19 Seagulls Party accuses LDC of 'sexing up' dodgy dossier.
24 Last day of postcard distribution, 37,000 so far.

MARCH
2 Interested parties receive notice of a decision on or by July 9th.

APRIL
14 Supporters walk from the Clock Tower to Sheepcote Valley to test the 25-minute claim in LDC's evidence.
24 Seagulls Party supporters begin distributing 11,000 election leaflets in four LDC wards.
25 Other clubs begin hosting a letter of support for the stadium on their websites.

26   FFA hands in a further 5,000 postcards to DCLG and Ruth Kelly. Attila hosts a Goldstone nostalgia night (ten years) at The Volunteer, Lewes, to raise funds for FFA.

MAY
4   Seagulls Party candidates take 21.5% of the vote in the four contested wards. David Neighbour loses out East Saltdean & Telscombe Cliffs.
13   Paul Samrah asks Gordon Brown, Chancellor, about the stadium in public QA session at The Dome.
28   Another 10 Downing Street website petition for the stadium closes with just 26 signatures.

JULY
2   Inspector's report into SDNP says that site at Falmer should not be included (because it was already designated for possible development).
4   Following Gordon Brown taking over as PM and reshuffle, decision moved back to on or before July 25th. Now responsibility of Hazel Blears.
24   Hazel Blears gives approval.

SEPTEMBER
4   Deadline for appealing against the permission expired.

2008

DECEMBER
1   Contractors move onto Falmer site.
17   Building formally starts on the stadium.

2009

MAY
18   Tony Bloom takes over as chairman of the club, Dick Knight becoming Life President.

2010

2011

JULY
16   First game at the Amex: Sussex Senior Cup Final, Brighton & Hove Albion 2 Eastbourne Borough 0.
30   Official opening of the American Express Community Stadium: Brighton & Hove Albion 2 Tottenham Hotspur 3.

AUGUST
6   First league game at the Amex Stadium: Brighton & Hove Albion 2 Doncaster Rovers 1.

Dick Knight about to save the Albion. A break during CEDR negotiations with Archer.

Dick Knight and Bill Archer deep in negotiation, 1997.

"The most ludicrous ground share in the history of football, anywhere in the world." The 'home' supporters entrance at Gillingham, 1997.

"The worst game of football I've ever seen." However, scorer of the last-ever goal at the Goldstone Stuart Storer makes up for it off the pitch at the second Fans United, 14th Feb 1998 at Gillingham.

Operation Morning Surprise. "The plan was to ensure that when everyone in Brighton and Hove woke up on the morning of the referendum day, all they saw was a mass of green balloons with 'Vote Yes' on them." The evening before the crucial referendum vote, 5th May 1999.

"He just got that campaign by the scruff of the neck... got people organised and got them running it..." Ian Morley and Adrian Newnham helping drive the 'Yes Yes' campaign, 1999.

Withdean gets ready.

Wycombe away, 7th February 2004. "500 people bought tickets at the last moment when it was confirmed that our campaign was in serious trouble." During the sit-in after the Wycombe game, the fans applaud the players returning to the pitch to join the protest.

The Clock Tower protest, February 2004. "We collected umpteen signatures at various times, but that alone wasn't going to get a stadium."

Roz South

Roz South

Getting the message out: a banner on a road bridge.

"A carpet of flowers in Whitehall outside Prescott's offices." Some of the bouquets from the 91 clubs who sent flowers to John Prescott.

The September 2004 Labour Party Conference march - a view from the street.

Roz South

Roz South

Roz South

"...the disabled supporters' banner saying 'Without Falmer we won't have a leg to stand on' just made you proud to be an Albion supporter."

"It was another of those moments when you said, all those years ago, watching the Albion from 1959 and it comes to this... singing on a top 20 hit record!" John Baine (Attila) leads (amongst others) Ed Bassford, Tim Carder and Paul Samrah in the backing vocals at the recording of Seagulls Ska.

Labour Party March, September 2005. Dick Knight, Des Lynam, Paul Samrah and Martin Perry among the marchers.

Tim Carder 7th December 2005. "So, back into campaigning again - the last thing I wanted." After Lewes appeal against Prescott's decision, over 5,000 signatures are collected in one week.

"Lewes told us that Sheepcote Valley was easy for transport. They said it was only 25 minutes' walk from the centre of Brighton." Thirty five fans in a timed walk from the Clock Tower to Sheepcote Valley prove Lewes wrong. A careful Bill Swallow keeps one hand on the steering wheel, 14th April 2007.

24th July 2007, Hazel Blears gives Falmer the green light. Paul Samrah, Fatboy Slim and Martin Perry celebrate – but note the crossed fingers.

Four fans celebrating in front of the field where the stadium will be built.

"If we don't do it we will die trying...we are never ever going to give up." Liz Costa with Ed Bassford and Paul Whelch.

Roz South

Roz South

"This stadium had a history before a game had been played... because of the huge, wonderful battle for it."

"I just felt it was a landmark building and a kind of symbol of rebirth in so many ways."

Chairman Tony Bloom at the unveiling of the Albion Mosaic in Dick's Bar, with Mosaic co-designer Warren Dudley.

They're on the bus – coming to Falmer. Ed Bassford and Roz South, 6th August 2011.

Roz South

Roz South

6th August 2011. "It was awesome in the literal sense – the scene that greeted me inspired awe. I can only compare it to the 1983 FA Cup final." The marvellous scenes as kick-off approaches on 6th August.

"A bunch of happy fans without a care". Supporters in the North Stand celebrate the Albion's fairytale injury-time winner against Doncaster Rovers.

Stadium conceals view of A27 shock.

JJ Waller